HABS HEROES

THE GREATEST CANADIENS EVER FROM 1 TO 100

Transcontinental Books
1100 René-Lévesque Boulevard West, 24th floor
Montreal (Quebec) H3B 4X9
Tel.: 514 340-3587
Toll-free 1-866-800-2500
www.livres.transcontinental.ca

Library and Archives Canada Cataloguing in Publication
Campbell, Ken, 1962-
Habs Heroes : The Greatest Canadiens Ever from 1 to 100

"The Hockey News".

ISBN 978-0-9809924-0-3

1. Montreal Canadiens (Hockey team) - Biography. 2. Hockey players - Québec (Province) - Montréal - Biography. 3. Montreal Canadiens (Hockey team) - History. 4. Montreal Canadiens (Hockey team) - Pictorial works. I. Hockey news (Montréal, Québec). II. Title.

GV848.M6C35 2008   796.962'64   C2008-941765-8

Project editor: Jason Kay
Copy Editing: Brian Costello
Proofreading: THN staff
Photo research: Sabina Lam, Glenn Levy/Getty Images
Page design: Karine Léger, Shared Production Centre of Montreal, Transcontinental Media
Cover design: Jamie Hodgson
Photo credits (cover): Getty Images

Printed in Canada
© Transcontinental Books, 2008
Legal deposit — 4th quarter 2008
National Library of Quebec
National Library of Canada

We acknowledge the financial support of the Government of Canada through the Book Publishing Industry Development Program (BPIDP) and the Government of Quebec through the SODEC Tax Credit for our publishing activities.

For information on special rates for corporate libraries and wholesale purchases, please call **1-866-800-2500.**

The Hockey News

Ken Campbell

HABS HEROES

THE GREATEST CANADIENS EVER FROM 1 TO 100

Transcontinental Books

To Ken and Inez Campbell and their other children
Jim, Bonnie, Susan, Dale and Tracy.

My dad was the biggest Montreal Canadiens fan
I've ever known and he left us far too soon.

_____

Acknowledgements

What seemed like a mammoth project at the beginning actually turned out to be one. But the writing of this book was possible and came to its fruition due to the efforts of some very special people.

THN editor-in-chief Jason Kay was instrumental with his support, encouragement, enthusiasm and the occasional kick in the pants.

THN publisher Caroline Andrews helped push the project ahead and believed it could work. Book publisher Jean Pare did much of the same.

THN colleague Brian Costello painstakingly edited this book and did his customary outstanding job. He's a man whom Herb Gardiner, ranked 95th on our list, would be proud to call his nephew.

The panelists who were vital in ranking the top 100 were Frank Orr, Eric Zweig, Ralph Mellanby and Scott Abbott in Toronto and Louis Jean, Jacques Demers, Yvon Pedneault, Bertrand Raymond, Chrys Goyens and Michel Vigneault in Montreal. Their dedication, passion and belief in the process were instrumental to its success.

THN interns Jordan Samery, John Grigg, Sabina Lam and Kevin Kennedy get enormous shout-outs for their work, which was tireless and without glamor, but essential to the finished product.

THN marketing/communications co-ordinator Carlie McGhee did all sorts of behind-the-scenes organizational work with her customary 1,000-watt smile and pleasant disposition. Her colleague, Janis Davidson-Pressick, is responsible for letting the world know about the project.

THN colleagues Mike Brophy, Ryan Kennedy, Ryan Dixon, Adam Proteau, Edward Fraser, Rory Boylen, Sam McCaig, Jamie Hodgson and Matt Filion were remarkably patient and understanding, and helped see the project through to the end.

Hockey historians Bob Duff, Ernie Fitzsimmons and Eric Zweig guided the author through the stories of many of the turn-of-the-century Canadiens and put their contributions into sharp perspective.

ACKNOWLEDGEMENTS

Rejean Houle of the Montreal Canadiens helped the author get in touch with many members of the Canadiens' alumni.

Miragh Addis of the Hockey Hall of Fame's resource center allowed the author to unfettered access to the facility and, most importantly, dug up every player file he needed.

Nic Chabot of Fantasy Sports compiled all of the statistics in his usual efficient manner.

And finally, to my wife, Lucie, and sons Connor and Lukas, for their cavernous well of love, support, patience and understanding. It simply could not have been done without you.

Foreword

When Butch Bouchard was trying out for the Canadiens almost 70 years ago, legend has it that every day of training camp he rode 35 miles on his bicycle from his home in Longueuil to the Canadiens' training facility in St-Hyacinthe.

I know how he felt. All right, that's a bit of a stretch. But on May 26, 1986, when I jumped on my BMX in St-Leonard bound for the streets of downtown Montreal, I did it with every bit of determination that Bouchard showed when he was trying to impress the Canadiens in the fall of 1940.

Three weeks before, I had celebrated my 14th birthday. Two nights prior, I had celebrated as the Canadiens won their 23rd Stanley Cup after dusting off the Calgary Flames in the final. It was Monday morning and suddenly, Grade 8 at math class at Ecole Saint-Exupery didn't seem all that enticing.

Getting to a Stanley Cup parade? Now that was a matter of life and death. So myself, my brother, Denis, and a couple of my friends figured we would bike to Montreal to see the parade. We took off out of school and rode right to the corner of Ste-Catherine and Peel and it was the greatest thing in our lives. It took about an hour biking through the streets for us to get there, but it was worth it. We had to watch out for a guy with a camera, though, because my dad, also named Denis, was the team photographer for the Canadiens.

We got into trouble big-time at school for that one. They called my parents the next day at home and, fortunately, my dad understood the mind of a hockey-crazed teenager and he was pretty good about it. "Come on, what do you expect?" he told the school. "The Canadiens just won the Cup. Give the kid a break."

Watching that parade gave me a chance to take part in something that has become a less frequent occurrence over the years. Long gone are the days when the Canadiens could be counted upon to win the Cup almost every year and follow the "regular" parade route through the streets of Montreal. When the Canadiens won in 1993, I was a pro rookie and had just finished playing my season in Utica. I went out and saw all the rioting and I didn't stick around very long for that.

As we sat on the corner that day, we saw all the Canadiens from Patrick Roy to Bob Gainey to Larry Robinson to Chris Chelios, all of whom are on the list of the top 100 Canadiens of all-time. When you look down the list, it's amazing how many great players have played for this franchise. And when you look at the Devils, it's no coincidence our franchise has been built precisely in the Canadiens' image.

Lou Lamoriello makes no secret of that. It's not just happenstance that we've won our three Stanley Cups with Jacques Lemaire, Larry Robinson and Pat Burns behind our bench. We've had guys such as Claude Lemieux and Stephane Richer in our lineup because they learned how to win with the Canadiens. Even in our scouting staff, we have Andre Boudrias and Pierre Mondou. Lou knows that winning follows these guys around and it all started for them with the attitude that was instilled in them by their experience with the Canadiens.

About the only thing we can't duplicate in New Jersey, or anywhere else in the NHL for that matter, is the cultural significance that Montreal places on its team. It's part of what drives the organization to win and its players to be great. Detroit likes to refer to itself as Hockeytown, but let's get serious here, there's only one Hockeytown in the NHL and that's Montreal. I know Detroit has been successful the past 10 years or so, but anytime I talk about hockey anywhere in the world, it always goes back to Montreal. What the Yankees are to baseball, the Canadiens are to hockey.

I realize it every time we play in Montreal and every time I come home during the summer. The other day I was at the gym and all anybody wanted to talk to me about was whether or not the Canadiens were going to get Mats Sundin. When I go golfing and hit my ball into the rough – on the very rare occasion that happens – if someone else is in there I know it won't take long before the conversation turns to the Canadiens. When the Devils are in town, my brothers beg me to have a good game because they know they have to go to work the next morning and hear about it all day if the Canadiens beat us.

We were playing against the Canadiens at the Bell Centre late in the 2007-08 season and we were getting our butts kicked in a game we would end up losing 4-0. With about two minutes left in the third period, I made a really nice kick save. Then at the next stoppage of play they took a TV timeout and suddenly everyone got on their feet and started cheering. I swear the whole building was shaking. I joked to my teammates after the game that everyone was cheering my save, but I knew. After that game, most of the guys on our team looked at each other in amazement saying, "Wow. Could you believe that?"

I guess my brothers heard about that one at work the next morning. It's nice to see people in Montreal have had more to cheer about lately, but I don't think it will ever be the same as it was in the past. It can't be because nobody will ever duplicate what this team has done on a consistent basis.

And the reason they did that is because of the great players they've had over the years, many of whom are in this book. You may not know who Newsy Lalonde and Didier Pitre are – I know I didn't – but you don't have to know them to understand what they and countless others have contributed to the success of this team.

Enjoy.

Martin Brodeur

June, 2008

Table of
Contents

Bruce Bennett Studios/Getty Images

p.71

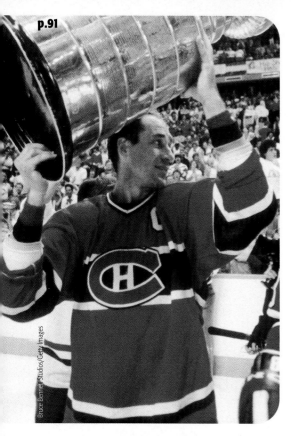

p.91

Bruce Bennet Studios/Getty Images

Bruce Bennett Studios/Getty Images

p.118

Elsa/Getty Images

p.270

Introduction

M ost of us don't choose the sports teams we support. Ninety-nine percent of the time they choose us.

More often than not, we're born into it, either by location or inheritance. We grow attached to the franchises in the cities in which we live; or as youngsters we align ourselves with the same favorite teams our parents or older brothers or sisters have already latched onto. If the sibling rivalry is particularly intense, we may gravitate toward the arch-rival.

Whatever the case, like gender, eye color and hair loss, our cheering preferences are usually pre-determined.

That's why so many of us puckheads are envious of Montreal Canadiens Nation; we want to be just like them, or even join their ranks, but the natural laws of sports fandom don't permit it.

I have my parents to blame for my tale of woe. We emigrated to Canada from England when I was an infant, traveling by boat to Halifax, then by train to Montreal. That's where the story could have ended happily ever after. Instead, my mom and dad thought it prudent to stick to their plans and proceed to...Toronto.

I suppose, from a hockey perspective, it didn't seem like such a bad idea at the time. The Maple Leafs had won three consecutive Stanley Cups earlier in the decade and had a veteran team that could, and did, make noise in the '67 post-season. With a little luck, the Leafs could start challenging the Habs for all-time supremacy.

It sounds funny in retrospect...if you're a Canadiens fan. Since that time, Montreal has won 10 more championships, Toronto none. Heck, the Leafs haven't even qualified for a Stanley Cup final in more than four decades.

While Canadiens supporters lined the streets for parade after parade, the most raucous Leafs celebrations came after Lanny McDonald helped upset the New York Islanders...in the first round. Or when Nikolai Borshevsky tipped home a shot to knock off the Detroit Red Wings in, you guessed it, the first round.

Fortunately, when I joined The Hockey News in 1989 I got to don a journalist's hat and claim objectivity. Deep down, however, the fire never completely dies for genuine sports fans, it just recedes to embers.

I suppose that's part of the reason I was so engaged and amazed while working on this project. The wannabe in me got stoked. Ken Campbell, senior writer at The Hockey News, did a Rocket Richard-like job in assembling the Top 100 list and writing all the stories and vignettes.

The order of the hundred greats was arrived at by consensus of 10 panelists, all experts on the history of the franchise. They are, in alphabetical order:

Scott Abbott, covered the Canadiens for Canadian Press in the 1970s; co-inventor of Trivial Pursuit; owner of the Brampton Battalion of the Ontario League

Jacques Demers, former NHL/Canadiens coach; RDS and CKAC radio hockey analyst

Chrys Goyens, Montreal-based author; co-wrote Habs history book *Lions in Winter,* and *My Life in Hockey* with Jean Beliveau

Louis Jean, former anchor for RDS; covers the Canadiens for Sportsnet

Ralphy Mellanby, former executive producer of Hockey Night in Canada; father of Scott Mellanby

Frank Orr, longtime hockey writer for the *Toronto Star;* noted hockey author; Elmer Ferguson Award winner for hockey reporting

Yvon Pedneault, longtime hockey writer for for *La Presse* and *Le Journal de Montreal;* longtime television analyst; Elmer Ferguson Award winner for hockey reporting

Bertrand Raymond, longtime hockey columnist for *Le Journal de Montreal;* Elmer Ferguson Award winner for hockey reporting

Michel Vigneault, Montreal-based hockey historian; authority on early Canadiens players

Eric Zweig, noted hockey historian whose work includes collaborating on *Total Hockey*

Each player's story is accompanied by biographical/statistical facts. For the skaters, their numbers include goals-assists-points; for goaltenders, it's wins-losses-ties or overtime/shootout losses. It's important to remember the rankings and statistics pertain only to the player's career with the Canadiens. That's why, for example, Frank Mahovlich who had a short but brilliant career in Montreal, didn't place higher.

It's important to note some of the major individual awards we cite in the player bios didn't come into existence until the NHL was well into its development, thus depriving some early era players the chance at swelling their hardware. For example, the Norris for top defenseman wasn't conceived until 1954; the Conn Smythe for playoff MVP in 1965; and the Selke for top defensive forward in 1978.

That's the fine print. Big picture, the Montreal Canadiens are the marquee franchise for the NHL and, as they celebrate 100 years of existence, we're adding our voice to the chorus of admirers through this book.

Jason Kay
Editor-in-Chief
The Hockey News

Pictorial Parade/Getty Images

Maurice **RICHARD**

A Raging Rocket

Bruce Bennett Studios/Getty Images

Right Winger
Born: Aug. 4, 1921, Montreal, Que.
Died: May 27, 2000
Habs Career : 1942-1960
8 Stanley Cups, 8 first-team all-stars,
6 second-team all-stars,
1 Hart Trophy
544-421-965, 1,285 PIM in 978 games
Hockey Hall of Fame: 1961

His younger brother, Henri, won more Stanley Cups. Jean Beliveau was a far more galvanizing force when it came to leadership. Guy Lafleur won more individual trophies and eclipsed his magical 50-goal mark five times. And when it comes to career points per game, he barely cracks the top 10 in the all-time history of the Montreal Canadiens.

"He also wasn't the best hockey player who ever played for the Montreal Canadiens," said longtime Canadiens broadcaster Dick Irvin, "and he admitted that himself."

But Maurice 'Rocket' Richard is simply the greatest Canadien of all-time. It has been that way since he retired in 1960 and there's a very good chance it will be that way in 2060. Richard's greatness goes far beyond the franchise-best 544 career goals and the eight Stanley Cups – and its reach goes far beyond the confines of hockey.

It was Richard who was instrumental in resurrecting a Canadiens' franchise that had fallen into such a state of disarray the team sometimes played before announced crowds of fewer than 2,000 and was not far from the precipice of extinction. In many ways, he raised the consciousness and self-realization of an entire province. Such was his hold over the general public that his suspension in 1955 caused a violent uprising that only subsided after the Rocket made a public plea for calm.

It was not just the talent the Rocket possessed, although that did set him apart from so many other players. What made Richard so imposing was his powder keg of emotions – a mixture of hunger and anger that could be explosive.

Maurice 'Rocket' Richard was famous for the fire that burned within and a piercing glare. Sometimes, he would stare down teammates for going offside.

Bruce Bennett Studios/Getty Images

Richard would stare down teammates if they went offside and do the same in the dressing room after losses.

Ray Getliffe, who gave Richard the most famous nickname in hockey history during Richard's rookie year, said the famed Richard eyes were every bit as intimidating as the legends say. When Richard retired, Terry Sawchuk was asked what he would remember most about Richard and without hesitating, Sawchuk responded, "His eyes."

"He was on another planet, in another world," Getliffe remarked in the book *Lions in Winter*. "He had that look in his eyes, like the other players against him weren't even there…like he was all by himself on the ice. I played with him and sometimes when I was on the ice with him and I saw him coming in my direction with that look on his face, I wanted to jump right over the boards out of his way. Can you imagine what the opposition felt?"

It was not always that way for Richard, whose two years with the Montreal Royals senior team and his first season in the NHL were so ravaged with injuries, GM Tom Gorman wondered whether Richard wasn't too brittle to play in the league.

"There's a scene in the movie they made about him where Gorman is trying to trade him and my dad (the Canadiens' coach Dick Irvin Sr.) is trying to talk him out of it," Irvin said. "That's true. That really happened."

Perhaps it was his resentment or anger over his treatment early with the Canadiens, but Richard seemed fuelled with an intense desire to prove Gorman and the others who doubted him wrong. Richard scored 32 goals the next season, then in 1944-45 scored his legendary 50 goals in 50 games to lead the league. He would lead the league in goal scoring four more times during his career, which would have earned him five times the trophy that now bears his name.

"Rocket Richard, from the blueline in, is still the greatest hockey player who has ever played in the world," former Detroit Red Wings' star Ted Lindsay said during the 2008 Stanley Cup final. "I don't care if they play hockey for 100 years, nobody will ever be better than the Rocket."

"Rocket Richard, from the blueline in, is still the greatest hockey player who has ever played in the world."
– Ted Lindsay

Many outside Montreal referred to Richard as a "wartime player," who benefited from so many people being overseas during World War II. Richard tried to enlist twice and was turned down and while he did score his 50 in 50 in 1944-45, the return of the soldiers did nothing to slow him down.

And through much of his career, Richard excelled as a marked man. Once against Detroit, Richard dragged defenseman Earl Seibert from the blueline in and scored a goal. His career was filled with violent confrontations, including famous one-punch victories over the notorious Bob Dill of the New York Rangers, Bill Juzda of the Toronto Maple Leafs and Lindsay.

During one training camp, there was a noted pugilist from the Quebec Senior League named Butch Stahan who, at 6-foot-1 and 210 pounds, was considered a behemoth. Intent on making an impression, he went after the 5-foot-10, 170-pound Richard in the first scrimmage and Richard punched him into unconsciousness and oblivion.

But just as often, Richard's temper and penchant for lashing out had disastrous consequences. Aside from being suspended for the playoffs in 1955 after a stick-swinging duel with Hal Laycoe that resulted in Richard manhandling a linesman, Richard was repeatedly fined for incidents with his stick.

And in 1951, he was fined $500 for assaulting referee Hugh MacLean in the lobby of a New York hotel. MacLean had penalized Richard in a game earlier that evening.

"It wasn't the penalty that got me mad," Richard told the *Detroit News* eight years later. "It was the way he laughed at me. And he laughed at me again in the hotel."

Richard's exploits are too many to mention, since he held 17 records when he retired. He arrived as a superstar when he scored five goals in a playoff game against the Leafs in 1944, cemented his reputation the next season when he scored five goals and three assists in a game after spending the entire day moving. His goal against the Boston Bruins in the 1952 semifinal, where he fought off two Boston defensemen and scored on 'Sugar' Jim Henry after suffering a head injury earlier in the game, produced a picture of a bloodied Richard and Henry shaking hands after the series. That photograph is ever-enduring and one of the most memorable in the game's history.

Richard's last years with the Canadiens were less than stellar. He played most of his final three seasons overweight and teammates resented that coach Toe Blake, a stickler for players maintaining an ideal body mass, didn't require Richard to weigh in regularly. In fact, Irvin maintains Richard's level of play had diminished so much he spent much of his last year hidden on the power play.

But that will never take the luster off the greatest Canadien player ever.

"When the Rocket scored, the cheer was just a little bit louder than anybody else," Irvin said. "(Jean) Beliveau and (Bernie) Geoffrion and (Guy) Lafleur could score big goals in big games and everyone would cheer, but there was just something about when Maurice scored, it would just be a decibel or two higher." ●

Bruce Bennett Studios/Getty Images

Jean **BELIVEAU**

A Legend Beyond Reproach

Bruce Bennett Studios/Getty Images

Center	
Born: Aug. 31, 1931, Trois-Rivieres, Que.	
Habs Career : 1951-1971	
10 Stanley Cups, 6 first-team all-stars	
4 second-team all-stars	
1 Art Ross Trophy, 1 Conn Smythe Trophy	
507-712-1,219,	
1,029 PIM in 1,125 games	
Hockey Hall of Fame: 1972	

Had Jean Beliveau not been a man of such unwavering principle, he just might have been remembered as the greatest Montreal Canadiens player of all-time.

One thing is certain. Beliveau's bank account would have been much, much larger, almost as imposing as the mystique that surrounds the man who embodies the class and dignity of the Canadiens like no other.

"The two greatest figures of the Canadiens in the past 60 years are 'The Rocket' and Jean Beliveau," former Canadiens goalie Ken Dryden once observed. "One of them evokes love, the other evokes admiration."

At 6-foot-3 and 205 pounds, Beliveau was difficult for the Canadiens to ignore. That he possessed a rare combination of power and grace and a wonderful, swooping stride made the Canadiens covet him all the more from the time Beliveau turned 18. But instead of joining the Canadiens, Beliveau played junior for the Quebec Citadelles for two years. Then, feeling a sense of obligation to the people of Quebec City who supported him as a junior player, he spent two years with the Quebec Aces of the Quebec Senior Hockey League.

Eighteen seasons after joining the Canadiens, Beliveau left the game for good following Montreal's unlikely Stanley Cup win in 1971. He recorded 76 points that year, one of the highest totals for a player in his final NHL season.

> "The two greatest figures of the Canadiens in the past 60 years are 'The Rocket' and Jean Beliveau. One of them evokes love, the other evokes admiration."
> – Ken Dryden

"I actually wanted to retire from the Canadiens the year before," Beliveau said. "But (GM) Sam Pollock and (owner) David Molson asked me to stay another year. We had a lot of young players in 1970 and Sam Pollock told me, 'Jean, I'll feel much better if I know you're in the room.' So I said, 'All right, Sam, I'll play another year, but it will be my last.' "

And this is where Beliveau's legacy comes into the picture. As it stands, Beliveau is third on the Canadiens all-time list for goals with 507, 37 behind Maurice Richard. He's second in points with 1,219, 27 behind Guy Lafleur and fourth in games played with 1,125, 131 behind Henri Richard.

Had Beliveau played the four years prior to joining the Canadiens and a couple more instead of retiring, there's no question he would have broken all three marks and easily be at the top of each category. Even if he had joined the Canadiens as a 20-year-old, he would have been around for their Stanley Cup win in 1952-53 and had he played longer, he would have been there for their Cup victory in 1973. That would have given Beliveau 12 Stanley Cups as a player, one more than all-time leader Henri Richard.

"Numbers to me are very secondary," Beliveau said, "compared to when people are honest with me. I have a very hard time to split with somebody who has been good to me."

Numbers in his financial portfolio were apparently secondary to Beliveau as well. Once he retired from the Canadiens, Beliveau turned down a four-year contract with the Quebec Nordiques of the World Hockey Association that would have paid him a reported $1 million. The Nordiques even told him that if he wanted to retire one year into the deal, he could fulfill the rest of the deal by working in the team's front office.

But Beliveau's loyalty to the Canadiens and his need to be true to himself prompted him turn the Nordiques down. In fact, he claims it wasn't even that difficult a decision.

Jean Beliveau grabbed the torch from 'Rocket' Richard (left) and sprinted with it. In 1964-65, Beliveau won the Conn Smythe Trophy as most valuable player of the playoffs and, as captain of the Canadiens, accepted the Stanley Cup.

Beliveau was known for his resovle and integrity, not to mention skill on the ice. Here, he attempts to beat Boston's Terry Sawchuk.

"The only thing I can say is that the offer of that four years was more than the 18 years I played in the NHL," Beliveau said. "I said, 'Whatever amount of money you offer me, the answer is no.' There is a quality type of game I enjoy playing and I told the Nordiques, 'I wouldn't be honest toward you, toward the fans, toward the game...

"I wouldn't be honest to myself. At 41, you cannot perform the way I would like to perform. Some people like (Chris) Chelios can do it, but he's the exception."

No player in the history of the franchise has carried himself with more class and dignity than Beliveau. When Canadien fans were booing the U.S. national anthem to protest the invasion of Iraq in 2003, Beliveau made a public plea for respect and the booing was replaced by people singing along with the anthem.

As the most decorated captain in the history of the Canadiens, Beliveau guided phenom Guy Lafleur as he struggled through his first three seasons and helped him become a superstar. When veteran Henri Richard railed against coach Al MacNeil during the playoffs in 1971, Beliveau managed to get Richard to stop by simply squeezing his arm.

Beliveau's resolve and integrity are stitched into Canadiens history; he never wavered, always following his own moral compass. The only time he felt the burden of expectation was when he entered the league in 1953-54. The lengths to which the Canadiens went to get Beliveau created enormous anticipation and instead of dominating, Beliveau struggled with injuries for much of his rookie season and scored just 13 goals and 34 points in 44 games.

"It was most difficult at the beginning," Beliveau said. "It was a long time the Canadiens were trying to sign me, so there was a lot of publicity surrounding the negotiations between the Canadiens and me. And there is nothing worse for an athlete than to be preceded by all this publicity. It put more pressure and tension on my shoulders."

Pressure also often brings out the best in some players and those shoulders were obviously big and strong enough to handle the obstacles that were ahead. He improved to 73 points in his second year, a league-leading 88 in his third. And even though Beliveau left the game with probably more to give, he refused to allow the world to watch as his speed and skills diminished.

"I just told you how I think," Beliveau said. "I could not do that." ●

Bruce Bennett/Getty Images

Doug **HARVEY**

Heroic and Tragic

Bruce Bennett Studios/Getty Images

Defenseman
Born: Dec. 19, 1924, Montreal
Died: Dec. 26, 1989
Habs Career : 1947-1961
6 Stanley Cups, 9 first-team all-stars
1 second-team all-star, 6 Norris Trophies
76-371-447, 1042 PIM in 890 games
Hockey Hall of Fame: 1973

The Hockey Hall of Fame still has two artifacts that are a testament to Doug Harvey's brilliance and his penchant for thumbing his nose at the establishment.

The first is a handwritten note from Harvey's wife Ursula, politely informing the Hall of Fame Harvey had not budged on his decision to refuse his induction in 1973.

The other is the Hall of Fame ring all members receive upon induction, a bauble Harvey never bothered to pick up because he never acknowledged he was in the Hall in the first place. Despite his objections, the Hall inducted him anyway.

It certainly wasn't because he didn't belong there, at least for his on-ice exploits. Harvey was the best defenseman of his era and, depending upon who is offering the opinion, the best of all-time. A superior first-passer and wonderful skater, Harvey could also excel in defensive lockdown or a back-alley brawl. There was no style of play in which Harvey was not confident and comfortable.

Many players can claim greatness, but precious few can be remembered for changing the landscape of the game. Harvey's game was so predicated on attacking that he opened the gap between defensemen and forwards and made his team a lethal offensive threat. His passing and rushing strengths, not to mention his ability to get back into defensive position when he did wander, stretched the ice for the Canadiens and allowed their talented forwards to devote more of their efforts to creating offense.

> "If you needed help, he would be there. When I lost my son (in a car accident in 1973), he was on the doorstep waiting for me at 6:30 in the morning."
>
> – Dickie Moore

"He would always say, 'It's easier for you guys to skate without the puck than with the puck,'" recalled former teammate and close friend Dickie Moore. "He'd say, 'Give it to me and I'll give it back to you.'"

Former teammate Billy Reay once said that, "When Doug put a pass on your stick, it was like a feather."

A native of Montreal who as a child delivered newspapers to Canadiens goaltending great Bill Durnan, Harvey won the Norris Trophy seven of the first nine years the award was presented, and was runner-up for it the first year it was awarded. He remains the only player in NHL history to win the Norris with two teams and was a first-team all-star for 10 of 11 seasons starting in 1951-52.

But Harvey could be as belligerent as he was brilliant. He often frustrated coaches and GMs with his attitude and work ethic and his involvement in the early days of the NHL Players' Association earned him a one-way ticket out of Montreal in 1961. Harvey was more than happy to shake hands after a playoff series if the Canadiens won, but would never do it if they lost.

"We were winning all the time, so that didn't happen too often," Moore recalled.

Harvey was also seen by those who knew him best as a fiercely loyal friend who had a kind heart and a soft spot, particularly for those who most needed help.

"People like to talk about his drinking episodes, but he was an ordinary man. He cared for people who were ordinary," Moore said. "If you needed help, he would be there. When I lost my son (in a car accident in 1973), he was on the doorstep waiting for me at 6:30 in the morning. I came from identifying my son and he was there."

But as brilliant as Harvey was on the ice and as gregarious as he was off, he had an enormous tragic flaw. His drinking often overshadowed his accomplishments. He never apologized for his vices, once telling a reporter, "When they drop this body into the ground, it won't rot for a long time. It's full of alcohol. It's got its own embalming fluid."

Getty Images/NHLI

Pictorial Parade/Getty Images

After being sent to the Rangers for Lou Fontinato in 1961, Harvey bounced around the NHL and the minors before retiring for good following a stint with the St. Louis Blues in 1969. The Canadiens won four more Stanley Cups from the time Harvey left to the time he retired and there are teammates who will tell you he should have been there for all of them and retired a Canadien.

But it was not to be. The Canadiens demanded a certain comportment both on and off the ice and Harvey simply was not the kind of personality to be restricted by such things.

"There always seemed to be two sides to Doug's life," Jean Beliveau said in 1986. "He was one of the greats of the game, always will be, but there is that tragic side."

Harvey was bypassed for induction into the

Doug Harvey was as comfortable playing a brawling, in-your-face game as he was leading an attack. But it's his offensive, change-the-landscape-of-the-game legacy for which he is best remembered.

Hall of Fame in 1972, three years after he retired, and a large part of the reason was his drinking. When Harvey learned of his fate, former Canadiens GM Frank Selke, who was also on the selection committee, told Harvey: "I can get you in next year, Doug, but you've got to help me."

Harvey took it as such a slap in the face that he refused to be included among the inductees in 1973, saying he was going on a fishing trip the day of the gala. He was also upset the Hall took so long to induct former Maple Leafs great Busher Jackson, who also fell on very hard times because of his drinking habits. Jackson retired in 1944, but wasn't inducted until 1971.

"What they're telling me is that they won't put me in because I'm not averse to sampling the nectar of the gods now and then," Harvey said in 1972. "The difference is that I'll hoist a few in full view of everyone where other guys will sneak around the corner to do theirs."

Harvey's drinking became more prominent as his life progressed to the point where there were reports he was destitute and living in a boxcar near the Connaught Race Track in Ottawa. It was actually a luxury car with all the amenities and Harvey was doing security at the track. The Canadiens took him back into the fold as a scout until he died of cirrhosis of the liver in 1989 at the age of 65.

"A lot of people, the team, tried to help," Rocket Richard told a reporter when Harvey died. "Most times, he wouldn't listen. He would do things his way. Everyone tried to put him on the right path, but there was nothing to be done." ●

Denis Brodeur /Getty Images

Guy **LAFLEUR**

Le Demon Blond

Bruce Bennett Studios/Getty Images

Right Winger	
Born: Sept. 20, 1951, Thurso, Que.	
Habs Career : 1971-1985	
5 Stanley Cups, 6 first-team all-stars	
2 Hart Trophies, 3 Art Ross Trophies	
1 Conn Smythe Trophy	
518-728-1,246, 381 PIM in 961 games	
Hockey Hall of Fame: 1988	

It was a hazy night, late summer of 1976, and some of the best hockey players in the world had assembled in Montreal for training camp for the first-ever Canada Cup tournament. Guy Lafleur was among them and the last physical exertion he had experienced was lifting the Stanley Cup over his head three months before.

Those who ran Team Canada thought a dryland training session would be a good way to start things and decided to have a fitness guru from the local YMCA put the players through their paces in the form of a grueling five-mile run. Remember, we're talking about the 1970s here.

We'll let Lafleur's former linemate, Steve Shutt take the story from here:

"So here we go, we take off," Shutt recalled. "Guy takes off and this guy from the YMCA can't catch him, no matter how hard he goes. So Lafleur does the five-mile run and comes back and he's in the dressing room having a cigarette waiting for the rest of us to come back."

For almost half the 14 seasons Lafleur played with the Canadiens, he made everything look so easy. At times, when he was at the height of his magic, Lafleur seemed to be toying with his opponents the way he toyed with the guy from the YMCA. In the six seasons between 1974-75 and '79-80, Lafleur scored 327 goals and 766 points in 462 games for an average of 128 points per season. In the history of the NHL, only Wayne Gretzky, Mario Lemieux and Phil Esposito have had more productive stretches of six consecutive years.

Steve Babineau/NHLI via Getty Images

For those six seasons, Lafleur was otherworldly, the best player on the planet. It was almost certainly the three seasons prior and the five that followed – almost all of them respectable, but certainly not up to the standard he set – that have prevented Lafleur from being indisputably remembered as the greatest Canadiens player of all-time. As it stands, he'll have to settle for being the franchise's all-time scoring leader.

When it comes to offensive flair and excitement, there are only two who merit consideration as the greatest ever – Rocket Richard and Lafleur. Where Richard was small and squat, combative and ill-tempered, Lafleur was slender, calm and graceful, with a sense of elan and finesse that made him far more ex-

Guy Lafleur was the NHL's dominant player for a period during the 1970s, adding a Conn Smythe Trophy in 1977 to his array of hardware.

citing than any other player ever could be. Teammates would marvel that the same player who chain-smoked and often lit up between periods could come back to the bench after a long shift and not even be breathing hard.

"Did you ever notice Guy Lafleur doesn't sweat?" former Canadiens defenseman Rod Langway once told THN. "He seems to walk on the red carpet all the time. No. 10, The Flower, that's it. He's in the garden all by himself."

For the first three seasons of his career, however, Lafleur played with such little direction or sense of urgency it looked as though he was wandering through the wilderness by himself. While fellow Quebec-born 1971 draft picks Marcel Dionne and Richard Martin were flourishing, Lafleur was regularly stunning people with his utter inability to have an impact on a game. In fact, Lafleur won his first Cup with the Canadiens in 1973 as a complete non-factor.

"He was just a part of the furniture," former Canadiens' broadcaster Dick Irvin said of Lafleur's three forgettable years.

The Canadiens were beginning to grow impatient with their prodigy. Lafleur appeared to be wilting under the pressure of playing in Montreal when so much was expected of him. When the Canadiens dealt for the No. 1 pick in the 1971 draft to get Lafleur, GM Sam Pollock was lauded as a genius. But after Lafleur's first three years, the hockey world was beginning to think Pollock had lost his magic touch.

> "Lafleur does the five-mile run and comes back and he's in the dressing room having a cigarette waiting for the rest of us to come back."
> – Steve Shutt

He hadn't. In Lafleur's fourth year, the prodigy showed up without headgear and with his head in the right place and 'Le Demon Blond' was born.

"After his third year, they had to sign him to a new contract and Sam Pollock called Scotty Bowman and Claude Ruel into his office and said, 'What are we going to do with this guy? Do we trade him or what?' and Ruel and Scotty talked him out of it," Irvin recalled. "And I'll never forget it. It was the start of the 1974-75 season and they were playing the Islanders on a Wednesday night to start the season at home and Lafleur didn't have his helmet on. And by the time the game was over, you were saying, 'Who was that guy? Who was No. 10 out there?' He was a totally different player. It was an amazing transformation."

The years that followed were among the best in NHL history both for one player and a team. With Lafleur as their superstar, the Canadiens won four straight Stanley Cups in the 1970s. In three of those years, Lafleur led the league in scoring and playoff points.

"There's absolutely no doubt about," Bob Clarke once told THN, "Lafleur was the best player in the league for about five years."

And just as the Canadiens dynasty subsided, so did Lafleur. Shutt once remarked that Canadiens superstars don't often enjoy 20-year careers because they end up playing a couple of extra seasons in playoff games. Lafleur's decline began in 1980-81 and as his career began to dwindle, the luster began to fade as well. In March, 1981, Lafleur made headlines after he narrowly avoided being decapitated when he drove his car off the road on his way home after a night of drinking. The photograph of a smashed car with a pole speared through the steering wheel into the headrest appeared in newspapers everywhere the next day.

By the time Lafleur retired for the first time in 1985, he was being benched by his former linemate-turned-coach, Jacques Lemaire. And Lemaire was privately telling people Lafleur was becoming a detriment to the team when he was on the ice.

Lafleur took a front-office job before clashing with the Canadiens and leaving the organization. He has since returned and is a team ambassador. He managed to find a measure of peace when he came back to play one season for the New York Rangers and two for the Quebec Nordiques.

"It wasn't an easy load to carry, being a god who was expected to act that way on and off the ice," Shutt told THN shortly after Lafleur retired from the Canadiens. "He was a very shy man who just wanted to play his game with no fuss or bother and it was tough for him to live with the load of people's expectations always on his shoulders." ●

Pictorial Parade/Getty Images

Howie **MORENZ**

HHOF Images

The Stratford Streak

Center
Born: June 21, 1902, Mitchell, Ont.
Died: March 8, 1937
Habs Career : 1923-1934, 1936-37
3 Stanley Cups, 2 first-team all-stars,
1 second-team all-star, 3 Hart Trophies,
2 Art Ross Trophies
256-156-412, 516 PIM in 460 games
Hockey Hall of Fame: 1945

Perhaps it's because he was the NHL's first true superstar, the first player to truly define the Montreal Canadiens and hockey's crown jewel in the golden age of professional sports.

Whatever the reason, no player in Canadiens history is as mythical a figure as Howard William Morenz. No player is as enveloped in mystique, romance and mystery as Morenz and, to be sure, the Canadiens have never had as tragic a figure as the kid from rural Ontario who begged the Canadiens to let him out of his contract so he could stay home and play amateur hockey.

There is much about Morenz and his career that can be up for debate, but one thing is indisputable. Morenz was an extraordinary player, one with uncanny speed and a motherlode of talent. Like most star players in the NHL's early years, Morenz was a 45-to-60 minute-per-game player for the majority of his career and when most of his teammates and opponents began to fatigue halfway through the game, Morenz had the stamina and conditioning to continue playing at an elevated level.

King Clancy, who spent almost 70 years in the game, called Morenz the greatest player he ever saw. Some hockey historians, however, speculate Clancy might just have been pumping his own tires and those of the players of his era to make such a claim.

"If you went to a baseball game and saw Babe Ruth powder one over the fence, you didn't need to know first base from the ass of your pants to realize that you had seen something special," Clancy was quoted as saying in *Lions in Winter,* a book about the Canadiens by Chrys Goyens and Allan Turowetz.

"It was the same thing with Morenz. You didn't need to know the difference between a hockey puck and your belly button to know that when you had watched Morenz play the game, you had seen something special."

To be sure, both the Canadiens and the NHL were in dire need of a star by the time Morenz was dominating junior and senior hockey in Stratford, Ont., in the early 1920s. Just a few years removed from rising from the ashes of the National Hockey Association, the NHL was something of a mom-and-pop operation with just four teams based in Montreal, Hamilton, Ottawa and Toronto and was eager to infiltrate the large American markets. The Canadiens, meanwhile, were trying to energize a dwindling fan base that had been in constant decline since star Joe Malone left in 1919. Although they had won one Stanley Cup in the NHA in 1916, the Canadiens had not won a single Cup in the six years the NHL had existed and has missed the playoffs three times by the time Morenz arrived in 1923-24.

Morenz's impact was immediate. Playing on a line with Aurel Joliat and Billy Boucher, Morenz scored seven goals in six playoff games in 1924 to help the Canadiens to the Stanley Cup. By the time the NHL allowed forward passing in all zones in 1930-31, Morenz was at the apex of his career and he took advantage of the new rules to cement his status as the best player in the game.

Morenz, nicknamed 'The Stratford Streak,' did indeed make his mark on the professional game beyond Montreal, but again his impact on the marketing of the game is open to debate.

The conventional story behind the emergence of the NHL in New York has always suggested Madison Square Garden president Tex Rickard, who later ran the New York Rangers, was lukewarm to the prospect of hockey and wasn't terribly eager to install expensive ice-making equipment into the new Madison Square Garden. That all changed, the story goes, when he and Charles Adams of Boston were invited to Montreal to watch Morenz play in the playoffs in 1924. Apparently the men came away so impressed they committed to NHL teams immediately.

However, some hockey historians beg to differ. They claim Adams had already purchased the rights to the Boston franchise by the time he had seen Morenz play and Rickard was very interested in putting another team in MSG to join the New York Americans. In fact, hockey historian Eric Zweig has meticulously researched the story and said Rickard was not even in Montreal that night, instead dispatching

> **"The doctor decided the problem could wait until the morning. The morning was too late."**
> – Howie Morenz III

36

HHOF Images

MSG vice-president John Hammond. A fight promoter, Rickard was actually in Washington testifying before Congress at an inquiry into the illegal exhibition of a fight film of the 1921 heavyweight championship bout between Jack Dempsey and Georges Carpentier.

Rickard is also credited with referring to Morenz as, "the Babe Ruth of hockey," and that term has been generally accepted over the years. However, Zweig said that is not the case.

"I've never seen anything from anyone, including Tex Rickard, referring to Morenz as the Babe Ruth of hockey in his playing days or while he was alive," Zweig said.

But perhaps the most mysterious Morenz story has to do with the circumstances surrounding his death at the age of 34, one that attracted thousands of mourners to the Forum. His career in decline, Morenz was dealt to Chicago in 1934 at 32 and foundered with the Black Hawks and Rangers before returning to the Canadiens in 1936-37. It has been well documented Earl Seibert of the Black Hawks hit Morenz into the boards in a Jan. 28, 1937 game that resulted in Morenz badly breaking his leg.

And that's where the story begins to take several different routes. Teammate and good friend Joliat contends Morenz was so despondent about what was a career-ending injury he said he'd rather die than not play for the Canadiens. Seibert, who was vilified by Montreal fans for years to come, claims friends and teammates, who fuelled Morenz's drinking binges by bringing alcohol to his hospital room, are to blame.

But Morenz's grandson, Howie Morenz III, offered a different perspective in a piece he wrote for the Society of International Hockey Research in 2005. Morenz died of a coronary embolism and Howie Morenz III said the leg was broken so badly that Morenz required a steel plate to be inserted in his ankle so a weighted pulley could be used to reposition the bone before a cast could be applied. He also said the night of his grandfather's death, the doctor on duty did an X-ray on the leg and saw several blood clots.

"People just don't seem to understand the severity of the injury and cannot accept the fact that an athlete can die of a broken leg," Morenz III wrote. "Blood clots are extremely dangerous and once loose in the blood stream, can be fatal. It's our understanding that, even in 1937, they had the means to dissolve blood clots. But the doctor decided the problem could wait until the morning. The morning was too late."

"It was basically a case of gross negligence," Morenz III added later. ●

Pictorial Parade/Getty Images

Making friends was not a priority for Jacques Plante, one of the most decorated goalies of all-time. Stopping pucks and winning hockey games was foremost on his mind.

Jacques **PLANTE**

A Brilliant Enigma

Goaltender
Born: Jan. 17, 1929, Shawinigan Falls, Que.
Died: Feb. 27, 1986
Habs Career : 1953-1963
6 Stanley Cups, 3 first-team all-stars,
3 second-team all-stars, 1 Hart Trophy,
6 Vezina Trophies
312-134-108, 2.23 GAA, 58 shutouts
Hockey Hall of Fame: 1978

Jacques Plante won the Stanley Cup six times during his career and his name is spelled five different ways on the trophy – appearing as J. Plante, Jacques Plante, Jac Plante, Jacq Plante and Jaques Plante.

It should really come as no surprise that the man the hockey establishment never really ever figured out would also flummox those who engraved the trophy.

Plante was a brilliant goalie to be sure and his place in hockey history as an innovator when it comes to playing the puck and facial protection is undeniable. But Plante was also a very different sort in a sport that was even less tolerant of individualism and eccentricities than it is today.

Legendary Canadiens coach Toe Blake often clashed with his star goalie, largely because Blake was an old-time hockey man who had little time for Plante's quirks. It has been debated how badly Plante suffered from asthma during his career, but it often rankled Blake that Plante would keep him guessing as to his status for games.

But nothing irked Blake more than Plante's insistence on wearing a mask in 1959. Plante was subject to every stereotype and insult imaginable, not just from opponents but from teammates as well.

"What he went through, the adversity he went through trying to bring in that mask, he went through hell," said former teammate Dickie Moore. "Real hell, it was amazing. Everybody made it difficult for him. We thought he was doing the wrong thing, but it was all right for us to say that. It wasn't fair to him. We were a bunch of kids."

His indoctrination into the Hab culture came in 1953 when he was thrown into the heat of the play-offs, Game 6 of the first round against the Chicago Black Hawks with the Canadiens trailing the series 3-2.

Plante was so nervous before the game, but his fears were subdued by the presence of Maurice Richard, who walked up to Plante in the dressing room and held out his shaking hands for Plante to see.

"Look at them," Richard said. "They always shake before a big game. You'll feel better when you get out on the ice."

Plante was about so much more than the mask. First of all, he could play at an incredibly high level. He won seven Vezina Trophies over the course of his career and pulled off the nearly unheard of feat for a goalie of winning the Hart Trophy in 1962.

Plante always seemed to be thinking on a higher level. As former Maple Leafs goalie Johnny Bower once told columnist Allen Abel: "He had a lot on his mind. But what he was thinking about, nobody knew."

Among his other innovations were being the first goaltender to raise his arm to indicate to his team-mates an impending icing and his penchant for barking out directions to his teammates from his goal crease. But it was in the mid-1950s that Plante started a trend that would have far-reaching effects into the game – the practise of venturing behind the net to get to pucks that had been dumped in and starting the rush the other way by dishing it off to a defenseman.

Plante was also the first goalie to come out of his net to smother loose pucks and get a stoppage in play.

"He's the guy who designed that play of coming out of the net and stopping the puck from going around the boards," Moore said. "That's what Detroit used to do when they were beating us and Plante would come out and stop the puck from going around. They'd send a big guy in like Vic Stasiuk or Marcel Pronovost to pick up the puck going around and (Gordie) Howe or (Ted) Lindsay would let it go. He figured we didn't have to play them the way we were playing them."

Moore said that contrary to popular belief, Plante was accepted by his teammates and was not as distant as many have been led to believe over the years. But there is no denying Plante had a reputation for aloofness, one he never tried to discourage.

George Silk/Time Life Pictures/Getty Images

"No, I never make friends, not in hockey, not else-where, since I was a teenager," Plante said at the apex of his career. "What for? If you are close to someone, you must be scheduling yourself to please them."

Long before there was video that broke down every minute aspects of an opponent's play, there was Plante, who kept a mental book on every player in the league. He would become so nervous the day before a game that he would ignore autograph seekers.

"I never intend to be unkind or ungrateful," he said at the time. "But I become very nervous and I have many things on my mind at least 24 hours before a game. I try to mentally review each player on the team we're about to play and get a picture in my mind of their formations."

That philosophy served Plante well throughout his re-markable career. He remains the only goalie in NHL his-tory to win the Vezina seven times (which was awarded at the time for the goalie with the lowest goals-against av-erage) and his Hart Trophy in 1962 would be the last for a goalie until Dominik Hasek was named MVP 35 years later. He is also the only goalie in NHL history to win five straight Stanley Cups.

Moore said he got to know Plante well be-cause Plante would always drive him home from the train station after road trips. He was al-ways an intensely difficult man to decipher, but there was a certain dignity about him.

"When we played, the money wasn't really big," Moore said. "I remember he used to knit his undershirts and he wore them and still walked tall in front of everybody. I was proud of him for that."

"He had a lot on his mind. But what he was thinking about, nobody knew."
– Johnny Bower

After being dealt to the New York Rangers in 1963, Plante bounced around with four more NHL teams and the Edmonton Oilers of the WHA. For health reasons, he moved to Switzerland after his play-ing career, where he died in 1986 of stomach cancer. ●

George Silk/Time Pictures/Getty Images

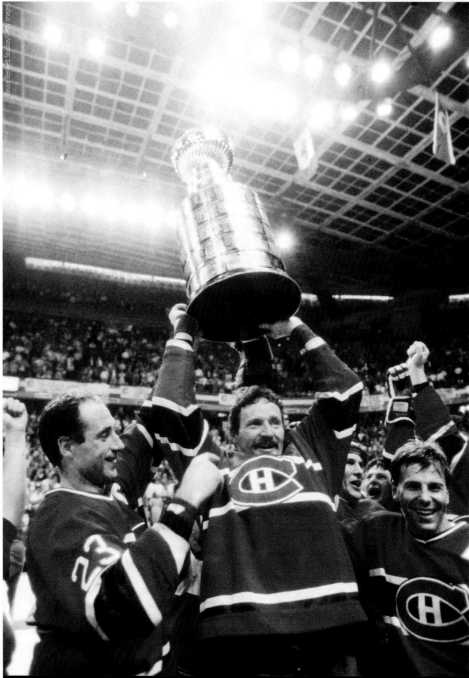

Larry Robinson, who excelled at every facet of the game, was an integral member of six Stanley Cup teams in Montreal. Here, he celebrates his final one, flanked by Bob Gainey (left) and Mats Naslund (right).

Larry **ROBINSON**

Tower of Power

Bruce Bennett/Getty Images

Defenseman
Born: June 2, 1951, Winchester, Ont.
Habs Career : 1972-1989
6 Stanley Cups, 3 first-team all-stars,
3 second-team all-stars, 2 Norris
Trophies, 1 Conn Smythe Trophy
197-686-883, 706 PIM in 1,202 games
Hockey Hall of Fame: 1995

As a coach in the NHL, Larry Robinson would often chew his fingernails until they became a bloody mess. He turned his back on one coaching job and was dismissed from another, largely because of the unbearable stress the position placed on him.

But as a player, Robinson was the rock-steady tower of strength for a dynasty, the best defenseman on arguably the greatest team in the history of hockey. That he forged a Hall of Fame career was all the more remarkable considering he did it in perhaps the toughest hockey market in the league and didn't even become a defenseman until he was 18.

Perhaps the most telling testament to Robinson's greatness came in 1984 when a fan vote was held to determine the all-time starting six in Canadiens history. Fans named Jacques Plante in goal, Doug Harvey and Robinson on defense and Rocket Richard, Jean Beliveau and Dickie Moore at forward. All were members of the five-Cup dynasty of 1956-60 with the exception of Robinson, a player who defined his career by being versatile and great at everything.

If you wanted to play a skill game, Robinson certainly wouldn't have looked out of place. If you wanted to impose a shutdown defensive philosophy on the game, Robinson could do that, too. You don't set the all-time career mark for plus-minus with plus-730 (plus-700 in 17 years with the Canadiens) without being an elite defensive defenseman. And if you wanted to play down and dirty, Robinson could do that too. The 6-foot-4, 225-pound son of a dairy farmer was as tough as any player in the league and his beating of notorious Philadelphia enforcer Dave Schultz in the 1976 Stanley Cup

> "Playing in Montreal can do one of two things – it can either make you or break you. For me, it made me."

final is seen as a major turning point, one in which the Flyers realized Robinson and the Canadiens weren't about to be intimidated by the Broad Street Bullies.

The importance of Robinson's handling of both Schultz and Don Saleski in that series, not to mention a thundering bodycheck on Gary Dornhoefer should not be understated. After that, the Flyers never seemed as big or tough and their reign of terror was effectively over.

"With the Schultz thing, it was just coincidental that he was the one who happened to be free when I came out," said Robinson, who played the remainder of the game with Schultz's blood on his sweater. "I had gotten clipped with a stick before that and I was in getting stitched up and they told me the benches had cleared. I ran back and tied my skates and went back on the ice and he was the only one who was free. I saw him going to try to pair up with Guy Lafleur and I didn't really like that situation."

Canadiens goalie Ken Dryden once joked that by the time Robinson became a veteran, all he had to do in order to thwart a fracas was to enter the scrum and wag his finger at the offending player.

The fact of the matter is Robinson should never have been a Canadien in the first place. He was taken 20th overall in the 1971 draft and had been passed over three times before the Canadiens selected him. That year, Guy Lafleur went first overall, but the Canadiens took Chuck Arnason seventh and Murray Wilson 11th overall before settling on Robinson, who had just one season of major junior with the Kitchener Rangers under his belt. But at least the Canadiens got Robinson, unlike the Flyers, Detroit Red Wings, Vancouver Canucks, New York Rangers, Boston Bruins and Buffalo Sabres, who all passed on Robinson twice.

The Canadiens draft in 1971 stands as one of the best ever and marked the first time a team had selected two Hall of Fame players in the same year. Since then, it has been accomplished three more times: twice by the Edmonton Oilers, who picked Mark Messier and Glenn Anderson in 1979, and Paul Coffey and Jari Kurri the following year; and once by the New York Islanders, who chose Bryan Trottier and Clark Gillies in 1974. It's a good bet that 1989 Detroit picks Nicklas Lidstrom and Sergei Fedorov will both be inducted.

Robinson won a Calder Cup with the Nova Scotia Voyageurs in 1972, then won the Stanley Cup as a rookie in 1973, the first of five he would win in his first seven years as an NHLer. Paired with Serge Savard those seven years, they formed two-thirds of 'The Big Three' along with Guy Lapointe and it could easily be argued no team in NHL history has had a better group of top three defensemen.

"They never put you in situations where you might fail," Robinson said of the Canadiens. "They always put you in situations where you learned and you learned by experience or you learned by watching or listening to people who knew what they were doing."

But as the years went by and the Canadiens sagged through parts of the 1980s, it got more difficult to play in Montreal. At one point during the 1982-83 season, Robinson was suffering the wrath of the Montreal faithful and said he would never allow them to chase him out of Montreal the way they did to Savard.

"I have never done anything to anybody," Robinson said at the time. "I haven't said a bad word about the fans. So why me? Why pick on me?"

"I'm not saying it wasn't warranted," Robinson said 25 years later. "I wasn't playing great and we didn't have a very good team, either. Playing in Montreal can do one of two things – it can either make you or break you. For me, it made me because it made me a stronger person and it made me a better person. It brought out the best in me."

Robinson would win one more Cup with the Canadiens in 1986, but his departure from the organization was bitter. A contract dispute with his former defense partner and Canadiens GM Savard prompted Robinson, who was once released from a junior team because he refused to cut his hair, to sign with the Los Angeles Kings in 1989. Savard later accused Robinson of trying to orchestrate the terms of his own sweater retirement.

Robinson's No. 19 was eventually raised to the rafters of the Bell Centre in 2007 and even though Robinson found his comfort level as an assistant coach with the New Jersey Devils, his emotional ties to the Canadiens remained strong.

"If anything, I don't want to be known as a great player," Robinson said. "I want to be known as a great teammate." ●

Steve Babineau/NHLI via Getty Images

Patrick **ROY**

The Messiah of Montreal

Steve Babineau/NHLI via Getty Images

Goaltender	
Born: Oct. 5, 1965, Quebec City, Que.	
Habs Career : 1985-1995	
2 Stanley Cups, 4 first-team all-stars, 2 second-team all-stars, 2 Conn Smythe Trophies, 3 Vezina Trophies, 3 Jennings Trophies	
289-175-66, 2.77 GAA, 29 shutouts	
Hockey Hall of Fame: 2006	

More than two decades after the fact and with the benefit of hindsight, it would certainly make for an interesting barstool conversation. You have the first overall pick in the 1984 entry draft. Who do you take, Mario Lemieux or Patrick Roy?

On the floor of the Montreal Forum on June 9 of that year, it was nothing short of a slam-dunk. Even though the two were born on precisely the same day in the same year in the same province, there could not have been a wider gap between them as NHL prospects. Lemieux was a superstar-in-waiting, coming off a season in which he scored 133 goals and 282 points in major junior. Roy, on the other hand, had given very few indications he would rival Lemieux as an NHL player. In three seasons in the same league, Roy compiled a record of 58-89-3 with a 5.33 goals-against average with the Granby Bisons. He played just four playoff games and lost them all.

Roy would later say it was in Granby he learned to deal with the frustrations of losing. It was also the last time he ever had to really deal with them.

Which is a rather obvious way of saying the Canadiens hardly knew what they were getting when they selected Roy 51st overall that day in a draft that turned out to be an embarrassment of riches since they had already picked Petr Svoboda, Shayne Corson and Stephane Richer prior to taking Roy. (The Canadiens took another goalie that draft, a guy from Verdun named Troy Crosby 240th overall. Three years later, Crosby would sire a son named Sidney.)

They couldn't have possibly known Roy would go on to become the most dominant goalie of his generation and perhaps the greatest of all-time, in large part due to the amazing accomplishments he accrued in 10 seasons in a Canadiens sweater.

"I'm not sure he was the most talented goaltender ever," said former Canadiens' coach Jacques Demers, who rode Roy to a Stanley Cup in 1993. "But I believe he had more desire and was the most competitive goalie who has ever played this game and that's what puts him over the top."

In their 2002 goaltending book *Without Fear,* authors Bob Duff and Kevin Allen rank Roy as the No. 1 goaltender of all-time, not because of his physical tools or athleticism, but because of his mental make-up.

"There is a sense he knows all and sees all in this sport," they wrote. "He has long been able to predict the movements of forwards before they actually occur. He is blessed with a sixth sense for locating the puck in traffic when others can't seem to find it. His focus is panoramic. While some goalkeepers struggle to maintain their concentration on the play, Roy seems to be able to take in every event in the building. His observation skills rival those of a New York City beat cop. Nothing escapes Roy's notice."

When people talk about unbreakable records in the game, a few come to mind. Wayne Gretzky's 2,857 points, Glenn Hall's 502 consecutive games, Bill Mosienko's three goals in 21 seconds are just a few that are surely impenetrable. But what about Roy leading the Montreal Canadiens to 10 overtime victories in the 1993 playoffs? The next best mark in NHL history is seven, which is just one more than the number of overtime wins the Canadiens had on the road that season.

> "They were so happy when the game ended up after three periods tied. They knew they were going to win."
> – Dick Irvin

"They were so happy when the game ended up after three periods tied," former Canadiens broadcaster Dick Irvin once observed. "They knew they were going to win."

Almost all of that knowledge came from the fact Roy was behind them. Prior to Game 4 of the final against the Los Angeles Kings, Roy told his teammates he was only going to give up two goals that night and as long as they scored three, they would win the game. The Canadiens won 3-2 in overtime before putting the finishing touches on the most recent Stanley Cup in franchise history and the last one on The Forum ice two nights later.

Patrick Roy's 10 overtime wins en route to the 1993 Stanley Cup is a record that may never be broken.

"All the Stanley Cups, the MVPs, the wins are good, but I really think his legacy and what will make him the greatest of all-time is winning 10 straight games in overtime in 1993," Demers said. "When we would go into overtime that year, nobody ever asked Patrick how he was doing. Nobody would ever, ever say a word to him. That's how intense his focus was."

But focusing too much on what Roy did in 1993 would be giving short shrift to his accomplishments in 1986, which were just as impressive and also resulted in the Conn Smythe Trophy. One year after coming off the bench as a professional rookie to lead the Sherbrooke Canadiens to the Calder Cup in the American League, Roy was spectacular in the playoffs backstopping the Canadiens to the Stanley Cup. In Game 3 of the Eastern Conference final against the New York Rangers, the Canadiens were outshot 13-2 in overtime, but still won the game on a goal by Claude Lemieux and went on to win the Cup.

"That was one of the greatest goaltending displays I had ever seen," said former Canadien Bobby Smith. "I think then was when we knew we had something special with this player."

But Roy was not all confidence and bravado. Behind the persona, he was one of the greatest technical goalies the game has ever seen. Very early in his career, Roy came to the realization fewer goals were scored high, so a goalie would have more success if he covered up the lower part of the net. It was then he adopted the butterfly style of goaltending that was copied by the hundreds of top-level Quebec goalies Roy's heroics spawned.

Even though Roy was enormously intense during his Montreal days, his career there was largely without the temperamental explosions that marked his tenure in Colorado and later, in his career as a junior hockey executive. The one time he did explode it resulted in his departure from Montreal. Both sides could have handled the situation better, but time has healed most of those wounds to the point where Roy was scheduled to have his No. 33 lifted to the rafters of the Bell Centre in 2008-09.

As of the summer of 2008, the Canadiens had not won, or even come close to winning, the Stanley Cup since the days of Roy. And if not for Roy, their Stanley Cup drought would have been almost 30 years, which would have made The Great Darkness of the 1930s and early '40s look like a minor annoyance.

"Let's face it, it takes an entire team to win a Stanley Cup," Demers said, "but I have a Stanley Cup ring on my finger because of him." ●

Bruce Bennett Studios/Getty Images

Henri **RICHARD**

His Own Man

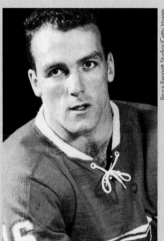

Bruce Bennett Studios/Getty Images

Center
Born: Feb. 29, 1936, Montreal
Habs Career : 1955-1975
11 Stanley Cups, 1 first-team all-star, 3 second-team all-stars, 1 Masterton Trophy
358-688-1,046, 928 PIM in 1,256 games
Hockey Hall of Fame: 1979

At one point during Henri Richard's rookie season of 1955-56, a reporter asked Canadiens coach Toe Blake whether the young Richard spoke any English.

"I don't think he can even speak French," was the reply. "I've never heard him talk."

Richard was so quiet that when his older brother, Maurice, marched him up to GM Frank Selke's office to sign his first contract, Henri left without even knowing his salary.

For the record, it was $7,000 in the first year and $8,000 in the second year.

"Mr. Selke asked Maurice, 'Is Henri ready?' and Maurice said, 'Yes, he's ready,' and he turned around and walked out of the room," Henri Richard said. "I couldn't speak English and they put this paper in front of me and I signed it. I didn't know what I was making, but I didn't care. I just wanted to play."

Such humble beginnings for a player who would carve out a Hall of Fame career even if his name were Joe Blow and his brother were a plumber instead of the greatest player ever to wear the Canadiens uniform. Dealing with the pressure of being Rocket Richard's little brother, Henri Richard instead became his own man and player, never resenting that his brother would always be more revered.

"We'd go places all the time after games and people would see Henri and the first thing they would say was, 'How's Rocket?'" recalled Dickie Moore, who was a linemate of both Richard brothers. "He always answered and was always courteous to people. It never seemed to bother him and he never once lost his patience because of it."

"It's still that way and Maurice has been dead for a few years now," Henri said in 2008. "Just the other day a man introduced me to his son and he said, 'This is Rocket Richard's brother.'"

In some ways, Henri was a superior player to his superstar brother. Rocket was a mercurial and dramatic player, who relied on instinct and reflexes and had a burning passion to score goals. Henri, on the other hand, was guided more by hockey intellect than passion and was a far better two-way player and playmaker.

He was also one of the best-conditioned athletes of his time. Henri Richard was a tireless worker who could skate a three-minute shift and come to the bench without a heaving chest. He always played a lot of tennis in the summer and credited that with his superior cardiovascular stamina.

"(Former Canadiens coach) Toe Blake used to yell at me all the time," Richard said. "He used to give me hell. 'Get off the ice and change!' But I wouldn't change, I think because I just loved playing the game so much."

The one area of the game where Henri usurped his brother was in championships. Henri's 11 Stanley Cups is unmatched by anyone in NHL history and is one of those records that surely will stand the test of time. Only Bill Russell, who won 11 titles with the Boston Celtics dynasty, has as many titles in North American professional sport as Richard.

Melchior DiGiacomo/Getty Images

And to hear Henri tell it, he was actually responsible for a good number of his brother's Stanley Cups.

"In 1955, Maurice had had enough of the game and was going to retire," Henri said, "but he decided to keep playing when he saw I made the team."

The Canadiens won five consecutive titles from 1956 through 1960, giving Henri five championships in his first six NHL seasons. The younger Richard was never a big conversationalist, but he did grow out of his shy demeanor as his career progressed.

> "I couldn't speak English and they put this paper in front of me and I signed it. I just wanted to play."

He became a strong-willed player as well as a fierce competitor. In 1968, Richard didn't show up for a team meeting and was suspended for a game by the Canadiens for challenging the authority of his employers. In 1972, he left the team briefly after a post-game confrontation with teammate Serge Savard resulted in Richard hitting Savard across the face with his open hand.

When Richard was offered a two-year contract worth $200,000 per season by the Houston Aeros of the World Hockey Association, he instead stayed with the Canadiens and was paid $165,000 for his last season.

"I've been happy with the Canadiens through the years," Richard said at the time. "Underpaid, but mostly happy."

But Richard's boldest stance came in the 1971 Stanley Cup final when the Canadiens, who had finished third in the East Division, were in the midst of an unlikely run to the Cup. After being benched for several shifts against the Chicago Black Hawks, Richard described first-year Canadiens coach Al MacNeil as, "the worst coach I've ever played for."

Despite the predictable French-English controversy that emanated from the confrontation, Richard went on to lead the Canadiens to the Cup by scoring both the tying and winning goals in Game 7 of the final.

"I met him (in 2006) and it turns out he was a hell of a good guy," Richard said of MacNeil. "We talked a little bit and he didn't hold anything against me. His wife wouldn't talk to me, though. I guess she was still mad."

Richard never scored more than 30 goals or 80 points in a season, but is remembered as one of the all-time great players. Former Canadiens GM Sam Pollock once said Henri Richard belongs in the same stratosphere as Maurice, Bobby Hull, Jean Beliveau and Bobby Hull. Henri Richard twice led the NHL in assists and made his mark with an all-around game that would have made him a multi-millionaire many years later.

Even though he grew out of his shyness later in his career, Richard was never comfortable being the center of attention. Intense interest was focused on his brother whether he liked it or not, but Henri Richard would not welcome the spotlight. When the Canadiens wanted to hold a Henri Richard Night in 1974, he only agreed to go along with it if the proceeds from the ceremony would go towards building a gymnasium for a local orphanage.

"My father worked 48 years in the Angus (railway) shops," Richard said at the time. "He never missed a day at work in all that time and they never held a night for him." ●

Newsy **LALONDE**

The First Torch Bearer

HHOF Images

Center/Rover
Born: Oct. 31, 1887, Cornwall, Ont.
Died: Nov. 21, 1970
Habs Career : 1912-1922
1 Stanley Cup, 2 Art Ross Trophies
231-62-293, 421 PIM in 179 games
Hockey Hall of Fame: 1950

They stare down from upper reaches of the dressing room, almost as though they are watching over the players, always reminding them of their responsibility to carry on the proud tradition of the Montreal Canadiens. Underneath the pictures of the Canadiens Hall of Famers is the famous line from the John McCrae poem, *In Flanders Fields,* a quotation that has become as synonymous with the Canadiens as it has for those soldiers to whom McCrae was paying tribute.

"To you from failing hands we throw the torch," it says, "be yours to hold it high."

No team in hockey weaves its past into its fabric as well as the Canadiens. That metaphorical torch the Canadiens speak of in hushed tones found its first carrier in Edouard 'Newsy' Lalonde, the franchise's first superstar player and the father of The Flying Frenchmen, even though his status as a Francophone is in doubt.

"In Montreal, they talk about passing the torch," said hockey historian Bob Duff. "Well, this guy ignited the torch."

Like most players at the turn of the century, Lalonde was a gun for hire, a mercenary who would play where the most money was being offered. In Lalonde's case, he actually chased the money as a lacrosse player since he was one of the best of his time. But also like so many others, he found a home with the Canadiens, who were eager to have French Canadians, or at least those with French Canadian names, in their lineup.

The problem was that at the time, hockey was viewed as a sport for the English and few French Quebecers played at a high level. Sports enthusiasts in Montreal were more prone to take part in snowshoeing than hockey, so the Canadiens had to chase their French Canadian talent largely in Ontario. Lalonde was originally from Cornwall, where he earned the nickname Newsy because as a youth he worked at a newsprint plant.

After stops in Cornwall, Woodstock, Sault Ste. Marie, Portage la Prairie, Toronto and Hailebury, Lalonde joined the Canadiens in 1909 and established himself as a star player and scorer immediately. In a time that would have made the pre-lockout Dead Puck Era look compelling by comparison, Lalonde was regularly a 20-plus goal scorer, recording a mind-boggling 37 in 1920 and 33 in 1921. One season, Lalonde scored winning goals in six straight games, a feat that has never been documented since.

"I think he was by far the best player of his era," said hockey historian Eric Zweig. "The other big scorer was Joe Malone who started a little later and lasted a little longer, but his career numbers are like half (of Lalonde's). Cyclone Taylor might have been a better all-round player, but he played mostly defense. Nobody scored near the goals Lalonde scored, but I don't think he backchecked much. That was the style of the game – forwards played forward and defensemen played defense."

Lalonde also possessed a nasty streak that made him downright scary as an opponent. His battles with 'Bad' Joe Hall were legendary in a time when hockey violence was not only accepted, but encouraged. Lalonde and Hall often engaged in vicious stick-swinging duals that left both battered and bloody. Legend has it in one such encounter, Lalonde implored Hall to drop his stick and fight like a man. When Hall complied, Lalonde allegedly kept his stick firmly in hand and used it to wallop Hall over the head.

The two would later become teammates when Hall joined the Canadiens in 1917-18 and they became good friends and roommates on the road.

The year after helping the Canadiens to their first-ever Stanley Cup, Lalonde and the Canadiens traveled to Seattle to defend their title and in the second game of a series the Canadiens would lose, Lalonde had five

> "He had a lot of courage and he scored a lot of goals, but I don't know that he ever backchecked in his life."
>
> – Hockey historian Ernie Fitzsimmons

> "In Montreal, they talk about passing the torch. Well, this guy ignited the torch."
> – Hockey historian Bob Duff

penalties, then was fined $25 for butt-ending the referee during a brawl. Not pleased with a salary that paid much less than he made playing lacrosse, Lalonde held out on the Canadiens twice. He also left the team once as a player-coach because he felt the players weren't following his instructions.

"He was like 'The Rocket' in that he would sometimes let his emotions get the better of him," Duff said.

"He was a guy who was extremely rough and violent," said hockey historian Ernie Fitzsimmons. "He had a lot of courage and he scored a lot of goals, but I don't know that he ever backchecked in his life."

Duff said during one playoff game against the Quebec Bulldogs, Lalonde was so upset that his check got away he slammed the puck into the Montreal net after the player had shot. The only problem was that the player had only hit the post and Lalonde, thinking he had scored, whacked it into his own net in frustration. That goal tied the game, so Lalonde promptly went out and scored the winner – this time on the Quebec net – in overtime.

Lalonde led the Canadiens in scoring six times and led all NHL scorers in 1918-19 and 1920-21. In 1920, he scored six goals in a game against Toronto and established a record that lasted just three weeks, ending when Joe Malone scored seven in a game for Quebec. He likely would have won a third Stanley Cup had the 1919 final not been cancelled due to the death of teammate Joe Hall from influenza. Lalonde was one of several Canadien players who were hospitalized during the outbreak of Spanish influenza, which is said to have taken more lives than World War I.

After a contract squabble with the new owners of the Canadiens in 1922, Lalonde was traded to the Saskatoon Sheiks of the Western Canada Hockey League for the unknown Aurel Joliat and $3,500. Fans in Montreal were outraged, but aside from his contract problem, it looked to many as though Lalonde was slowing down and was being usurped as the No. 1 center by Odie Cleghorn.

The deal turned out to be a boon for both teams. Joliat and Howie Morenz took the torch from Lalonde and carried it to greatness, while Lalonde proved he was far from finished as a player and went on to star in Saskatoon before returning to the NHL to play one game with the New York Americans in 1926.

Three years later, The Great Depression swept away $100,000 in life savings and instead of retiring a rich man, Lalonde found work in a liquor store. But hard times could not keep Lalonde down or take the luster off the earliest spectacular career in Canadiens' history. ●

Dickie **MOORE**

The Proud One

Bruce Bennett Studios/Getty Images

Left Winger
Born: Jan. 6, 1931, Montreal
Habs Career : 1951-1963
6 Stanley Cups, 2 first-team all-stars,
1 second-team all-star,
2 Art Ross Trophies
254-340-594, 575 PIM in 654 games
Hockey Hall of Fame: 1974

When the Montreal Canadiens retired Dickie Moore's No. 12 in 2005, team owner George Gillett presented Moore with a toilet as a gift. It was intended as a harmless joke from Gillett, who thought he was poking some innocent fun at Dickie Moore Rentals, which provides construction companies with everything from washroom facilities to heavy equipment.

Moore was not amused by the gesture and made sure Gillett found out he had been offended. That Gillet, a very rich and powerful man, was honoring Moore by retiring his number did not make up for the fact Moore had been slighted.

"I made sure he got the message," Moore said. "I'm a proud guy. I'm as good as anybody. Don't push me too far."

It was that kind of stubborn resolve that marked Moore's Hall of Fame career and made him one of the greatest two-way left wingers of all-time. Moore was tough and unyielding as a player and has often been described as the heavy lifter on a dynasty of superstars. But that blanket perception does not give enough credit to Moore's hockey talents. An authority no lesser than Maurice Richard said Moore was the best left winger with whom he ever played.

For his part, Moore twice won the NHL's scoring title and his 96 points in 1958-59 was the most recorded in history at the time and would stand as the league's single-season benchmark for seven years. Moore also twice led the Canadiens and the league in playoff points.

> "I'm a proud guy. I'm as good as anybody. Don't push me too far."

But there was a very quiet confidence in Moore, a kid from the working-class Park Extension neighborhood in Montreal. Moore often instructs young players to continually tell themselves they are the best, but never tell anyone else the same thing.

"I used to talk about how lucky I was," Moore said. "If I scored a goal, I was lucky to be in the right place at the right time or I made a play where the goalie went the other way. But today they want you to talk about how good you are. I'll ask you a question. Have you ever seen a good person lose? Of course. But have you ever seen a lucky person lose?"

It's interesting that Moore, given all his accomplishments, would refer to himself as lucky. Shoulder and knee injuries plagued him during much of his playing career; and as a youngster Moore was hit by a car, almost had his lip chewed off by a dog and broke both his legs. Shortly after he retired from the Canadiens, his kneecap was destroyed by a grinding machine and after being told by the doctor it would have to be removed, he begged the doctor not to do it.

"And I still have that kneecap today," Moore said in 2008.

Nothing ever seemed certain for Moore, either. In 1953-54, Moore was not yet a full-time NHLer, but thrived in the playoffs that spring on a line with Jean Beliveau and Bernie Geoffrion. Moore led all NHLers in assists and points that post-season and Beliveau was the top goal-scorer. But when Moore reported for camp the next season, he was told by coach Dick Irvin there was no way he was going to be playing with those linemates again. After that season, Irvin would retire and give way to Toe Blake, who guided the Canadiens to five straight Stanley Cup championships and installed Moore on a line with Rocket Richard.

Moore then carved out a career as one of the most responsible and productive left wingers to ever play the game. Along with his two scoring championships, Moore was named a first-team

Bruce Bennett Studios/Getty Images

all-star twice and a second-teamer once. And if the Selke Trophy for top defensive forward had existed in those days, his name would have likely been on it as often as Bob Gainey's or Guy Carbonneau's.

Moore was nothing if not industrious on and off the ice. The unpredictability of pro hockey and his own insecurity about his place in it prompted Moore to work the off-seasons in construction. And in 1961, behind one of the three Dairy Queen outlets he owned in suburban Montreal, Moore started a company that rented tools and garden equipment such as tillers and lawn mowers. He started the business with a $2,000 loan and the bank later forced Moore to either liquidate the business or find a new lender. He managed to get the money together to keep the business going.

> "I looked at him and said, 'Mr. Selke, I'll tell you one thing. Nobody trades me.' And I stuck my hand out and said, 'Thank you for everything,' and I walked out."

"I picked up the check that morning and threw it at the bank manager and said, 'Give me everything back,'" Moore recalled. "That's how it all started."

But unlike many of the Canadiens' greats of the 1950s, Moore's parting with the franchise was not exactly amicable. After six Stanley Cups in 12 seasons, Moore was called into GM Frank Selke's office in training camp in 1963 to discuss a trade. Thinking he was being unfairly blamed for the Canadiens first-round ouster to the Toronto Maple Leafs the previous season, Moore was indignant. But he also knew the Canadiens were trying to replace him with a less expensive rookie, the way Moore displaced Bert Olmstead on the Canadiens roster 12 years before.

"I looked at him and said, 'Mr. Selke, I'll tell you one thing. Nobody trades me,'" Moore said. "And I stuck my hand out and said, 'Thank you for everything,' and I walked out."

Moore made two comebacks, with the Maple Leafs in 1965 and the St. Louis Blues in 1968, where he scored 14 points in 16 games before the Blues lost the Stanley Cup final to the Canadiens.

Much of his life has been charmed, but Moore has also had to deal with horrible tragedy. The worst came in 1973 when his beloved son, Richard Jr., was killed in a car accident at the age of 16.

"He was so clever. He put together my parts department when he was 13," Moore said. "He sat at my desk when he was 15 and said, 'Dad, I'm going to take this company right across the country.' He never had the chance." ●

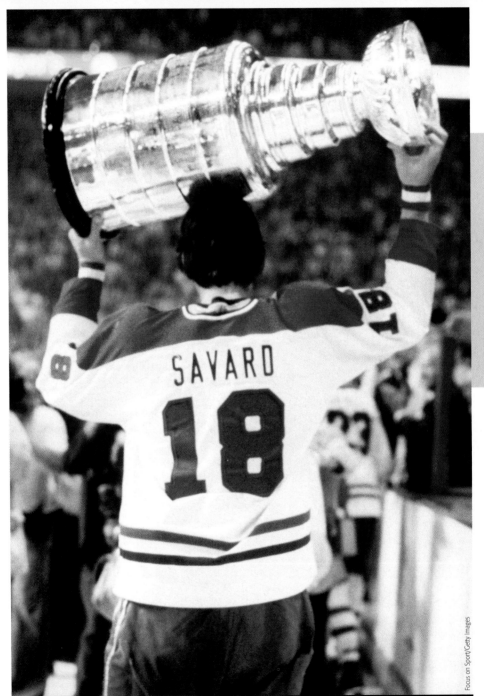

Serge Savard has won more Stanley Cups than any defenseman in NHL history, including this one in 1979.

Focus on Sport/Getty Images

Serge **SAVARD**

The Great Galoot

Steve Babineau/NHLI via Getty Images

Defenseman
Born: Jan. 22, 1946, Montreal, Que.
Habs Career : 1966-1981
8 Stanley Cups, 1 second-team all-star, 1 Conn Smythe Trophy, 1 Masterton Trophy
100-312-412, 537 PIM in 917 games
Hockey Hall of Fame: 1986

No defenseman in the history of the Canadiens, or any other team for that matter, has won as many Stanley Cups as the eight gathered by Serge Savard. But if not for his persistence in the face of the organization's ambivalence, Savard might have been exiled to mediocrity in Detroit.

The Canadiens managed to get Savard into their fold in 1961 when he was just 15. He was almost six feet tall when he was 11 and by the time he caught the Canadiens' eye he was 6-foot-3 and 200 pounds. That year, Cliff Fletcher was running youth hockey in Quebec for the Canadiens and moved Savard from his team in Amos to a midget team in Rosemont in Montreal.

Things did not start well.

"After a while, the Rosemont coach told me he knew how he could save the organization a lot of money," Fletcher remembered years later. " 'Send this big, clumsy galoot back to Amos. He can't play.' "

A couple years later, Savard showed up for training camp with the Montreal Jr. Canadiens only to discover the organization had essentially forgotten about him. Luckily for the Canadiens, Savard didn't take the snub personally and in an even more fortuitous stroke of luck, ignored the overtures the Detroit Red Wings were making.

That Savard emerged from such humble beginnings to become the greatest defensive defenseman in franchise history is a testament to his talent. But to do so after suffering two career-threatening breaks in his left leg less than a year apart is a testament to his drive, determination and on-ice intellect.

The first occurred in March, 1970, when he crashed into a goalpost trying to strip the puck from Rod Gilbert. Savard dived for the puck and his left leg doubled under him. He suffered five separate fractures, underwent three operations and was immobilized for three months. The second occurred in February, 1971, when he crumpled to the ice after being hit by Bob Baun. This time, surgeons took a piece of bone from his right hip for a graft to the tibia.

To that point in his career, Savard was establishing himself as an offensive defenseman, but the days of headlong rushes up the ice ended for him shortly after his 25th birthday.

"I don't think I ever recovered 100 per cent," Savard said. "I didn't take as many chances and I really became a defensive defenseman. I think, too, it forced me to become a smarter player."

It also helped that Savard played most of his career with Larry Robinson, a tandem he said "fit together like a pair of gloves." Robinson's forays up the ice were always executed with the knowledge Savard was watching his back. In fact, there were years Robinson won the Norris Trophy and acknowledged Savard should have been the winner.

One thing the injuries did not do was prevent Savard from perfecting his signature move in which he would use his big body to protect the puck and spin around to avoid forecheckers. Canadiens' broadcaster Danny Gallivan coined the term 'The Savardian Spin-a-rama,' after taking a walk in Los Angeles one day and seeing a plethora of stores and businesses that ended with "a-rama."

"Doug Harvey was great at it, but I don't think he did it as often as I did," Savard said. "For me, it was natural. I did it right at the last split second when the guy was almost on me. I used to do it all the time in practice with Rejean Houle and even he didn't know what I was doing. I was always able to keep the puck because it was not in my feet."

> "Doug Harvey was great at (the spin-a-rama), but I don't think he did it as often as I did."

With the exception of becoming the first defenseman to win the Conn Smythe Trophy when he was named MVP of the playoffs in 1969, Savard's career was generally bereft of individual awards. It seems amazing now Savard was a postseason all-star just once in his career, when he was named to the second team in 1979.

Of all his on-ice exploits, however, Savard is most proud of playing for Team Canada in the 1972 Summit Series. His leg was just healing from the second break when John Ferguson, who had

> ## "I'm proud of what I did as a player, but I'm also proud of what I did as a GM."

lost defensemen Bobby Orr, J-C Tremblay and Jacques Laperriere due to various circumstances, invited Savard to camp. Savard was a standout for the team, appearing in five games, none of them losses.

Another thing that set Savard apart was his passion for business and politics away from the rink. His father, Laurent, was an entrepreneur and the mayor of the village of Landrienne. A keen student before he played in the NHL, Savard used his idle summers to establish his business career. At one time, he had exclusive distribution rights of Loto-Quebec tickets in three areas of Quebec. He later owned a 132-unit apartment complex in Longueuil, had a minority interest in a resort in Cuba and established a company in which he invested all his fees from public appearances.

"When I was about 22, I got very interested in real estate," Savard said. "I looked at it in a very simple way. If I had a 20-year mortgage, I looked at it like putting money in the bank for 20 years."

While most of his teammates would rifle through the sports pages in hotel lobbies on the road, Savard could be found reading *The Wall Street Journal*.

Melchior DiGiacomo/Getty Images

"We are a new generation of athletes," Savard once told legendary Montreal hockey writer Rejean Tremblay. "We will not be content to become former idols with no future."

As Savard got older and his game began to deteriorate, fans in Montreal turned on him. He was often booed mercilessly at home and made the decision to retire at 35 in the summer of 1981 when he was jeered after showing up for an arena dedication to Houle in Rouyn-Noranda. Ferguson, who was then GM of the Winnipeg Jets, lured Savard out of retirement and he played two more years.

As soon as he retired for good, Savard was named GM of the Canadiens and served for 12 years, putting together Cup-winning teams in 1986 and 1993 under circumstances that were much more challenging than his Cup-winning predecessors.

"I'm proud of what I did as a player," Savard said, "but I'm also proud of what I did as a GM." ●

Yale Joel//Time Life Pictures/Getty Images

13

Bernie **GEOFFRION**

Superstar Talent, Second Banana Status

Right Winger
Born: Feb. 16, 1931, Montreal
Died: March 11, 2006
Habs Career : 1950-1964
6 Stanley Cups, 1 first-team all-star,
2 second-team all-stars, 1 Hart Trophy,
1 Calder Trophy, 2 Art Ross Trophies
371-388-759, 636 PIM in 766 games
Hockey Hall of Fame: 1972

Bruce Bennett Studios/Getty Images

One day after practice late in his career, Bernie 'Boom-Boom' Geoffrion limped up the stairs of his home, only to have his young son, Robert, ask why he continued to play.

"I love it son," he told the boy. "It's like a woman crawling back to a man who beats her. But sometimes I wish I didn't have to take that awful beating."

On any other team in the league, Geoffrion would have been the focal point and the most feted player of his era, but he happened to play on the same team as Rocket Richard, and later Jean Beliveau. No matter what Geoffrion did, he could never measure up to Richard and when he did do anything to usurp the Rocket, it was met with derision and resentment by The Forum faithful.

In fact, Geoffrion has been likened at times to Roger Maris, whose pursuit of Babe Ruth's single-season home run record in 1961 earned him little more than the ire of Ruth loyalists. ("You know what I have to show for 61 home runs? Nothing. Exactly nothing," Maris once said.)

Geoffrion received much the same treatment as Maris six years earlier when he won the scoring championship at the expense of Richard, who had been suspended the remainder of the regular season and the playoffs for striking an official. Some fans pleaded with Geoffrion not to pass Richard and others threatened him, but Geoffrion did not apologize for putting up a better season than their hero.

Bernie 'Boom Boom' Geoffrion, (No. 5), has been compared to baseball's Roger Maris.

Bruce Bennett Studios/Getty Images

In fact, even after Richard retired, there seemed to be a coldness between the two. Geoffrion once told a reporter he didn't receive as much as a phone call from Richard when he scored 50 goals in 1961, which he found odd since Richard apparently sent Bobby Hull a congratulatory telegram after Hull scored 50 the next season.

After his career, Richard was also quoted as saying Geoffrion was short on desire, which elicited this response from Geoffrion: "Ever since I was a kid, there was only one hockey player for me. Always he was my idol. When (Richard) says these things about the Boomer, it does not change anything. He was always the greatest with me. But I am disappointed…very disappointed. There is nothing more to say."

That Geoffrion was an outstanding player in his own right is beyond dispute. He acquired his nickname, which was shortened simply to 'Boom' later in life, by reporter Charlie Boire of the Montreal *Star* while Geoffrion was playing junior hockey for the Laval Nationale in the late 1940s.

And it didn't take Geoffrion long to use his booming shot to make an impact on the game. In his first full season in the league in 1951-52, for which he earned the Calder Trophy as top rookie, Geoffrion scored 30 goals playing right wing on a line with Beliveau at center and Dickie Moore at left wing. It was a mark that had never been attained before by a freshman and stood as a record for rookies until after the league expanded to 12 teams.

That prompted Canadiens' coach Dick Irvin to predict great things for Geoffrion and created, perhaps, unrealistic expectations.

> ## "Someday that kid is going to become one of the game's greatest."
> ## – Dick Irvin

"Someday that kid is going to become one of the game's greatest," Irvin told The Hockey News. "He can score goals with the best in the league and he's got a shot that rates above Charlie Conacher's. When Maurice Richard hangs up his skates, that youngster will take over as the greatest player in the NHL. Already he's scoring goals that veterans of 10 years have been unable to do."

But as productive as Geoffrion was, he was prone to long slumps that seemed to affect almost all aspects of his life. Geoffrion had a terrific voice and once sang on a CBC television variety show and when he would get down, his wife would put him in a chair and have him listen to Mario Lanza records.

But Geoffrion certainly took his scoring droughts to heart. He was, in the words of one sportswriter, "one of those finely tuned athletes whose moods rise and fall with the content of the fine print on the Canadiens' scoring summary."

In 1961, Geoffrion told Milt Dunnell of The Toronto *Star:* "When goals don't come, there is no song. That is a mistake, I know, but how can I sing when I am not happy?"

Geoffrion suffered a number of disappointments over the course of his career. After supporting Doug Harvey to succeed Richard as captain in 1960, Geoffrion wanted to be captain when Harvey was traded the next season. A vote among Geoffrion, Beliveau, Moore and Tom Johnson resulted in a tie between Geoffrion and Beliveau. Coach Toe Blake ordered another vote and Beliveau won easily.

In 1957-58, Geoffrion collided with teammate Andre Pronovost in practice and ruptured his bowel on the left side of his abdomen so badly that he called for a priest to be by his bedside. But weeks later he was back in the playoffs for another Canadiens Stanley Cup run.

One of the few scoring stars of the team that won five consecutive Cups not to finish his career as a Canadien – he retired in 1964 but made a comeback with the Rangers two years later – Geoffrion succeeded Scotty Bowman as coach of the Canadiens in 1979, but stepped down 30 games into the season after clashing with management.

More than 40 years after his career with the Canadiens ended, his No. 5 was finally raised to the rafters of the Bell Centre, alongside the No. 7 worn by Howie Morenz, the father of Geoffrion's wife, Marlene. Geoffrion's son, Dan, would later briefly play for the Canadiens. Dan's son, Blake, was a second-round pick of the Nashville Predators in 2006, creating the possibility of four generations of NHL players.

Sadly, Geoffrion died of stomach cancer March 12, 2006, hours before his number was raised to the rafters.

"This is the realization of Dad's dream and brings closure to his career," Dan Geoffrion told the crowd. "I know Dad wanted to celebrate it with all of you." ●

Bruce Bennett Studios/Getty Images

Ken **DRYDEN**

Not So Different After All

Goaltender
Born: Aug. 8, 1947, Hamilton, Ont.
Habs Career : 1970-1979
6 Stanley Cups, 5 first-team all-stars,
1 second-team all-star, 1 Conn Smythe
Trophy, 1 Calder Trophy, 5 Vezina Trophies
258-57-74, 2.24 GAA, 46 shutouts
Hockey Hall of Fame: 1983

It turns out Ken Dryden had us fooled all that time. Right down to how he leaned on his stick, Dryden always led us to believe he was so ridiculously composed, so intellectual in his approach to the game, so above it all.

Nothing could have been further from the truth. Former teammate Pierre Bouchard once compared Dryden to a duck, a creature that appears to be calm and serene above the surface, but one whose legs are furiously pedaling underwater in an effort to remain upright and buoyant.

It's not a comparison with which Dryden disagrees.

"Most of the time," Dryden said, "you're just trying to survive."

Dryden did so much more than that in eight off-the-charts seasons with the Canadiens, only two of which he didn't finish by attending a Stanley Cup celebration. The other season he became one of the first players in history to hold out when he felt he deserved more than the $90,000 he was making for the Canadiens. Instead, he went to a Montreal law firm and articled for $125 a week in 1973-74 and Canadiens GM Sam Pollock later admitted he made a mistake in not renegotiating Dryden's deal.

And it all started so innocuously for both Dryden and the Habs. In fact, Dryden was well into his career before he learned he actually wasn't drafted by the Canadiens in the first place. He thought he had been because that's what he was told by the manager of his Jr. B team. But what the 17-year-

> "Most of the time, you're just trying to survive."

old Dryden didn't know was he had actually been selected by the Boston Bruins 14th overall in 1964 and was immediately traded to the Canadiens along with the second overall pick, Alex Campbell. In exchange, Boston received defenseman Guy Allen, whom the Canadiens took 12th overall, and Paul Reid, whom the Canadiens had picked 18th.

And had the Canadian national team not disbanded, Dryden wouldn't have signed with the Canadiens minor league team in 1970-71 and wouldn't have been called up for the last couple weeks of the season.

With three games remaining in the campaign, the Canadiens were already locked into a first-round playoff match-up with the Boston Bruins and speculation was swirling around which goalie would start the playoffs for the Canadiens – Phil Myre, Rogie Vachon or the 23-year-old unflappable goaltender who was studying law at McGill University.

Teammate Pete Mahovlich said during one of Dryden's first practices, he and John Ferguson looked at each other and said, "He's got to be the guy." The two took Dryden out for lunch later that day and told him they thought he should be their goalie through the playoffs.

"I was just over the moon," Dryden said.

Two of the last three games that season were against the Bruins, with one against the New York Rangers sandwiched between them. Coach Al MacNeil gave the first Boston game to Vachon and the second, the last game of the season, to Myre. Dryden got the Ranger game and assumed he was the odd man out.

"After (MacNeil) told us about the arrangement, he pulled me aside and said, 'Look, don't read anything into this. I'm working on something,'" Dryden said.

Both Vachon and Myre were dismantled by the high-powered Bruins and Dryden won his game handily against the Rangers. MacNeil installed Dryden as his goalie and Dryden rewarded him by stopping the Bruins, one of the most dominating offensive teams in the game's history, in the first round in seven games.

Steve Babineau/NHLI via Getty Images

> "Ken hated to let a goal in, even during practice. If you scored on Ken in practice, you knew you earned it."
>
> – Yvan Cournoyer

His dominance continued in a six-game triumph over Minnesota in the second round and a seven-game victory over the Chicago Blackhawks in the Stanley Cup final, which earned him his only Conn Smythe Trophy as playoff MVP.

Years of brilliance would follow with Dryden backstopping perhaps the most complete and least flawed team in the history of the game. In his eight seasons with the Canadiens, he earned five first-team all-star berths and one second-team berth and either won or shared five Vezina Trophies.

"Ken hated to let a goal in, even during practice," said teammate Yvan Cournoyer. "If you scored on Ken in practice, you knew you earned it."

Through it all, Dryden could never really shake the perception he was different from those around him. He never saw it that way. He was just as close to a hard-living extrovert as Peter Mahovlich as he was to Bill Nyrop, a graduate of Notre Dame whose father served under President Truman and was chairman of the board of Northwest Airlines.

"I get that question a lot and I never quite have been able to understand where it comes from," Dryden said. "So much of what we did was the same. I grew up idolizing the same players as they did. I wanted to live that dream just as badly as they did. There was about a five per cent difference between me and Pete Mahovlich."

But there was no disputing the fact Dryden separated himself from his peers, even in the 1970s, simply because he was not beholden to an NHL career the way many of them were. That's essentially why he retired after Montreal's run of four straight Stanley Cups. He went on to become an acclaimed author, president of the Toronto Maple Leafs and an elected member of the Canadian parliament.

But for those eight seasons, Dryden held the torch of excellence very high. As good as he was and as outstanding as his teammates were, Dryden has a clear explanation why he and his teammates were able to remain grounded in reality while so many others were granting them rarified status.

The way Dryden figures, it had a lot to do with the faces of the Hall of Famers who adorn the Canadiens dressing room and look down upon the players every time they get ready to play. There's something humbling, he said, about living up to the legends that were set by the players before them.

"It was the same for all of us. No matter what he did, Guy Lafleur could never been Jean Beliveau or Rocket Richard. Larry Robinson could never be Doug Harvey and I could never be Jacques Plante," Dryden said. "You're just not good enough. You will never be good enough to be them." ●

Bruce Bennett Studios/Getty Images

Yvan Cournoyer wasn't just lightning fast, he could control the puck at top speed and had a knack for finding the net.

Yvan **COURNOYER**

Beep-Beep!

Melchior DiGiacomo/Getty Images

Right Winger
Born: Nov. 22, 1943, Drummondville, Que.
Habs Career : 1963-1979
10 Stanley Cups, 4 second-team all-stars,
1 Conn Smythe Trophy
428-435-863, 255 PIM in 968 games
Hockey Hall of Fame: 1982

When Yvan Cournoyer was 14, his father bought a machine shop in Lachine and moved his family from Drummondville to the Montreal suburb.

It was there Cournoyer thought he was carving his own path as a machinist, but it turned out he was forging his future in the NHL. It was while working part-time in that shop Cournoyer made 10 steel pucks ranging in weight from 16 to 18 ounces. (A standard pucks weighs 5.5 to six ounces.)

"I would go to the garage every day and I would shoot 10 left, 10 right and 10 backhand…10 left, 10 right, 10 backhand…I would just keep doing that," Cournoyer said. "When I used a real puck, it felt like nothing to me. That's how I learned to shoot both ways. And it was really good for my legs and wrists."

The move to Montreal allowed Cournoyer to blossom. Not only did his hockey career flourish, Cournoyer played a number of other sports, among them football. His English wasn't strong enough for him to be involved in intricate offensive plays, so his team made the 5-foot-7, 165-pounder into a linebacker.

"I liked the body contact, but it was a difficult way to learn English," Cournoyer told *Sport* magazine in 1973. "If I had to do it over again, I would go to Berlitz."

The obvious calling card for Cournoyer was his speed – at the height of his career he reckoned he could skate 50 miles per hour – but what made that speed so lethal was Cournoyer's ability to control the puck at top speed and his unwillingness to allow anyone to separate him from it.

Think Alexander Mogilny.

As a young man, Cournoyer had to have his pants tailor-made because his legs were so big. The wide trunk and big legs came early in life, the result of shoveling wet, heavy snow off the outdoor rink in Drummondville and later, from working three summers delivering beer for Labatt's.

"That was kind of illegal because I was underage," Cournoyer said. "But if they wanted to know how old I really was, all they had to do was check where I was playing hockey."

For the better part of the first four years of his NHL career, Cournoyer would win three of his 10 Stanley Cups as a part-time player. Canadiens coach Toe Blake, who demanded all his players have a two-way element to their game, had almost no trust in Cournoyer's ability to backcheck, so he played Cournoyer almost exclusively on the power play.

Crowds at the Forum would often chant, "On veut Cournoyer!" (We want Cournoyer), but aside from the power play and the occasional shift with Jean Beliveau at center and John Ferguson at left wing, Cournoyer found himself watching a lot of hockey from the bench.

"I played with Jean Beliveau in those days and I would tell him, 'Hey Jean, let's not score in the first minute, let's wait until the second minute,' " Cournoyer said. "That way I would get more ice time."

It was then Cournoyer also established himself as a clutch scorer. He scored just 18 goals in 1965-66, but 16 of them were goals that tied the game, put the Canadiens ahead or were the first goal of the game.

But when Blake retired and was replaced by Claude Ruel, Cournoyer exploded for 43 goals in 1967-68, the first of his four 40-goal seasons. The Cups kept coming and Cournoyer turned in his most dominant playoff performance in the 1973 post-season.

Despite playing with pulled stomach muscles, he set a playoff record with 15 goals, including the Cup-winner in Game 7 against the Chicago Black Hawks. Cournoyer was heading back on defense when Jacques Lemaire stole the puck at the Chicago blueline, his shot hit the glass and bounced out into the slot, by which time Cournoyer had turned around and caught up to it before knocking it past Chicago goalie Tony Esposito.

The Black Hawks, and much of the rest of the league for that matter, had almost no response for Cournoyer's speed. After the 1971 season when Beliveau retired, Cournoyer was desperate to prove he could thrive without Beliveau's

> "I always said the best day in my life was when I signed with the Canadiens and the worst day in my life was when I had to retire."

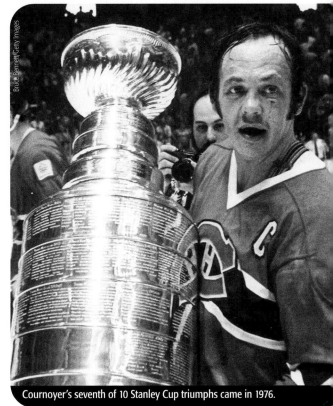

Cournoyer's seventh of 10 Stanley Cup triumphs came in 1976.

help and despite playing with two rookies who struggled in Guy Lafleur and Steve Shutt, scored a career-high 47 goals in 1971-72.

The speed that earned Cournoyer the nickname 'Roadrunner' was something to behold through the early 1970s.

"I went out a few times during the playoffs and it felt like I was flying out of my body," Cournoyer told *Sport* magazine after the 1973 playoffs. "I don't skate at top speed that often because I would lose the element of surprise and wear myself out...I have never lost a race – and I've been challenged a lot – but I've never been timed. I hear a stopwatch wouldn't be fast enough. It would be fun to have a series of races for television with electronic timers. I would take on all comers."

Cournoyer continued to thrive and was named captain of the Canadiens after Henri Richard retired in 1975. He went on to win four more Cups with the Canadiens to bring his total to 10, just one fewer than Richard and the same number as Beliveau.

But what Cournoyer thought was a pulled muscle in his leg turned out to be a serious disc problem in his back that required two major surgeries before ending his career in 1979 at the age of 35. Despite playing only 15 regular season games and none in the playoffs in his final season, Cournoyer received special dispensation from the league to have his name placed on the Stanley Cup for the 10th time in his career.

Retirement did not come easily for Cournoyer, who was bitter the Canadiens apparently asked him to quit after his first surgery in 1978.

"It took me a good five years before I was able to accept my retirement," Cournoyer said. "I always said the best day in my life was when I signed with the Canadiens and the worst day in my life was when I had to retire. But it's hard enough to play the game when you're healthy – it's almost impossible to play it in that kind of pain." ●

Bruce Bennett Studios/Getty Images

Bill Durnan won the Vezina Trophy six times during his seven years with the Habs.

Bill **DURNAN**

Perfection or Bust

Goaltender
Born: Jan. 22, 1916, Toronto, Ont.
Died: Oct. 31, 1972
Habs Career : 1943-1950
2 Stanley Cups, 6 first-team all-stars,
6 Vezina Trophies
208-112-62, 2.36 GAA, 34 shutouts
Hockey Hall of Fame: 1964

Bruce Bennett Studios/Getty Images

Among the pantheon of legendary men who have played goal for the Montreal Canadiens over the years, two stand out as enigmas.

Both emerged as NHL stars later than most and showed few signs they would ever develop into dominant players before joining the Canadiens, both had Supernovae careers chock full of individual honors and Stanley Cups that were spectacular and short and both left the Canadiens never to return while still at the top of their professions. Both were odd by hockey standards and difficult to decipher and both were considered something of loners among their peers.

One of them is Ken Dryden and the other is Bill Durnan. It's little wonder, then, that although their careers were more than two decades apart, they are mirror images of one another.

"(Durnan) and Dryden, to me, are almost the same player," said hockey historian Ernie Fitzsimmons.

And if other teams had been as sharp at spotting talent as the Canadiens were, both would have forged their Hall of Fame careers for other teams. Dryden was originally drafted by the Boston Bruins in 1964, but was immediately traded to the Canadiens. Durnan, a native of Toronto, was originally property of the Maple Leafs, but was let go after he was injured.

Durnan once said the idea of playing in the NHL after being released by the Leafs, "was about as far from my mind as swimming on Mars."

> "He was just an ultra-perfectionist. He was driven by the need for perfection and I think that's probably what destroyed him."
> – Bob Duff

In fact, Durnan only began to emerge as a goaltending talent when he went to Kirkland Lake, Ont., during the 1930s to play softball. Durnan was one of the best softball pitchers in the province and during the Depression, northern Ontario mining towns provided good jobs to talented athletes who were willing to play for the company team. That's how Durnan hooked up with the Kirkland Lake Blue Devils to play hockey in the winter and it was there he established himself as a top senior amateur goalie. At 24, Durnan led the Blue Devils to the 1940 Allan Cup, then played three more years of senior hockey with the Montreal Royals before reluctantly signing with the Canadiens in 1943, becoming an NHL rookie at 28.

But even then, there was no indication Durnan would join the Canadiens and not only own their net, but emerge as the top goaltender in the league.

"The year before he went to the Canadiens, he led the Quebec Senior League in losses," Fitzsimmons said. "Really, he didn't show any signs he was going to be this major superstar."

In just seven seasons with the Canadiens, Durnan was both dominant and brilliant. He won the Vezina Trophy six times and was a first-team all-star six times. But for all his accomplishments during the regular season, Durnan won only two Stanley Cups with the Canadiens and in four of his seven seasons the Canadiens failed to get out of the first round of the playoffs.

"The two great goalies of that era were him and (Turk) Broda (of the Maple Leafs)," said hockey historian Bob Duff. "You look at their numbers and Durnan had the great regular seasons and Broda had the great playoffs. The knock against (Durnan) has always been that Broda was the money goaltender."

Durnan stands out for a host of other reasons, not the least of which was that he was the only known ambidextrous goalie in NHL history and he served as captain of the Canadiens in 1946-47. Durnan's ability to catch with either hand was honed when he played in a church league in Toronto as a youngster and was encouraged by a coach who felt Durnan could be more effective playing that way. Durnan said at first switching from hand to hand made his stick feel like a telephone pole, but got easier as he continued to do it. In the NHL, Durnan would often switch hands depending upon which way his opponent was shooting, leaving his catching hand for the big part of the net. In fact, he had his gloves tailor made so he could catch with either hand. On one occasion Gordie Howe had as breakaway and Durnan switched hands, only to have Howe switch hands and score.

Perhaps bearing the scars of being dumped by the Leafs early in his career, Durnan was plagued by self-doubt. He would often prepare for a game by getting dressed by himself in a space adjacent to the Canadiens dressing room and frequently struggled with the stress of playing in the NHL. That was exacerbated when The Forum faithful booed him.

"Durnan's personality in some ways reminds me of (Terry) Sawchuk because he didn't seem to think he was that good," Duff said. "He was just an ultra-perfectionist. He was driven by the need for perfection and I think that's probably what destroyed him. Numbers that would have been satisfactory for most goalies weren't good enough for him. I think the Vezina became an obsession for him, too. He had to win the Vezina."

Durnan, shaking hands here with Toronto's Turk Broda, was given the captain's 'C' in 1946-47.

Things came to a head for Durnan in the playoffs in 1950 when he pulled himself from the Canadiens first-round series against the New York Rangers with the Canadiens down 3-1. It was then he decided to retire from hockey for good. He was just 34. Durnan said later hockey started to become difficult for him in the late 1940s. He had broken his hand at one point and suffered badly from the pain it caused.

Durnan would later say he retired from hockey mainly because of the injuries and because the money wasn't that good, but also told THN, "My nerves are shot and I know it. It got so bad that I couldn't sleep the night before a game. I couldn't even keep my meals down. I felt that nothing was worth that kind of agony."

Durnan's depature created an opening for Gerry McNeil, the next in a long line of great Canadien goaltenders.

"A lot of people thought it was a nervous breakdown, but it wasn't," Durnan later told an interviewer about his retirement. "To this day, people still won't believe me." ●

Frank Prazak HHOF Images

Elmer **LACH**

A 'Rocket' Launcher

Bruce Bennett Studios/Getty Images

Center
Born: Jan. 22, 1918, Nokomis, Sask.
Habs Career : 1940-1954
3 Stanley Cups, 3 first-team all-stars,
2 second-team all-stars, 1 Hart Trophy,
1 Art Ross Trophy
215-408-623, 478 PIM in 664 games
Hockey Hall of Fame: 1966

One of the enduring conceptions surrounding the Canadiens is much of their pre-expansion success could be attributed to their unfettered access to every player born in the Montreal area.

And while that might have been true for the 1950s dynasty team that featured a roster more than 70 per cent Quebec-born, it didn't apply to the Canadiens teams of the 1940s and early '50s. Of the 22 players who were on Montreal's Cup-winning teams in 1944 and '46, only 11 were Quebec-born players. Of the 22 who were on the 1953 Cup winner, just 10 were from Quebec.

In those days, the Canadiens had to beat the bushes for players just as hard as everyone else and arguably the greatest one they found during the era was smooth-skating and slick-passing fellow from Nokomis, Sask., by the name of Elmer Lach. (The only serious challenge would come from Toronto native Bill Durnan.)

To hear it from Lach, who in the spring of 2008 became the oldest living former Canadien after the death of 94-year-old Ray Getliffe, the move to Montreal almost never happened. That's because Lach was enjoying life in Moose Jaw too much to worry about the NHL. He had a good job in the late 1930s as a meter reader for National Light, Heat and Power and was playing senior hockey for the Moose Jaw Millers in the winter and baseball in the summer.

In fact, Lach had already turned down a tryout with the New York Rangers when Paul Haynes, who was injured and dispatched on a scouting mission to western Canada, spoke to Lach about trying out for the Canadiens.

"I didn't pay much attention to it because I had a good job in Moose Jaw and I was happy," Lach said. "I talked to the management in Moose Jaw and they said, 'Why not go, Elmer? You won't be able to skate in Moose Jaw until it gets cold enough that the river freezes.' "

Lach went to the Canadiens' camp in 1940 and, as it turned out, hell would have frozen over before they would let him go back. Lach ultimately developed into one of the greatest and most courageous playmaking centers of his era and the centerpiece and defensive conscience of one of hockey's greatest all-time lines – The Punch Line with Toe Blake at left wing and Rocket Richard on the right.

Consider that when Richard turned in the most spectacular performance of his career by scoring 50 goals in 50 games in 1945, it was Lach who was named the winner of the Hart Trophy as MVP, not Richard. Although Lach is quick to defer to his more famous linemate for most of his success, it's clear Richard would not have had the early fortune he had if not for Lach.

"I've always said, Rocket Richard put me in the Hall of Fame," Lach said. "If he hadn't scored the goals, I would have never got the points."

> "He's been out, had bones broken, he's been bloody and half dead, but he's never quit. That's what makes him the greatest centerman that ever came into this league."
> – Dick Irvin

Lach was sometimes referred to as a "wartime player" – a derogatory term for a player who put up his best seasons when many of the other top players in the league were fighting in World War II. And while it's true Lach had by far his two best offensive seasons in 1943-44 and '44-45, he won the scoring championship in 1948 and earned two first-team all-star berths after the war.

And anyone who questioned his courage never witnessed the injuries he endured. Lach had his nose broken seven times, won the scoring title the season after suffering a fractured skull, suffered such a badly broken arm he was turned down for military service and suffered a badly broken jaw in 1948-49 that limited him to 31 games.

It's no coincidence Richard endured one of the worst offensive seasons of his career without his playmaking center that season.

> "I've always said, Rocket Richard put me in the Hall of Fame. If he hadn't scored the goals, I would have never got the points."

In fact, Lach had such a penchant for getting injured, the front page of The Hockey News on Feb. 2, 1952 featured a cartoon of a scrum of players with a head emerging from the fracas and sliding along the ice and the referee saying, "Oh-oh, there goes Elmer, hurt again."

"Year in, year out, that guy has been climbing over the boards to get into the play," former Canadiens coach Dick Irvin told THN in 1953. "I've never heard a peep out of him as far as beefs go. He's been out, had bones broken, he's been bloody and half dead, but he's never quit. That's what makes him the greatest centerman that ever came into this league."

And for a short time he was the greatest offensive player ever in the league. In 1952-53, Lach scored his 549th point to pass Bill Cowley for No. 1 on the NHL's all-time scoring list, only to be later usurped by Richard.

But it was Lach's all-round game that made him such an outstanding player. His passing and scoring skills were well-documented, but he also played both ends of the ice equally effectively and was a pioneer of the quick transition game, gaining the puck in the neutral zone and getting it up to the blazing Richard, who had already turned towards the offensive zone.

"We played our system to a 'T' and that's why we were so successful," Lach said.

Lach retired in 1954, two years before the Canadiens dynasty of five straight Cups, but not before winning three Cups of his own and bridging the gap and helping the Canadiens get back to respectability after falling on extremely hard times in the 1930s and early '40s.

At 90, Lach said he still follows hockey and is a particularly avid fan of Sidney Crosby, a player who reminds Lach a little of himself sometimes.

"He's really aggressive, just like the way I was, I guess," Lach said, "but sometimes I think I might have been a little too aggressive."

Lach said he personally responds to the dozen or more autograph requests he receives a day, but now only sends back those that come with a self-addressed and stamped envelope. The Canadiens keep him stocked with an unlimited supply of hockey cards just for that purpose.

He also tries to get out golfing three or four times a week, but his game isn't quite as good as it was when he was a four handicap in the years following his retirement when he worked in public relations for a trucking company and would entertain clients on the golf course.

"I'm trying to shoot my age, but it's not going very well," he said. "It will get easier in a couple of years." ●

Bruce Bennett Studios/Getty Images

Aurel **JOLIAT**

Little Man, Big Legend

Bruce Bennett Studios/Getty Images

Left Winger	
Born: Aug. 29, 1901, Ottawa, Ont.	
Died: Jan. 2, 1986	
Habs Career : 1922-1938	
3 Stanley Cups, 1 first-team all-star,	
3 second-team all-stars, 1 Hart Trophy	
270-190-46-, 771 PIM in 665 games	
Hockey Hall of Fame: 1947	

There is no dispute Aurel Joliat was a spectacular little hockey player, a magnificent talent, a truly great two-way player who, along with linemate Howie Morenz, was integral in laying the foundation for the legend the Montreal Canadiens would become. He was a hockey cocktail concocted with equal parts of skill, nastiness and flamboyance.

But Joliat also played at a time when people played loose and fast with the facts, so many of the legends surrounding Joliat are so preposterous it's a little difficult to believe all of them are true.

Then again, you never know…

Legend has it that while playing for the Iroquois Falls Flyers in 1922, he was approached by two rather sinister looking types prior to a championship game and offered $500 to throw the game. (What two big-time gamblers were doing in small-town northern Ontario betting that kind of money on intermediate amateur hockey is never explained.) The story goes Joliat asked to see the $500, then grabbed it and ran off with the money.

That night he scored six goals to lead Iroquois Falls to the championship and, with the gangsters apparently in pursuit with murder on their minds, immediately left the rink and boarded the night train headed west to Saskatchewan, where he played for the Saskatoon Sheiks of the Western Canadian Hockey League before being traded to the Canadiens.

Credible hockey historians, however, maintain that although Joliat had a contract to play in Saskatoon, he never reported to the team. But it is true his rights were traded by the Sheiks to the Canadiens for Habs fading superstar Newsy Lalonde and $3,500 in a deal that was considered a blockbuster and was so controversial that team owner Leo Dandurand had to have his phone disconnected after the transaction.

"To put that trade into perspective," said hockey historian Bob Duff, "it would have been like if they had traded (Jean) Beliveau in 1971 to get Guy Lafleur. Lalonde had been the greatest player in franchise history to that point and people were pretty resentful that the team had traded their star for this kid nobody had ever heard of."

Joliat quickly soothed the faithful by scoring twice in his first game as a Canadien and went on to become a bona fide superstar of the NHL's early years. The year after Joliat arrived, Howie Morenz joined the Canadiens and teamed with Billy Boucher (and later Johnny Gagnon) to form the greatest line in the game.

Joliat played 16 seasons with the Canadiens and was integral in their three Stanley Cup wins in 1924, '30 and '31. He led the team in scoring four straight seasons, won the Hart Trophy in 1934 and was a member of the first-ever first all-star team in the NHL.

But it was his style of play and relentless approach to the game that made him so popular. A former star kicker for the Ottawa Rough Riders who turned seriously to hockey after breaking his leg, Joliat was as tenacious as he was talented. He played at about 5-foot-7, 135 pounds and often willingly took on players who were tipping the scales at 200 pounds.

"He was a consistently good goal-scorer, a guy who scrapped for every inch of the ice he got," said hockey historian Ernie Fitzsimmons. "He'd be sort of a Theoren Fleury type of player. He would just outwork and outskate the opposition."

HHOF Images

> "He was a consistently good goal-scorer, a guy who scrapped for every inch of the ice he got."
> – Ernie Fitzsimmons

Perhaps fitting given his reputation as something of an irascible on-ice character, Joliat wore a signature black skull hat whenever he played. The hat covered a bald spot that the ever-conscious Joliat was eager to protect. Opponents would sometimes make off with it to try to throw Joliat off his game, but were often repaid with a two-hander.

And it was Joliat's legendary toughness that made him so difficult as an opponent. He played 13 of his 16 seasons with two displaced vertebrae and many of them with painful stomach ulcers. Prior to his death, Joliat estimated he suffered separated shoulders six times, broken ribs three times and had his nose broken on five occasions.

Joliat once told a story about how Boston Bruins defenseman Eddie Shore hit him with a blindside check that left him being carried off the ice with a separated shoulder. After seeing Shore carrying the puck up ice after the play, Joliat recalled, "Forget the shoulder. I jumped over the boards and intercepted the big bugger. Hit him with a flying tackle that was so hard he was out cold on the ice. He had it coming, I'd say."

Another legend apparently occurred in 1970 when the league arranged a reunion of hockey legends in Boston and prior to the event, Joliat, 69, and Punch Broadbent, 78, were embroiled in a heated argument about something that had happened between them on the ice more than 50 years before. The two took their argument up a notch and went toe-to-toe, battering and bloodying each other so badly NHL president Clarence Campbell apparently banned them from the group photo and told them to go order room service at their hotel and stay away from the celebratory dinner.

The next morning, Joliat was apparently looking for Broadbent so the two of them could go for a drink if they could only find a bar that was open.

During the 1925-26 season, he got into an argument with Hall of Fame writer Elmer Ferguson during a game. Ferguson, who was a beat writer covering the team, was also the official scorer and neglected to award Joliat an assist on a goal. After laying into Ferguson while the game was still going on, Joliat skated away in disgust, got the puck and went in and scored. After the goal, he skated by Ferguson and glared at him.

When the Canadiens celebrated their 75th anniversary in 1984, they invited Joliat to take part in the festivities. At the age of 83, he took to the ice in skates and full gear – complete with black hat – and skated around stickhandling and waving to the crowd with a burning cigarette in his mouth. When he fell to the ice after a nimble display of moves, there was hush amongst the Forum crowd.

The player nicknamed 'The Little Atom' and 'The Little Giant' regularly skated on the Rideau Canal in his native Ottawa through most of his life and died June, 2, 1986, just months after his beloved Canadiens won their 23rd Stanley Cup. ●

Bob Gainey was brilliant in Montreal's 1979 Cup run, recording 16 points and earning MVP honors.

19

Bob **GAINEY**

To Protect and Respect

Bruce Bennett/Getty Images

Left Winger
Born: Dec. 13, 1953, Peterborough, Ont.
Habs Career : 1973-1989
5 Stanley Cups, 1 Conn Smythe Trophy,
4 Selke Trophies
239-262-501, 585 PIM in 1,160 games
Hockey Hall of Fame: 1992

Perhaps it began with the Flying Frenchmen. Certainly it was perpetuated by the long line of Stanley Cups and the longer line of offensive superstars the Canadiens produced from Howie Morenz to Guy Lafleur.

But probably the most enduring identity the Canadiens carved for themselves, certainly during the first 80 years of their existence, was one of supreme skill, offensive elan and explosive talent.

But the fact is every successful Canadiens team has also been anchored in a defensive conscience that was almost always unequalled by their opponents.

And nobody embodies that notion with the Canadiens more than Robert Michael Gainey. There were a number of snickers around the NHL when GM Sam Pollock used the eighth overall pick in 1973 on the relatively unknown Gainey, but Pollock knew his team of budding stars required the defensive presence other great Canadien teams had.

"Lots of good things happened to me, like going from an average teenage player to getting drafted, so I had lots of reasons to buy into what I was doing," Gainey said. "And the brilliance was really with the Canadiens because they were what I needed and I was what they needed and they had the guts to do that."

Few kids grow up aspiring to be the best two-way winger the Canadiens have ever had, but Gainey had spent years prior to joining the Habs preparing for that very role. Many players who turned out to be defensive/two-way stars for the Canadiens were offensive players who had to adapt their games in order to find a place in the lineup. Gainey never had to do that because he was always a conscious defensive player.

"There are a couple of reasons for that," Gainey said. "I played as a defenseman until I was about 15, so I had that kind of mindset. And then when I did start to play forward, Roger Neilson was my coach."

Although Gainey was a sub-par offensive player with a weak shot early in his career, his offensive game got much better as his defensive game reached new heights of excellence. Because of his defensive play, it's easy to forget Gainey had four 20-goal seasons and exploded for 16 points in 16 games en route to the Conn Smythe Trophy in 1979. He didn't score a lot of goals, but had a penchant for scoring big ones, both in NHL and international play.

And all the while he was taking defensive play to an art form. A very good skater for a big man, Gainey was able to nullify opponents by using superior body position, foot speed and angling rather than draping himself over the player he was supposed to be checking. As a result, he often was able to create offensive chances for himself and his teammates off his good defensive play.

Gainey's play prompted Canadiens' defenseman Larry Robinson to opine during the 1970s, "Bob Gainey is just as important to the Canadiens as Guy Lafleur."

In his own unique, self-deprecating way, Gainey shows he clearly isn't comfortable having his contributions mentioned with the same impact as Lafleur's.

"It's not really good to mix apples and oranges like that," Gainey said. "(Lafleur's) ability level was so high, that he could do the things that would allow me to participate because I could come in and protect. Sometimes it was like having a good closer, but never getting to the last inning."

One of the aspects of Gainey's game that was also overshadowed by his defensive play was his leadership capabilities. Late in the 1985-86 season, there was something of a player revolt against coach Jean Perron and GM Serge Savard refused to fire him. Observers say Gainey, then a 32-year-old, 13-year veteran, took control of the dressing room and galvanized the effort so well the Canadiens went on to win the Stanley Cup.

> "There couldn't have been a better captain in the history of the game than Bob Gainey."
> – Chris Chelios

Focus on Sport/Getty Images

And as stern and disciplined as Scotty Bowman was as coach, he almost always allowed the players to sort out issues for themselves and that was where Gainey shone.

"As a captain, Bob was like E.F. Hutton," said former Canadiens winger Murray Wilson. "He didn't say much, but when he did, it had impact."

"Anytime you needed advice, Bob Gainey was the guy," said former Canadiens' defenseman Chris Chelios. "As close as he was to Larry (Robinson) and Rick Green and Guy Lafleur, when he spoke he was very stern. Everybody listened and nobody went outside the boundaries. There couldn't have been a better captain in the history of the game than Bob Gainey."

To be sure, Gainey had some outstanding templates to draw upon in the form of former captains of the Canadiens. But Gainey also came into the captaincy during a time in which, for the first time in more than 30 years, the Canadiens were not the class of the NHL.

"It was like a skyscraper with deep, deep foundations," Gainey said. "The older players who were there had been taught by the older players, who had been taught by the older players and it was like we were still sucking on the fumes of the 1950s in the early 1970s. But by the time I got into a leadership position, we were going through some more difficult times. And it wasn't always the most fun being in that role in Montreal. There were some years that weren't a lot of fun."

But the Canadiens, as they always did, turned things around in the mid-1980s with an improved lineup and Gainey was a more mature leader and was able to better do the job.

But it always comes back to Gainey's defensive play. Perhaps he wasn't that much better than players such as Pit Lepine, Claude Provost, Ralph Backstrom and Gilles Tremblay before him or Guy Carbonneau after. But the advent of the Selke Trophy – which he won each of the first four seasons it was awarded – and legendary Soviet coach Anatoli Tarasov saying he was the most complete player in the world gave tangible recognition to what was once a more anonymous role.

Actually nobody is quite sure exactly what Tarasov said about Gainey, but as Gainey once said, "It has been interpreted a few different ways, but I sure got a lot of mileage out of it." ●

(20) Jacques **LEMAIRE**

Unselfish and Unsure

Center
Born: March 7, 1945, LaSalle, Que.
Habs Career : 1967-79
8 Stanley Cups
366-469-835, 217 PIM in 853 games
Hockey Hall of Fame: 1984

If there's anyone who shouldn't have suffered from a crisis in confidence as an NHL player, it was Jacques Lemaire. After all, here was a guy who was blessed with incredible speed, a lethal shot and uncanny hockey instincts.

But for much of his brilliant 12-year career with the Montreal Canadiens, Lemaire lived with the dreadful feeling it was just a matter of time before it was all going to fall off the rails. Even Lemaire admits he struggled with confidence for years and it didn't help he was sensitive to criticism and playing in a city where the fans take being judgmental to an art form.

Once, during the 1974-75 season, Lemaire reacted to a perceived prejudice from media members who chose the three stars by refusing to acknowledge a third-star selection and later announced his intention to keep doing so.

"I don't know, I really don't," Lemaire said in 2008 when asked why he had such problems with confidence. "Maybe it's how you're raised. I really don't know. I was always afraid I was going to lose my spot on the team. It wasn't until my last couple of years that I felt, 'I'm here now.' "

Lemaire began his career in Montreal as a left winger, but was moved to center early and developed into one of a long line of Canadiens pivots who were elite players at either end of the ice. But there was no shortage of observers who speculated moving Lemaire to the middle might be a waste of his talents given his ability to shoot the puck off the rush. In 1969-70, Lemaire's third season in the league, no lesser an authority than Jean Beliveau had this to say to THN: "Lemaire is the big goal-scorer on this club now."

That season, Lemaire gave every indication he was emerging as an elite scorer in the NHL. He became the first player in the league to hit the 20-goal plateau, doing so in his 36th game. When it was suggested he might score 50 that year, Lemaire responded to THN by saying, "Fifty? Who do you think I am, Bobby Hull?" He then proceeded to score just 12 goals in the remaining 33 games.

Lemaire played briefly as a center on Henri Richard's line between Dick Duff and Bobby Rousseau when Richard suffered an injury in 1967-68, prompting Richard to briefly leave the team once he returned because Lemaire had taken his spot. But it was another move to center that would make an indelible impact on the franchise. Guy Lafleur had been drafted as a center and was playing between Frank Mahovlich and Yvan Cournoyer in his rookie season of 1971-72. But coach Scotty Bowman realized Lafleur was not cutting it down the middle and put Lafleur at right wing and replaced him with Lemaire on the top line. Lemaire would later be Lafleur's center on one of the best lines in the history of the game.

Even though it sometimes seemed Lemaire didn't want to score too many goals, there were few players in his era who performed better when it mattered most. Seven times Lemaire registered double figures in points in the post-season and led all players in goals (11) and points (23) in the Canadiens fourth straight Cup victory in 1979. He is one of only a

Bruce Bennett Studios,Getty Images

handful of players to score two Cup-clinching goals and was Montreal's best player in a 3-3 tie against the Soviet Red Army team on New Year's Eve in 1975, a game some observers contend was the best hockey ever played.

"He'd only want a certain number of goals," said former linemate Steve Shutt. "He could take a slapshot and hit your finger and all of a sudden, those shots would be a little wider. But once he got into the playoffs, he was probably one of the best playoff players I've ever seen."

As the center with Mahovlich and Cournoyer, Lemaire also regularly killed penalties and his short-handed work with Mahovlich in the early 1970s were sights to behold. He later moved to a line with Shutt and Lafleur, replacing Pete Mahovlich, and there is no doubt he was both a prime puck distributor and the defensive conscience for the line.

"He hated playing with us at first," Shutt said.

"I didn't mind playing with Lafleur," Lemaire countered with a laugh. "I used to joke with Shutt all the time that once he got the puck, the only way I was going to get it back was to go to the front of the net because he wasn't going to pass it."

That was not a problem for Lemaire, who admitted he took more pleasure from setting a teammate up for a goal than scoring one himself. It was that approach that sometimes bothered fans who thought Lemaire should be using his blistering shot to score more. Lemaire never scored fewer than 20 goals in a single season and scored 30 or more goals in six of his 12 seasons.

> "He was probably one of the best playoff players I've ever seen."
> – Steve Shutt

"One year (1972-73) I scored 44 goals, but I was not that type of player," Lemaire said. "My mind was not on scoring. My mind was on everything. Backchecking and making a play was huge for me, even more than scoring. I saw a lot of guys who had tough times to score and I just got really happy when I could make that guy score. You know, bring the goalie on your side, pass it across and the guy puts it in. That, too, is a skill."

Lemaire has since gone on to become one of the best – and not surprisingly, most defensive – coaches in the game. After retiring from the Canadiens, he coached them briefly before moving on to the New Jersey Devils, where he won a Stanley Cup in 1994-95, and the Minnesota Wild.

When Lemaire was inducted into the Hockey Hall of Fame as a player in 1984, he was in his first full season as an NHL coach and one of his players on the Canadiens shared this observation of Lemaire with THN: "Jacques really keeps his expectations for his players at a realistic level. After all, he knows what it's like when they're unrealistic." ●

Bruce Bennett Studios/Getty Images

Guy **LAPOINTE**

The Crown-Wearing Clown

Bruce Bennett Studios/Getty Images

Defenseman
Born: March 18, 1948, Montreal
Habs Career : 1968-1982
6 Stanley Cups, 1 first-team all-star,
3 second-team all-stars
166-406-572, 812 PIM in 777 games
Hockey Hall of Fame: 1993

It was an off day during the 1976 Canada Cup and Guy Lapointe was not only running late for practice, he'd also committed a serious fashion faux pas, or so his teammates thought.

What a bunch of unsuspecting pigeons.

Players on that team were ordered to wear a team-issued off-ice uniform right down to the black shoes and socks. This day in Ottawa, however, Lapointe bounded into practice wearing a pair of brown dress shoes and brown socks, and boy, did he hear about it.

As his teammates dressed and hit the ice, Lapointe stayed behind and proceeded to drop all the shoes and socks in the room, including his own, into a barrel that was in the middle of the dressing room.

"I mixed them all up with mine," Lapointe recalled. "Everybody is going through the shoes and I said, 'Boy, I'm lucky I've got mine here.' "

Yup, Lapointe had a million of 'em. Legend has it that in games in which the Canadiens had a big lead late, which was pretty much every one during Lapointe's career, he would intentionally take a late penalty in order to get into the dressing room to cause mayhem.

One time in junior hockey, each player was issued a team hat that had to be worn. During one practice, Lapointe snuck back into the dressing room and cut the top off all the hats, including his own and those belonging to future NHLers Gilbert Perreault, Marc Tardif, Rejean Houle and Pierre Bouchard. He left only one unscathed, making it look as though unsuspecting teammate Bernie Gagnon was the perpetrator.

Lapointe used his sense of humor to diffuse the pressure that came with playing in Montreal and for an organization that, both internally and externally, was expected to win every game in which it played. His physical gifts were far more on display for the paying public and they were plentiful. Part of the fabled "Big Three" with Larry Robinson and Serge Savard on the Canadiens blueline, Lapointe was probably the most offensively gifted of the trio and definitely had the best shot from the blueline.

And while Robinson and Savard played with each other for the first seven years of Robinson's career, Lapointe was paired primarily with the likes of Pierre Bouchard, Gilles Lupien, Brian Engblom and Rod Langway. But Lapointe put up some remarkable numbers. He scored 10 or more goals nine straight seasons, including three seasons of 20-plus goals. All told, he scored 158 goals in those nine seasons for an average of 18 goals a season.

Makes you wonder what he might have accomplished had he been regularly paired with Savard or Robinson for his prime years.

"I think those guys were just as skilled as I was," Lapointe said. "But I think most people would say they were more disciplined than I was because I was forcing the issue a lot."

Lapointe managed to tame the wandering on-ice ways he had early in his career, but when he did get caught out of position, he had the speed to get himself back into the play and the smarts and ability to put himself in a good defensive spot. But there is little doubt his most prominent attribute was his ability to move the puck and create offense.

"He's like an extra forward on defense," Canadiens coach Scotty Bowman once said of Lapointe.

Lapointe's early days in the Montreal Canadiens organization certainly didn't seem to reveal any portents that would be the case, much less that he would forge a career that would include six Stanley Cups and a ticket to the Hall of Fame. By the time Lapointe turned 19, he had set his sites on becoming a police officer in Montreal, but that changed when the Canadiens invited Lapointe to training camp in 1967.

> "He's like an extra forward on defense."
> – Scotty Bowman

The Canadiens at the time were notorious for hording Quebec-based talent and, as usual, invited about 100 teenagers to camp. Lapointe managed to impress the team enough to have him play with the Montreal Jr. Canadiens and after one year of major junior and two years in the minors, Lapointe emerged in time to win a Stanley Cup in his rookie season of 1970-71.

Lapointe cites his involvement in the Summit Series as a major turning point in his career. Although he only had two full seasons of NHL experience, he made the team, in large part because Bobby Orr was injured, Jacques Laperriere's wife was having a baby and the fact Canadiens teammate J-C Tremblay had bolted for the World Hockey Association.

In fact, Lapointe was so insistent on playing in the series, he missed the birth of his son while playing in Moscow. But playing with the best players in the world and excelling in his role gave Lapointe the confidence he needed to take the next step in his career.

Lapointe was named a first-team all-star once and a second-teamer three times, but he never received the accolades afforded to a number of his superstar teammates. He seemed firmly entrenched as the No. 3 among "The Big Three," and might have piled up more impressive offensive credentials playing for another team.

But then again, he wouldn't have won six Stanley Cups and Lapointe says he might not have been able to accomplish what he did had he not been surrounded by the great players who were his teammates in Montreal.

Perhaps his lack of stature has something to do with the fact Lapointe so willingly played the role of court jester. But his contribution to the team dynamic in that respect shouldn't go unnoticed either.

In the spring of 1973, the Canadiens were playing the Philadelphia Flyers in the second round of the playoffs and had split the first two games at home, both in overtime. The Canadiens were appearing vulnerable entering a two-game set in Philadelphia and when Lapointe joined his teammates on the pool deck the day of Game 3, he looked skyward and said, "Let us pray." The Canadiens cracked up and the tension was broken. The series was over and the Canadiens went on to win the Stanley Cup.

Another time a Montreal radio station erroneously reported Lapointe had been killed. When Lapointe appeared for practice that day, he declared, "I am very pleased to deny that I am dead."

Once Lapointe stepped on the ice, however, the time for joking was over.

"That was just my personality to do things like that," Lapointe said. "But on the ice, I was just as serious as everybody else." ●

HHOF Images

Toe **BLAKE**

A Two-Time Legend

HHOF Images

Left Winger
Born: Aug. 21, 1912, Victoria Mines, Ont.
Died: May 17, 1995
Habs Career : 1934-1948
3 Stanley Cups, 3 first-team all-stars,
2 second-team all-stars, 1 Hart Trophy,
1 Lady Byng Trophy
235-292-527, 272 PIM in 577 games
Hockey Hall of Fame: 1966

Toe Blake was such a successful and innovative coach with the Montreal Canadiens it's some-times difficult to remember he was inducted into the Hockey Hall of Fame as a player, not a builder.

But Blake is one of a very small group of men who would have been inducted as players had they never coached or managed a single game after their careers, or gone into the shrine as builders had they not played a single minute of high-level hockey before that.

The only others who share that distinction are Lester Patrick, Jack Adams and Dick Irvin. But it cer-tainly wouldn't be a stretch to suggest Blake was the best player of them all. Blake's nickname, The Old Lamplighter, pretty much says it all.

(Note to reader: Blake's ranking among all-time Canadiens is based only on his playing career with the organization. His coaching record was not taken into account.)

A six-time 20-goal scorer in an era when goals were harder to come by, Blake was making a se-rious run for Bill Cowley's all-time career points record of 548 when a double ankle fracture ended his career in 1948.

Blake was born in 1912, one of 11 children, in Victoria Mines, Ont., just outside Sudbury. Legend has it Blake would skate to school and leave his skates on in class, "because recess was too short to change from boots."

Bruce Bennett Studios/Getty Images

The 1956 Stanley Cup was Toe Blake's first of eight as a coach, but people often forget he built a Hall of Fame career as a player before ever stepping behind a bench.

Blake actually started his career with the Montreal Maroons, who were the established favorite of English-speaking Montrealers in the 1930s. The Maroons and Canadiens were bitter rivals and there was a time the Maroons were getting more attention and having more success than the Canadiens. It had always been assumed one of the teams would ultimately have to move, but in the early 1930s there was a very real question concerning which one it would be.

The Maroons traded Blake to the Canadiens after just one season along with Bill Miller and Ken Gravel for goaltender Lorne Chabot and two years later they were out of business.

Blake would begin to assert himself right away as an impact player, an accomplishment that was even more impressive considering the Canadiens were going through perhaps their bleakest on-ice period in history. They had not won the Stanley Cup since 1931 and would not win another until 1944. Those who wax poetic about the long and storied history of the Canadiens conveniently forget they were a terrible team for the better part of a decade during The Depression.

> "A practice was like a game to him. He didn't fool around."
>
> – Elmer Lach

But Blake emerged as a beacon of hope on an otherwise fairly dismal team. He led the NHL in points with 47 and captured the Hart Trophy in 1939, despite the fact the Canadiens finished sixth in the seven-team league with a winning percentage of just .406.

Legend has it after that season, the Toronto Maple Leafs offered the Canadiens seven players in return for Blake, but were rebuffed.

During his career, Blake held or shared five scoring records, four of them in the playoffs. He was a first-team all-star three times and won the Art Ross,

> "Recess was too short to change from boots."

Hart and Lady Byng Trophies. He won the Lady Byng in 1946 with just two penalty minutes in 50 games, which was considered a remarkable transformation for a player who neither gave no quarter nor surrendered one.

Elmer Lach arrived in Montreal in 1940 and Rocket Richard would join the team two years later. Not long after that, the three players formed The Punch Line, one of the most dominant of its era.

Lach said one of the keys to the success of the line was all three were very different players who had a similar approach to the game.

"We worked great together," Lach said. "(Blake) was a great player. A practice was like a game to him. He didn't fool around. When he took over as coach of the Canadiens, I told him, 'Toe, you'd be too strict. I wouldn't be able to play for you.' Of course I was retired by then."

Blake posted four straight 20-goal seasons with Richard and Lach and aside from digging pucks out of the corners for his two flashier linemates, Blake also provided a measure of security for the young – and, early in his career, injury-prone – Richard.

"He led the league in scoring, he has won every trophy," Lach said of Blake. "He worked out great for the Rocket and me because he was a little slower. He wasn't a very good skater, but he was always there. The system we played, he worked out great."

But it was in the playoffs that Blake, like so many other great players, provided his highest level of play. He scored Cup-winning goals in 1944 – the year he led all playoff scorers with 7-11-18 totals in just nine games – and 1946. His average of two points per post-season game in 1944 was the highest ever recorded to that point and remained intact until Wayne Gretzky broke the mark in 1983. Blake's benchmark has been surpassed a total of four times, three times by Gretzky and once by Mario Lemieux.

All told, Blake recorded a total of 62 points in 58 playoff games and is one of those rare players whose point-per-game production in the playoffs was higher than in the regular season.

As Blake's career came to a close, he told Montreal sportswriter A.W. O'Brien he hoped he could remain in hockey in some capacity because, "living wouldn't mean much without hockey."

After forging one of the greatest coaching careers in NHL history, Blake retired in 1967-68 having led the Canadiens to eight more Stanley Cups.

Blake was ravaged by Alzheimer's disease in the final years of his life and died in 1995. Almost four years earlier, former Canadien Floyd Curry, who would also subsequently be afflicted with Alzheimer's, brought legendary Montreal hockey writer Red Fisher with him to visit Blake and had a care package of cookies. Blake did not recognize either man.

"It's a damned shame, isn't it?" Curry said at the time. "Look at his hands, he still has hands like a bear. Geez, he looks strong. Look, he's finished all his cookies." ●

HHOF Images

(23) Georges **VEZINA**

Mr. Cool

Bruce Bennett Studios/Getty Images

Goaltender
Born: Jan. 21, 1887, Chicoutimi, Que.
Died: March 27, 1926
Habs Career : 1917-1926
2 Stanley Cups, 3.41 GAA, 15 shutouts
175-146-6,
Hockey Hall of Fame: 1945

One of the enduring ironies of Georges Vezina's career with the Montreal Canadiens is despite the fact he played 15 seasons with the storied franchise, he would have won the award bearing his name only four times.

But it was never about goals-against average or shutouts for Vezina, it was more about winning games. Vezina was so poised in the Montreal net, he earned the nickname 'The Chicoutimi Cucumber.' But he was also so quiet and introverted that when the Canadiens signed him at 23 prior to the 1910-11 season, they also signed his brother just so they could get him to come to Montreal.

The Canadiens discovered Vezina in 1909 when they went to Chicoutimi as part of an annual barnstorming tour. The idea was the Canadiens would travel to small-towns all over Quebec, rub elbows with the locals and hold a dinner to raise money for the team, but only after laying a beating on the local amateur club.

> The Canadiens discovered Vezina in 1909 when they went to Chicoutimi as part of an annual barnstorming tour.

But in the exhibition game that year, the Chicoutimi Sagueneens shocked the Canadiens by beating them with Vezina supplying spectacular goaltending. Vezina, who was a leather tanner by trade when he wasn't playing amateur hockey, was instantly and zealously pursued by the Canadiens.

He ended up posing something a dilemma to Joseph Cattarinich, a part owner of the team who knew Vezina would be great for business. But Cattarinich was also the Canadiens' goalie.

"(Vezina) had played the Canadiens a few times before that and had given them fits every time," said hockey historian Bob Duff. "Joe Cattarinich said, 'We've got to sign this guy.'"

Vezina won only two Stanley Cups for the Canadiens, but was one of the few to play for Cup champions for Montreal both in the National Hockey Association and the NHL.

Through most of his career, NHL rules prohibited goalies from dropping to the ice to stop the puck, leaving Vezina no choice but to be an outstanding stand-up goalie.

Not only did Vezina not finish among the top goalies in goals-against average on a regular basis, he also finished his career with more than 100 losses. But to define Vezina's career by numbers would not do his legacy justice.

> "He gave you a chance to win every game. He wasn't too worried about how many goals he gave up as long as his team won."
> – Ernie Fitzsimmons

"He had the ability to come up big when the situation was on the line," said hockey historian Ernie Fitzsimmons. "He gave you a chance to win every game. He wasn't too worried about how many goals he gave up as long as his team won."

One season in which Vezina probably doesn't receive enough credit is 1923-24, the first in which the Canadiens won the Cup as a member of the NHL.

The team was in transition after bringing in a number of new players including future Hall of Famers Sylvio Mantha, Aurel Joliat and Howie Morenz. But the club struggled coming together and had a world of trouble scoring. They were barely a .500 team through the first half of the season and Vezina's goals-against average was just under 2.00. Had Vezina not played so well early on, the Canadiens likely wouldn't have been good enough to make the playoffs.

Vezina held the Canadiens in the race with some spectacular goaltending and when the sticks finally came alive, the Canadiens rallied to finish second in the four-team league. They dispatched the powerful Ottawa Senators – with stars Cy Denneny, George Boucher and King Clancy – in two straight games, then defeated the Vancouver Maroons of the Pacific Coast Hockey League in two straight and

Bruce Bennett Studios/Getty Images

the Calgary Tigers of the Western Canadian Hockey League two straight to take the Stanley Cup.

Just two years later, though, Vezina was forced to leave the team in one of the most tragic stories in the history of the franchise.

After playing 328 consecutive games and 39 more in the playoffs and establishing himself as an extremely durable player, Vezina, then 38, began sweating profusely during training camp workouts in 1925 and was dropping weight at an alarming rate. His level of performance, however, remained high and Vezina started the season against the Pittsburgh Pirates.

It was the Canadiens first game of the season and Vezina began running a high fever and collapsed in the net. He was coughing up blood and left the game. In the next few days, he was diagnosed with late-stage tuberculosis. Always an early arriver to practice, Vezina came to the rink without telling anyone he was sick and told team owner Leo Dandurand not to tell anyone. The team's trainer assumed Vezina was there to practice and put out all of his equipment.

Vezina simply slumped into his stall and wept. He then took his sweater and left The Forum, never to return.

Vezina lost his battle and died in March, 1926 at 39. A year later, the owners of the Canadiens donated a trophy to the league in Vezina's name that would be awarded to the goalie(s) posting the lowest goals-against average each season. Since 1981, it has been awarded to the league's best goaltender as chosen by the league's GMs.

An interesting side story to Vezina is that it has been reported that he fathered 22 children.

But there is some dispute to that claim. Some hockey historians claim Vezina actually only had two children and the lore of 22 came shortly after his death when a reporter was doing his obituary and his wife's English wasn't very good and told the reporter they had 22 children instead of two.

Others have said it's possible Vezina and his wife had 22 children, but many of them either died in infancy or were stillborn and Vezina actually had just four or five children. ●

Jacques Laperriere wasn't flashy, but was an incredibly consistent two-way defenseman who prided himself on his defensive acumen.

(24) Jacques **LAPERRIERE**

Passion and Poise

Bruce Bennett Studios/Getty Images

Defenseman
Born: Nov. 22, 1941, Rouyn, Que.
Habs Career : 1962-1974
6 Stanley Cups, 2 first-team all-stars,
2 second team all-stars, 1 Calder Trophy,
1 Norris Trophy
40-242-282, 674 PIM in 691 games
Hockey Hall of Fame: 1987

Jacques Laperriere averaged a Stanley Cup every other year he played. He was a multiple all-star and was the first, and one of only five, players in NHL history to win both the Calder Trophy as the league's top rookie and the Norris Trophy as the best defenseman.

But more than 40 years after the fact, something still rankles him. Whenever anyone mentions Canadiens' dynasties, the five straight Cups in the 1950s and the four straight in the late 1970s always come to mind. Very seldom do the Canadiens of the 1960s receive their due. That team was less star-studded, but more complete and came one agonizing playoff loss away from winning five Cups in a row itself.

And it's the one that got away that bothers Laperriere the most.

"Losing the Cup in 1967 was a disgrace," Laperriere spat. "We had the team. There's no way we should have lost that final. Everyone kept talking about how the Stanley Cup would be at Expo '67 and we got distracted. Next thing you know, we got beaten. It still bothers me to this day."

Passion is undeniably an important part of Laperriere's make-up. But so, too, is poise. Throughout his 11-year career as one of the most quietly effective defensemen in team history, Laperriere always exuded calm, rarely making the kind of play that got his team in trouble and often bailing it out with his long reach and quick stick. Beneath the calm countenance, however, an extremely fiery and proud man existed.

When Laperriere joined the Canadiens for good in 1963-64, he had visions of being the offensive wizard from the blueline that Doug Harvey was. Laperriere idolized Harvey as a youngster and wore his No. 2, hoping he'd carve a similar career path. That notion was put to rest in record time by Canadiens' coach Toe Blake.

"One of the first things he said to me was, 'We have enough guys here who can score goals. Your job is to keep the other team from scoring them,' " Laperriere said. "I guess it was pretty good advice and it worked out pretty well. We won lots of Cups."

Laperriere obviously caught on very quickly, parlaying his new style of play into rookie-of-the-year honors in 1964. For a franchise that has had as much success as the Canadiens have enjoyed over the years, their crop of Calder Trophy winners is shockingly small. Just six Canadien freshmen have ever been named top rookie and Laperriere remains the only one in franchise history who has won it as a defenseman. That year, Laperriere was also named to the second all-star team, marking the first time since World War II a rookie had been named to a post-season all-star team.

> "Everyone kept talking about how the Stanley Cup would be at Expo '67 and we got distracted. Next thing you know, we got beaten. It still bothers me to this day."

"I was tall and skinny and I had good speed and I had good anticipation of the play," Laperriere said. "When you've got that, it's a big plus for you. And when you have the passion to win, that helps. And I was with a group that had that passion."

Laperriere admits, though, that it was more than skill and passion that drove him early in his career. As a young player, much of his motivation came from fear – the fear of losing his spot in a six-team league where any one of a hundred players could replace you, and the fear of the repercussions of losing in Montreal.

"That's why we had success," Laperriere said. "Because the only thing we knew in Montreal was to win. There was no other word for us. Win, win, win…that's it. In those days, you had no choice because when you looked behind you there were a bunch of guys ready to replace you. Sometimes, you were even scared of getting hurt because you might lose your spot."

The accolades and awards continued for Laperriere through much of his career. Although he was never flashy, Laperriere was mind-boggling in his consistently high level of play. He perennially scored between 20 and 30 points and his mobility and defensive acumen were pivotal in the 1960s Stanley Cup triumphs.

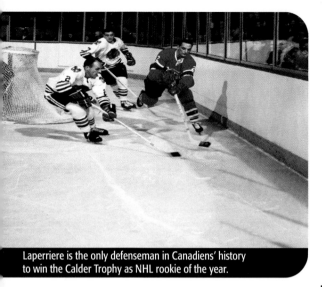

Laperriere is the only defenseman in Canadiens' history to win the Calder Trophy as NHL rookie of the year.

His greatest individual moments may have come in 1971 when the Canadiens stunned the hockey world by beating the powerful Boston Bruins in the first round en route to the Stanley Cup. Laperriere was a key defensive cog against both the high-powered Bruins and Chicago Black Hawks in the final and it was also by far his best playoff, with four goals and 13 points in 20 post-season games.

It wasn't long, however, before things started to decline for Laperriere. Scotty Bowman took over after the Canadiens won the Cup in 1971 and although Laperriere and Bowman won a Cup together two years later, they often clashed. Things were good at first. In fact, Bowman gave Laperriere credit for the part he played in the Canadiens six-game triumph over Chicago in the 1973 final after Laperriere missed the first part of the series.

"We were so disorganized in our own zone and there was no way we would have won if that had continued," Bowman told THN at the time. "The return of Jacques Laperriere changed all that."

But after a loss to Detroit in 1974, it was reported in THN Bowman said to Laperriere, who had been hobbled by knee injuries, "You can't skate anymore." Later that season, THN again reported that Bowman told Laperriere, "You're finished. Hang up your skates. Don't ruin your life and don't try to ruin mine." Three knee surgeries finally ended Laperriere's career in 1974 before Bowman could force him out.

More than 30 years later, Laperriere sees himself as just one in a long line of players who didn't mesh well with Bowman.

"Whoever played with Scotty at that time, (Jacques) Lemaire and everybody, you always had something," Laperriere said. "But the bottom line is we had success and that's it."

Laperriere turned to coaching after his career, but his days as a head coach ended abruptly in 1976 after his Montreal Jr. Canadiens and Sorel Blackhawks became involved in a vicious pre-game brawl. It was a sight Laperriere had seen too many times and the gratuitous violence repulsed him.

"I will never return behind a players' bench," Laperriere told THN at the time. "Not in junior hockey nor at the professional level. I can't do it anymore."

Four years later, Laperriere was convinced to join the Canadiens as an assistant coach and spent the next 25 years as an assistant with the Canadiens, Boston Bruins, New York Islanders and New Jersey Devils, picking up two more Stanley Cup rings in 1986 and 1993. ●

Bruce Bennett Studios/Getty Images

Butch **BOUCHARD**

Chiseled From Stone

Bruce Bennett Studios/Getty Images

Defenseman
Born: Sept. 4, 1919, Montreal, Que.
Habs Career : 1941-1956
4 Stanley Cups, 3 first-team all-stars,
1 second-team all-star
49-144-193, 863 PIM in 785 games
Hockey Hall of Fame: 1966

Butch Bouchard didn't have a pair of skates to call his own until he was 16, but five years later, having a pair of wheels was just as important to making the Canadiens as having a pair of blades.

The year was 1940 and Bouchard was 19. He had played only a few years of high-level competitive hockey in Verdun before catching the eye of the talent-depleted Canadiens, who invited him to training camp. Bouchard wanted so badly to make the team that each morning he would get on his bicycle at his home on Longueuil and pedal 35 miles to the team's training facility in St-Hyacinthe.

As it turned out, Bouchard was just getting warmed up. He was 6-foot-2 and 205 pounds, regarded as a freak of nature at the time, and had built up his muscle mass by lifting railway ties with steel plates added for more weight. Once he got to practice, his youthful enthusiasm took over and the young Bouchard was making an impression on his future employers and a more lasting and tangible one on his future teammates.

And he certainly didn't pick his spots. His penchant for hitting veterans as hard and as often as young players didn't always go over well with his older teammates.

In fact, Murph Chamberlain, a tough and durable forward who did his best work along the boards, told coach Dick Irvin one day after practice: "If I were you, I would order this young elephant to calm down and show less aggressiveness because if he keeps on going the way he is going, a few more days and you will find yourself without a player to open the season."

Bruce Bennett Studios/Getty Images

The Canadiens, though, were delighted. At the time they were two years removed from what still stands as the worst season in franchise history and were in the process of remaking the club with players who had both NHL talent and a desire to win. In previous years, the Canadiens had not only languished near or at the bottom of the league standings, their players had learned to accept losing. In 1939-40 the Canadiens were a dismal lot, going just 10-33-5. They would regularly get pounded in front of 3,000 fans, or fewer, and coach Pit Lepine would come into the dressing room, put on his coat and say, "See you tomorrow, boys."

They found exactly what they were looking for in the young Bouchard. He became an integral part of the new generation of Canadiens who not only saved the franchise from oblivion, but set the foundation for the dynasty teams that would follow. He was a classic defensive defenseman, scoring more than 10 goals just once in a 15-year career. And despite the fact he might have been the most imposing physical player in the league at the time, the highest penalty minute total he ever registered was 88.

> "He had the biggest shoulders and the smallest waist I had ever seen."
> – Dickie Moore

Bouchard spent much of his career as the steady, defensive influence on the blueline and after starting his career with Leo Lamoureux, was partnered with Doug Harvey, the best ever in moving the puck up the ice and using his skill to create offense from the back end. Much of Harvey's ability to freelance was due to the fact he knew Bouchard was always behind him.

And Bouchard was hockey's indisputable strong man. Although he wasn't terribly mobile and skating was not his forte, he managed

He refused to use his physical advantage to be anything more than a peacekeeper.

to get around the rink well enough not to be a liability. He used his size and strength to his advantage, but didn't fight much and refused to use his physical advantage to be anything more than a peacekeeper.

Of course, opponents probably realized it was a good idea not to provoke Bouchard. He often used his enormous hands to pull combatants apart.

"It was like he was chiseled out of stone," former teammate Dickie Moore once said. "He had the biggest shoulders and the smallest waist I had ever seen."

Bouchard was also years ahead of his time when it came to being an entrepreneur. In the 1930s and early 40s, most hockey players were regarded as small-town bumpkins or lunkheads who had few abilities outside the confines of the rink. But early in his career, Bouchard ran an apiary (where beehives are kept) that produced enough money to buy a home for his family and finance the start-up of a tavern in Montreal that was not far away from The Forum.

After a short stint in the minors, Bouchard landed in the NHL for good in 1941-42 and became a regular on the blueline in 1942-43 as the Canadiens tried to find a replacement for Ken Reardon, who left to join the effort in World War II.

And it wasn't long before Stanley Cups followed. The Canadiens ended a 13-year drought with a Stanley Cup in 1944 and won the Cup again two years later. Goalie Bill Durnan took over the captaincy of the team for a short time after Toe Blake retired, but then the 'C' was handed to Bouchard in 1948-49 and he held it for eight full seasons. As of 2008-09, only Jean Beliveau had enjoyed a longer tenure than Bouchard as captain of the Canadiens. (Bob Gainey was also captain for eight seasons and the 2008-09 season would be Saku Koivu's ninth.)

Bouchard was a member of two more Cup winners as captain, including his final season, which was the first in the Canadiens' five-Cup dynasty of the late 1950s. After playing only half the season in 1955-56, Bouchard missed the entire playoffs with a knee injury, but Blake dressed Bouchard for Game 5 of the Stanley Cup final against the Detroit Red Wings. He sat on the bench for most of the game, but with the Canadiens leading 3-1 in the series and 3-1 late in Game 5, Blake sent Bouchard out for the last shift of his career and was on the blueline when the buzzer sounded in the deciding game.

Bouchard's legacy with the Canadiens continued when his son, Pierre, joined the team in 1970-71. Pierre, who had his father's exact height and weight, went on to win five Cups with the Canadiens, making the Bouchards the most Stanley Cup-decorated father-son combination in NHL history. Brett and Bobby Hull are the only other father-son duo to have their names on the Cup as players. ●

Steve **SHUTT**

The Left Wing Rock

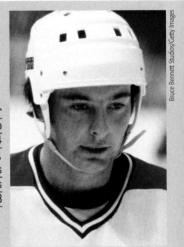

Bruce Bennett Studios/Getty Images

Left Winger	
Born: July 1, 1952, Toronto	
Habs Career : 1972-1984	
5 Stanley Cups, 1 first-team all-star,	
2 second-team all-stars	
408-368-776, 400 PIM in 871 games	
Hockey Hall of Fame: 1993	

Like his future linemate Guy Lafleur, Steve Shutt came to the Canadiens with mind-boggling junior credentials and the potential for superstardom. Blessed with stunning speed and accuracy on both his slapshot and wrist shot, Shutt teamed with Billy Harris and Dave Gardner to form one of the most devastating lines in the history of junior hockey in 1971-72. The three scored 173 of the Toronto Marlies 363 goals that season.

Shutt jumped directly to the Canadiens the next season, but any thoughts he would duplicate his scoring feats right away were dashed in record time. First of all, Shutt showed up to his first camp overweight. He was something of a free spirit, which wasn't an attribute coach Scotty Bowman found all that amusing. Shutt scored just eight goals his first season and even though the Canadiens won the Stanley Cup in 1973, Shutt played just one shift of one game that entire playoff.

For the first time in his life, the happy-go-lucky Shutt was miserable.

"(Canadiens GM) Sam Pollock said right off he would give us a hard time because he believes the hard road is the best road to the top," Shutt told The Hockey News later in his career. "Maybe it is, but it's the worst way to live. You get discouraged. Guy and I took turns consoling each other."

> "There hasn't ever been a hockey team that I couldn't make before and it's not going to start now."

Steve Babineau/NHLI via Getty Images

Things were so bad Shutt considered asking for a trade. The Canadiens were loaded with depth at forward and things were looking bleak for Shutt. The player who had always found scoring goals so easy had just 23 in his first 120 games. But it was then Shutt also experienced something of an epiphany.

"In that summer of the second year, I sat down and said, 'Well, I can maybe go somewhere else and make a go of it,' " Shutt said. "And then I thought, 'No. There hasn't ever been a hockey team that I couldn't make before and it's not going to start now.' "

Steve Babineau/NHL via Getty Images

Both Lafleur and Shutt took a couple of seasons to hit their strides, but when they did, the results were spectacular. In Shutt's third season and Lafleur's fourth, Bowman decided to play them with Pete Mahovlich and the two players began to reward the legendary coach. That was 1974-75 and Shutt broke out with a 30-goal season, while Lafleur exploded for 53. Mahovlich, meanwhile, recorded 117 points, by far the highest total of his career.

"Pete was the big star and he was the leader of our team," Shutt said. "Pete just took us under his wing and it was almost like, 'OK, you guys, I'm going to look after you now.' And he did. He gave us the opportunity to really get some confidence in ourselves. There's no doubt he was the one who jump-started our careers."

Once the two wingers began to show potential, Bowman knew he needed to place them with a center who could both get them the puck and be the defensive conscience on the line and he installed Jacques Lemaire into that role. It turned out to be a stroke of genius and for a five-year period that line was one of the most feared in the game.

Once Shutt began to establish himself as a scorer, he recorded nine consecutive 30-goal seasons and scored at least 40 four times. In 1976-77, he led the NHL with 60 goals and broke Bobby Hull's record for goals in a season by a left winger, one that stood for 16 seasons until it was surpassed by Luc Robitaille (63). With Alex Ovechkin collecting 65 goals in 2007-08, Shutt's total remained the third-highest ever by a left winger. ●

J-C **TREMBLAY**

Prince of Puckhandling

Defenseman	
Born: Jan. 22, 1939, Bagotville, Que.	
Died: Dec. 7, 1994	
Habs Career : 1959-1972	
5 Stanley Cups, 1 first-team all-star, 1 second-team all-star	
57-306-363, 204 PIM in 794 games	

Graphic Artist/HHOF Images

After winning the Stanley Cup in 1965 and finishing second in voting for the Conn Smythe Trophy, J-C Tremblay went to his hometown of Bagotville in the Saguenay region of Quebec.

People were lined up from his house to the City Hall building 12 miles away. Once the parade arrived at City Hall, the mayor declared the day J-C Tremblay Day.

"Amazingly, I found myself a folk hero in the town," Tremblay told THN years later. "I have to say, it made me feel wonderful."

But Tremblay's play in the 1965 playoffs, in which he finished second in playoff MVP voting to Roger Crozier, also created a level of expectation Tremblay was never able to match. Instead of that playoff being a jumping-off point for a brilliant career, fans in Montreal vilified Tremblay for not being physical enough in his own end and for what seemed like a constant string of giveaways.

There was no arguing Tremblay's talent level. He possessed the ability to slow the game down to his pace, particularly when he had the puck. It was not uncommon for him to get the puck in the neutral zone, not be able to find a suitable play and then start wheeling backward into the Canadiens end.

Opponents such as George Armstrong had a tough time separating J-C Tremblay from the puck.

> **"In his time, there were few to match his puckhandling skills and none who surpassed him."**
>
> – Red Fisher

Sometimes the results were disastrous. Other times, when he used the time and space to make a wonderful pass out of the zone, the results were spectacular. Twice in his career with the Canadiens, Tremblay topped 50 assists, including 1970-71 when he had 52 assists and a career-high 63 points.

"In his time, there were few to match his puckhandling skills and none who surpassed him," Red Fisher wrote in his nomination of Tremblay for the Hockey Hall of Fame.

But Tremblay often drew the ire of fans for his slow, methodical style of play and from management for his lack of a physical presence. In one game in 1969, two giveaways led to goals and Tremblay was being booed mercilessly as he carried the puck end to end to score. Instead of lifting his stick in celebration, he jabbed it in the air as a gesture of contempt for the fans.

"I think a player's performance depends a lot on confidence and that's a very hard thing to define," Tremblay told THN. "All I know is that when a guy has it he's capable of playing some very good hockey and he'll keep playing that way as long as the confidence lasts. When the confidence is lost, a player is in trouble. Don't ask me what causes it or why it comes and goes. All I know is that you feel sure of yourself in some games and in others you don't."

Tremblay became one of the first prominent NHL players to jump to the World Hockey Association and he did it because the Quebec Nordiques offered him a five-year deal worth double the $70,000 per year the Canadiens were dangling. Tremblay flourished in the WHA and was named top defensemen in the league twice. But like Bobby Hull, Tremblay was barred from playing for Canada in the 1972 Summit Series because he didn't have an NHL contract.

His brilliance in the WHA made him the envy of many teams and in Quebec he earned the nickname J-C Superstar. After one game in Toronto, Toros GM Buck Houle described Tremblay like this: "I think they should give J-C Tremblay one puck and the rest of the players on the ice have another one."

Tremblay died in 1994 at the age of 55, from cancer of the kidney, after spending several years scouting in Switzerland for the Habs. ●

> "I think a player's performance depends a lot on confidence and that's a very hard thing to define."

Frank **MAHOVLICH**

Finally, Happy Days

Melchior DiGiacomo/Getty Images

Left Winger
Born: Jan. 10, 1938, Timmins, Ont.
Habs Career : 1971-1974
2 Stanley Cups, 1 first-team all-star
129-181-310, 145 PIM in 263 games
Hockey Hall of Fame: 1981

It could be argued no player in the history of the Canadiens had such a large impact in such a short time as Frank Mahovlich.

To be sure, Mahovlich was never happier as an NHLer than he was when he was wearing the Canadiens sweater.

In almost 11 seasons with the Toronto Maple Leafs, Mahovlich established himself as one of the greatest players in franchise history and the team won four Stanley Cups, but was miserable and the experience nearly crushed his psyche and spirit. With the Detroit Red Wings, he was again brilliant and out of the clutches of Leafs GM Punch Imlach, he was never happier. But the team was terrible and his talents were largely wasted.

It was only when he reluctantly went to Montreal in 1971 that Mahovlich experienced true personal happiness, combined with individual and team success.

"It was the greatest part of my career," Mahovlich said, "and it showed on the scoresheet."

It certainly showed on the scoresheet shortly after he arrived in Montreal. He led the league with 14 goals in the 1971 playoffs, which was then an NHL record, as the Canadiens marched to one of their most unlikely Stanley Cups. With the Canadiens, Mahovlich had full seasons of 43, 38 and 31 goals and with his younger brother Pete on the team, enjoyed hockey more than he ever had in his career.

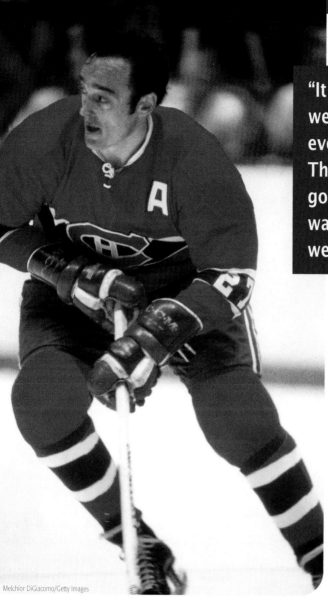

Melchior DiGiacomo/Getty Images

> "It seemed like we were doing everything right. The coaching was good, the managing was good. Everything went so smoothly."

Frank would always tell his younger brother to take the game and life more seriously and Pete would respond by telling Frank to lighten up a little. But it was a happy, productive time for both. The two would sometimes be sent out to kill penalties and, "the other team just dreaded seeing us kill penalties," Mahovlich said.

"They didn't know what to do. They were supposed to go on the offense and we stymied them right off the bat. We always had possession of the puck and it was really tough for them to get it back."

Mahovlich got a ton of ice time with the Canadiens and a variety of centermen of the ilk he had never seen before. Known primarily as a goal-scorer before coming to the Canadiens, Mahovlich rounded out his game with two seasons of 50-plus assists and one with 49.

Pictorial Parade/Getty Images

Melchior DiGiacomo/Getty Images

"The kind of style the Canadiens played was perfect for me," Mahovlich said. "It seemed like we were doing everything right. The coaching was good, the managing was good. Everything went so smoothly."

Perhaps Mahovlich appreciated the Canadiens so much because of what he had endured, particularly as a Maple Leaf. Despite being one of the most talented players Leaf fans had ever seen, Mahovlich was often booed for a perceived lack of effort and maligned by Imlach. Mahovlich would be treated for depression as a Maple Leaf and said he felt as though the weight of the world was lifted from his shoulders when he was dealt to the Red Wings in 1968.

With the Canadiens, Mahovlich was stunned that Canadiens executives Al MacNeil and Ron Caron greeted him at the airport in Minneapolis after his trade. He had seriously considered not reporting to Montreal, but that changed quickly once he learned how much he would be cared for and appreciated.

After two seasons of 90-plus points and one with 80, Mahovlich left the Canadiens to play in the World Hockey Association. Had he stayed with the Canadiens, there's a good chance he would have remained for the four-Cup dynasty of the late '70s.

"The WHA was the only place I ever made any money," Mahovlich said. "I sure didn't make any in the NHL." ●

Didier **PITRE**

An Original Big Shot

HHOF Images

Right Winger/Defenseman
Born: Sept. 1, 1883, Valleyfield, Que.
Died: July 29, 1934
Habs Career : 1909-1913, 1914-23
1 Stanley Cup
220-59-279, 344 PIM in 256 games
Hockey Hall of Fame: 1962

Didier Pitre will always hold the distinction of being the first player the Montreal Canadiens ever signed. He was also the first one to land the team in court.

It was early in the 20th Century and hockey players were notorious for signing and breaking contracts at the first hint of making more money. After starring in his hometown of Sault Ste. Marie, Ont., Pitre was coveted by both the Canadiens, who were starting their first season in the pre-NHL National Hockey Association, and the Montreal Nationals of the Federal Amateur Hockey League. Pitre signed a contract with both teams and even though the Nationals inked him first, a Montreal judge sided with the Canadiens. The Nationals folded after just four games and Pitre went on to star with the Canadiens as part of an opening night roster that included Jack Laviolette and Newsy Lalonde at forward.

> "He was kind of the Bobby Hull of his era, just really fast with an amazing, hard shot."
> – Bob Duff

The group was dubbed The Flying Frenchmen, but it's uncertain where Pitre was actually born. The Society of International Hockey Research has him listed as being born in Valleyfield, Que., while the Hockey Hall of Fame lists his birthplace as Sault Ste. Marie, Ont. Records indicate he is buried at a cemetery in Sault Ste. Marie, Mich.

"When you think of it, you could almost say (Pitre and Lalonde) were responsible for pro hockey as we know it today," said hockey historian Ernie Fitzsimmons. "If he hadn't stayed and the NHA had jumped around from place to place, I don't know what would have happened."

Pitre, though, is known better as an elite player, part of a small group of players who made up the first superstars of the game. Pitre was nicknamed 'Cannonball' and 'Bullet Shot' because of his devastating shot. And even though he battled a weight problem through much of his career, he was one of the fastest skaters the early pro game had seen.

"He was kind of the Bobby Hull of his era, just really fast with an amazing, hard shot," said hockey historian Bob Duff. "He was known to sometimes put the puck right through the net."

It took some time for that first team to find its stride, but there is little doubt Pitre and Lalonde combined to give the Canadiens an offensive presence other teams simply could not match.

Pitre won just one Stanley Cup with the Canadiens, but his offensive panache was always on full display. Nine straight seasons he was among the top seven scorers in the NHL and he was a consistent goal-scorer in both the NHA and NHL.

> "When you think of it, you could almost say (Pitre and Lalonde) were responsible for pro hockey as we know it today."
> – Ernie Fitzsimmons

With records from that era incomplete and sketchy, there is also some dispute over whether Pitre was a tough player. "He didn't take any bullshit," Fitzsimmons said.

But in a story about Pitre in the Montreal *Gazette,* an incident was recounted when Canadiens GM George Kennedy was livid because Pitre shrugged off a butt-end from Montreal Wanderers winger Gordie Roberts, who was also a doctor.

"How can I hit him back?" Pitre said to Kennedy. "Roberts is very polite. Each time I fall, he helps me get back up and apologizes, saying it was an accident. Can I hit a man who is apologizing to me? No, never. It is not done." ●

HHOF Images

Ken **REARDON**

The Intimidator

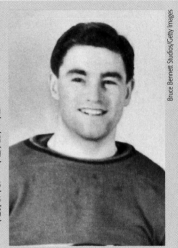

Bruce Bennett Studios/Getty Images

Defenseman
Born: April 1, 1921, Winnipeg, Man.
Died: March 15, 2008
Habs Career : 1940-1950
1 Stanley Cup, 2 first-team all-stars,
3 second-team all-stars
26-96-122, 604 PIM in 341 games
Hockey Hall of Fame: 1966

It should come as no surprise Ken Reardon volunteered for military duty in World War II as his promising NHL career was just getting started.

That's because Reardon never met a battle – on or off the ice – he didn't relish. For his efforts overseas, Reardon received a Certificate of Gallantry by Field Marshall Montgomery for bravery and in the NHL, he earned one Stanley Cup, two first-team all-star berths and three second-team honors.

But none of them came easily to Reardon, who was left orphaned at 13 when his parents were killed in a car accident near Winnipeg. Much of his career was played in debilitating pain, mostly in his back.

Perhaps that's why Reardon was such an ornery opponent. His battles with Cal Gardner were legendary, but Reardon certainly didn't pick his spots. He was charged with assault with a deadly weapon in 1949 when he went after a fan in Chicago Stadium and he even knocked senseless the man who was most responsible for getting him into the NHL.

That was Paul Haynes, a Canadiens veteran who was sent to western Canada during the 1939-40 season on a scouting mission while he was recovering from an injury. He saw Reardon playing in Edmonton and signed him immediately after learning the New York Rangers had temporarily dropped him from their protected list.

Haynes and Reardon developed a close friendship, one that was immediately put aside during the first scrimmage of training camp in 1940.

"I snaffled off the faceoff, passed to Toe Blake, who carried it over the blueline and whipped it back to me," Haynes later remembered. "At that identical moment, an earthquake hit. I found myself dazedly staring up at the roof lights. Players were looking down in sympathy. Reardon hit me with the most blistering check I ever received in 10 years in the big time."

Despite his rambunctiousness, Reardon was universally loved by his teammates and universally despised by the rest of the league. Fans at Madison Square Garden formed a Hate Reardon Fan Club and once threw a turkey at him. In 1950, he was forced to put up a $1,000 peace bond with the league after an altercation with Gardner left him with 14 stitches and he later told *Sport* magazine: "I am going to see that Gardner gets 14 stitches in the mouth. I may have to wait a long time, but I'm patient. Even if I have to wait until the last game that I ever play, Gardner is going to get it good and plenty."

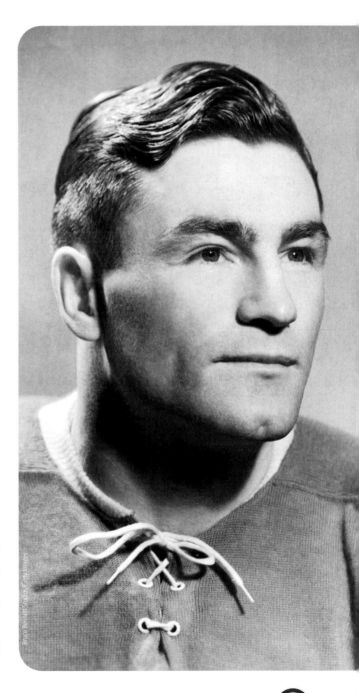

Bruce Bennett Studios/Getty Images

"Reardon hit me with the most blistering check I ever received in 10 years in the big time."
– Paul Haynes

After aggravating a back injury in the 1947 playoffs, Reardon was advised to have back surgery and retire. He asked Canadiens' GM Frank Selke if the team would pay for his operation after his playing days ended in return for him continuing to play. He then bought a leather belt to strengthen his back and went into the bush in northeastern Quebec and Labrador to map the course of a railroad to connect the huge iron ore deposits of that area to a port on the St. Lawrence River. When he came back the next season, he was better than ever.

But Reardon never lost his ability to intimidate and irritate his opponents.

"That Reardon is the most demoralizing player in the game," Toronto Maple Leafs coach Hap Day once said. "He can knock a whole National Hockey League team off balance – get them thinking of everything but hockey." ●

Bruce Bennett Studios/Getty Images

Peter **MAHOVLICH**

A Free Spirit

Steve Babineau/NHL via Getty Images

Center	
Born: Oct. 10, 1946, Timmins, Ont.	
Habs Career : 1969-1977	
4 Stanley Cups	
223-346-569, 695 PIM in 581 games	

Peter Mahovlich doesn't mind much he probably gets short shrift when it comes to his place in Canadiens history. The way he sees it, he wasn't the most committed player of all-time.

"Some people live to work and other people work to live," Mahovlich said. "I would count myself among the latter. But yeah, maybe I was a little too much of a free spirit."

That nature got him a ticket out of Detroit in 1969, the team with which he broke into the NHL and where he had a tough time finding his niche. Fortunately for the Habs, he blossomed in Montreal. At 6-foot-5 and 205 pounds, Mahovlich was a behemoth, yet was a terrific skater for a big man, a deft stickhandler, played the point on the power play and killed penalties.

And just as importantly, Mahovlich provided the driving force for his brother Frank, who joined the Canadiens in 1971 and had some of the best years of his career with the Habs.

Mahovlich enjoyed five 30-goal seasons in Montreal and in 1974-75 recorded 82 assists, which still stands as a team record.

> "Some people live to work and other people work to live. I would count myself among the latter."

Steve Babineau/NHLI via Getty Images

That season, he centered a line with Steve Shutt and Guy Lafleur and the wingers responded with 30 and 53 goals, respectively. Shutt credits Mahovlich with jump-starting both his and Lafleur's careers which, until that time, had been flagging.

But that didn't stop coach Scotty Bowman from taking Mahovlich off that line and replacing him with Jacques Lemaire, in part because the two young stars needed someone who could get them the puck more. Throughout his career, Mahovlich was called Peter Puckhog by his teammates and Pierre Bouchard once referred to his line as 'The Donut Line', because it had no center.

It didn't seem to bother Mahovlich then, nor does it now, although there is a touch of resentment in his voice when he points out an interesting historical tidbit.

"Here's my barometer," said Mahovlich, a pro scout with the Atlanta Thrashers. "I played in the 1972 Summit Series and I played in the first Canada Cup in 1976. I was one of only nine guys who played in both those series and I'm the only one of that group who never got to the Hall of Fame. Jacques Lemaire wasn't on either of those teams and he's in the Hall of Fame."

Steve Babineau/NHLI via Getty Images

(Rick Martin, who is not in the Hall, was on both rosters but saw no action in 1972. Bobby Orr was on both rosters and didn't play in the '72 series because of injury.)

While Mahovlich, whose trade request for the Habs landed him in Pittsburgh in 1977, doesn't let his preclusion from the Hall gnaw at him, he believes he would have had a smoother time in Montreal had he not had such a prickly relationship with some of the members of the Francophone media.

"Things might have been different if my name had been Pierre Mahovlich, if you know what I mean," Mahovlich said in 2008. "But some of the things that happened to me were my fault. I could have been a better conditioned athlete and I could have been more serious about the game." ●

In 1974–75, Mahovlich recorded 82 assists, which still stands as a team record.

Guy **CARBONNEAU**

A True Chameleon

Robert Laberge/Allsport

Center

Born: March 18, 1960, Sept-Iles, Que.

Habs Career : 1980-1994

2 Stanley Cups, 3 Selke Trophies

221-326-547, 623 PIM in 912 games

Every fall, Guy Carbonneau would come to the Canadiens training camp and every year he'd be dispatched either back to junior or the minors with the same words of advice.

Work on your defensive game, kid.

"Everybody told me that," Carbonneau said. "I think I took it to heart."

As the kids say these days, "Well, duh." Three Stanley Cups (two in Montreal), three Selke Trophies and one of the greatest defensive careers in NHL history later, the whole notion seems almost as laughable as Carbonneau being ranked the 210th best prospect for the 1979 entry draft.

When Carbonneau came to the Canadiens organization as a 19-year-old, he did so as a dazzling offensive player who had little regard for his own end of the ice. In fact, in six years of junior and minor pro hockey, he scored almost as many points as he would in 18 seasons in the NHL; he once had 70 goals in junior with the Chicoutimi Sagueneens.

Carbonneau endured his share of trials the first season and a particularly lackluster set of games in Carbonneau's rookie season prompted coach Bob Berry to opine, "If he doesn't want to do the job, we'll put someone in there who does. If he wants to play more, then he'd better put out a better effort when he does play."

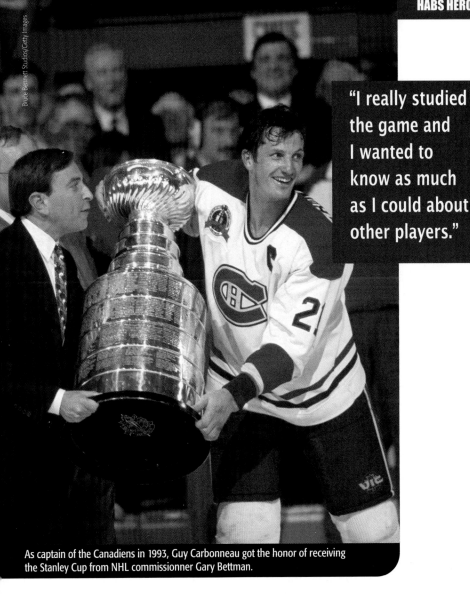

Bruce Bennett Studios/Getty Images

"I really studied the game and I wanted to know as much as I could about other players."

As captain of the Canadiens in 1993, Guy Carbonneau got the honor of receiving the Stanley Cup from NHL commissionner Gary Bettman.

But Carbonneau had two qualities in abundance that would serve him in terrific stead – intense competitiveness and top-notch hockey sense. His two years in the minors had helped his defensive game, but it really began to emerge when he was installed as the center on the Canadiens checking line with Bob Gainey and Chris Nilan.

"I always thought I had pretty good hockey sense," Carbonneau said. "And by getting hooked up on a line with Bob and Chris, we were a really good defensive line. And by playing on that line, I was able to play 20 or 25 minutes a game."

> "A player who scores can't score goals every game, but a player who plays well defensively can do that every game."

The native of the Montreal suburb of Sept-Iles grew up watching the likes of Jean Beliveau, Yvan Cournoyer, Guy Lafleur and Henri Richard and during his formative hockey years, the Canadiens were winning four straight Stanley Cups.

Carbonneau was not a one-dimensional shutdown player, as evidenced by his five 20-goal seasons with the Canadiens. And Carbonneau did not accomplish his mission with dogged checking or shadowing. Like Gainey, his was a far more intellectual approach to defensive hockey, based primarily on studying his opponents and superior defensive positioning and angling.

"One thing that I learned was that a player who scores can't score goals every game," Carbonneau said, "but a player who plays well defensively can do that every game."

Carbonneau quickly learned the value of being a strong defensive player, a trait that served him well in the 1986 Stanley Cup final when the Canadiens knocked off Joel Otto and the Calgary Flames.

Bruce Bennett Studios/Getty Images

And Carbonneau did it every game against the likes of Peter Stastny, Mario Lemieux and Wayne Gretzky.

"I really studied the game and I wanted to know as much as I could about other players," Carbonneau said. "I did it by memory a lot based on games that I had played against them, good plays you made and bad plays you made. Everyone has tendencies and obviously the best players have fewer than others, but if you can get to know them, you're able to stay a couple of seconds ahead of them."

The Gainey-Carbonneau tandem produced two of the best defensive forwards in the history of the game and seven Selke Trophies between them. In 2008, they were still inextricably linked as GM and coach of the team. ●

John **FERGUSON**

Iron Fists With a Twist

Bruce Bennett Studios/Getty Images

Left Winger	
Born: Sept. 5, 1938, Vancouver, B.C.	
Died: July 14, 2007	
Habs Career : 1963-1971	
5 Stanley Cups	
145-158-303, 1,214 PIM in 500 games	

Twelve seconds into John Ferguson's first-ever NHL game, he got into a fight. Two weeks later, he leaped over the boards to rescue a teammate who was being beaten badly in a fracas.

Lore has it teammate Boom-Boom Geoffrion told him just before he went over, "Don't bother. They'd never do that for you." Ferguson turned to Geoffrion with a near-maniacal look and said, "I'll never need anyone to help me."

In his brief but eventful career with the Canadiens, Ferguson held true to his word. He never did need anyone to help him, but likely could have used a better publicist. Ferguson will go down as one of the greatest enforcers of his era, but those who think he was strictly a hired gun should take note of two things. One, Ferguson led the NHL in penalty minutes only once during his eight-year career and, second, the guy could play.

> "I think the perception people had of him frustrated him sometimes. It only bothered him when people forgot he could play hockey, too."
> – John Ferguson Jr.

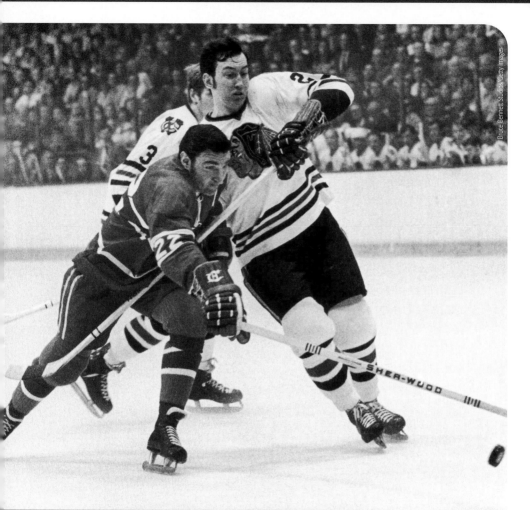

John Ferguson was known as one of the game's original enforcers,
but he was a talented player with the puck, too.

"I think the perception people had of him frustrated him sometimes," said Ferguson's son John, a former Canadiens' farmhand and former GM of the Toronto Maple Leafs. "It only bothered him when people forgot he could play hockey, too."

Of course, that's bound to happen when a guy enters the league vowing to be, "the meanest, rottenest, most miserable cuss ever to play in the NHL," then proceeds to go about doing just that. In fact, Ferguson once told Brian McFarlane for a profile in *Star Magazine* that, "at least half of the nasty letters I receive are simply addressed to: John Ferguson, Penalty Box, Montreal Forum."

But unlike most modern enforcers who are a liability in almost all other areas, Ferguson had some talent in his hands when they weren't balled into a fist. He also came by his 1,214 PIM honestly.

"It used to bother him to see guys who padded their totals with 10-minute misconducts for yapping to the referees. He called those cheap minutes," John Ferguson Jr., said. "He certainly earned his minutes."

Ferguson earned a first-team all-star berth in the American League in 1962-63, the season before he joined the Canadiens and in 1968-69, scored a career-high 29 goals. All told, Ferguson scored fewer than 15 goals only once during his career. In his first season in the NHL in 1963-64, he led all rookies in scoring with 18 goals and 45 points in 59 games and finished second in voting for rookie of the year to teammate Jacques Laperriere.

Ferguson once said he retired at the relatively early age of 32 because he was afraid he was going to do irreparable harm or even kill someone out on the ice, but the younger Ferguson finds that difficult to believe. Ferguson took his role very seriously and feared no one, but it wasn't as though he lost control of his faculties when he was playing the role.

"I know he had some injuries that were bothering him," the younger Ferguson said. "But, quite frankly, he was making more money away from hockey than he was in hockey. He had a textile business and horses and he was doing quite well." ●

Bruce Bennett Studios/Getty Images

Ferguson was feared by opponents around the league and sometimes, he once said, was even scared himself at the potential damage he could inflict on others.

George HAINSWORTH

A Master Technician

HHOF Images

Goaltender
Born: June 26, 1895, Toronto, Ont.
Died: Oct. 9, 1950
Habs Career : 1926-1933, 1937
2 Stanley Cups, 3 Vezina Trophies
167-97-54, 1.75 GAA, 75 shutouts
Hockey Hall of Fame: 1961

"I'm sorry I can't put on a show like some of the other goaltenders... I guess all I can do is stop pucks."

In an era when goaltenders were every bit as much showstoppers as they were puckstoppers, George Hainsworth was a master technician. He rarely made a spectacular save because he almost never needed to and, hey, it wasn't exactly like he was a darling in front of the camera either.

But man, could he play.

"He looks like one of these dumpy guys whom it would be impossible to believe he could be great at anything," said hockey historian Eric Zweig. "He looks like he's 50 when he's 30. But you can't deny the numbers."

Even though Hainsworth posted his most mind-boggling numbers in an era when goals were scarce and forward passed weren't allowed, he had no equal. Hainsworth came to Montreal from Saskatoon of the Western Canada Hockey League in 1926 on the recommendation of former Canadien Newsy Lalonde, who felt Hainsworth would be a worthy replacement for Georges Vezina. As it transpired, Hainsworth didn't just fill Vezina's skates, he won the first three trophies bearing his predecessor's name.

In 1928-29, Hainsworth allowed just 43 goals in 44 games and recorded 22 shutouts to establish a record that will never be broken. In fact, if you add Hainsworth's career shutouts from the NHL (94) and the WCHL (10), he has 104, one more than the all-time career leader Terry Sawchuk.

"And it's not like counting the WHA (World Hockey Association) and saying it was on par with the NHL," Zweig said, "because those leagues (NHL and WCHL) really were (on par)."

The year after Hainsworth recorded his 22 shutouts, the NHL changed the rules to allow forward passing and he finished that season with just four shutouts and his GAA went from 0.92 to 2.42, so it's obvious the style of play had something to do with Hainsworth's success. But if it were that easy to stop the puck, why wasn't every goalie in the league putting up those kinds of numbers?

> **"He looks like one of these dumpy guys whom it would be impossible to believe he could be great at anything."**
> – Hockey historian Eric Zweig

"I don't know how they got the fans out in 1926, '27 and '28," said hockey historian Ernie Fitzsimmons. "Every goal was a major occurrence."

Hainsworth owns the two best single-season GAA marks in history and won two Stanley Cups with the Canadiens, but was just as well-known for his textbook goaltending style as his ability to stop the puck.

"He was very unspectacular, a real technician," said hockey historian Bob Duff. "He didn't get a lot of credit because he wasn't acrobatic. In that era, goalies tended to be very athletic and were sprawling around making spectacular saves and he was a guy who always just seemed to be in the right spot."

Hainsworth explained his goaltending style in 1931 this way: "I'm sorry I can't put on a show like some of the other goaltenders. I can't look excited because I'm not. I can't shout at other players because that's not my style. I can't dive on easy shots and make them look hard. I guess all I can do is stop pucks."

Hainsworth played seven seasons for the Canadiens before being dispatched to the Toronto Maple Leafs for Lorne Chabot prior to the 1933-34 season. He played three-plus seasons in Toronto, returning to the Canadiens in 1936-37 to finish his career.

Thirteen years later, Hainsworth was killed in a car accident in Kitchener, Ont., where he was a municipal politician. ●

HHOF Images

Sylvio **MANTHA**

Two-Way Gem

HHOF Images

Defenseman	
Born: April 14, 1902, Montreal, Que.	
Died: Aug. 7, 1974	
Habs Career : 1923-1936	
3 Stanley Cups, 2 second-team all-stars	
63-78-141, 669 PIM in 538 games	
Hockey Hall of Fame: 1960	

Sylvio Mantha had never played defense in his life prior to joining the Canadiens in 1923. That he would go on to become one of the best two-way defensemen of his era is a testament to how truly underrated Mantha is among the pantheon of Canadiens former legends.

That Mantha joined the Canadiens the same season as Howie Morenz likely took a little luster off his arrival. But along with emerging stars such as Morenz and Aurel Joliat, Mantha helped usher in a new and productive era for the Canadiens, one that would see them win three Stanley Cups from 1924 to 1931.

The Canadiens were serving notice they were beginning to emerge as a power in the NHL. Winners of just one Stanley Cup in the old National Hockey Association in 1916 prior to their first Cup win as an NHL franchise in 1924, the Canadiens were starting to establish themselves as a perennial contender and were beginning to lay the groundwork for the foundations of the franchise.

In fact, it was Mantha's emergence as a defensive presence that allowed the Canadiens to trade the aging Sprague Cleghorn and Billy Coutu and begin to build their defense around him.

"He did for them on defense what Joliat did at forward," said hockey historian Bob Duff. "He was part of that next generation of players."

HHOF Images

Mantha was a strong defensive player and was able to also contribute offensively. After averaging just eight points per season his first six years, Mantha's totals ballooned to 13-11-24 in 44 games in 1929-30, likely as much a result of rule changes that allowed forward passing as his playing ability. It was also that season he set a career high for penalty minutes with 108. But Mantha was recognized as one of the league's top defensemen in subsequent years, earning second-team all-star spots on the first-ever all-star team in 1931 and again the next season.

"Here's a guy who, by today's standards, would have scored 20-some goals from the defense post and had 200 minutes in penalties," said hockey historian Ernie Fitzsimmons. "That should give you some clue as to what kind of player he was. He was hard-nosed and steady defensively and he also had the ability to score points in an era when they didn't have too much going on."

Mantha almost became part of Stanley Cup lore for all the wrong reasons. After their Cup triumph in 1924, the Canadiens were feted at a reception at the University of Montreal and Mantha was part of a group that headed to GM-owner Leo Dan-

> "By today's standards, (he) would have scored 20-some goals from the defense post and had 200 minutes in penalties."
> – Ernie Fitzsimmons

durand's home to keep the party going. The car in which they were traveling got stuck on a hill and the occupants got out to push the car.

Only after Dandurand's wife asked about the trophy they were talking about did they realize they had left the Cup on the curb when they got out to push the car. They went back to get it and in a stroke of luck, the Stanley Cup was still in the same spot.

Mantha served two stints as captain of the Canadiens and had a disastrous stint as a player-coach in 1936. But his achievements, while not apparent to those who don't follow the Canadiens closely, went a long way toward giving the Canadiens credibility and Cups in the early years of their existence. ●

Defenseman Sylvio Mantha, left, who had two stints as captain of the Canadiens, was a steadying influence for a franchise still trying to find its way.

Bruce Bennett Studios/Getty Images

Mats **NASLUND**

The Little Pioneer

	Left Winger
	Born: Oct. 31, 1959, Timra, Swe.
	Habs Career : 1982-1990
	1 Stanley Cup, 1 second-team all-star, 1 Lady Byng Trophy
	243-369-612, 107 PIM in 617 games

Bruce Bennett Studios/Getty Images

The night was Dec. 3, 1984 and it marked Guy Lafleur's first public appearance in the Montreal Forum after concluding his Hall of Fame career with the Montreal Canadiens. Through much of the game, the capacity crowd lustily chanted, "Guy! Guy! Guy!" and the guest of honor gratefully accepted the adulation.

But as the game progressed and the night wore on, the points kept coming and coming for little Mats Naslund. By the time the Habs had completed a 9-3 dismantling of the Hartford Whalers, the first European ever to play for the Canadiens had four goals and two assists. Not only that, the chants changed to, "Mats! Mats! Mats!"

More than 23 years later, Naslund can't say he remembers that night. But that's not to say he doesn't cherish his accomplishments with the Canadiens. Naslund admits he still follows the Canadiens closely, if for no other reason than he's checking to see whether anyone will usurp him as the last 100-point scorer for the franchise. He also checks the summaries after each All-Star Game to see whether anyone has broken his NHL record of five assists in one game.

"I'm always pretty happy when I see that no other guy has scored 100 points," Naslund said. "I'm pretty proud of that one."

Naslund played only eight seasons with the Canadiens, but there is no debating his impact. He was the first European player ever to find full-time work with the organization and he earned the respect of his teammates and fans by establishing a franchise record for points by a rookie with 71 in 1982-83. Kjell Dahlin matched that total three years later, but is considered to be the highest rookie scorer in franchise history because he had 32 goals, compared to 26 for Naslund.

It's hard to believe Naslund, along with fellow rookie Guy Carbonneau, was a healthy scratch for the first three games of the season. It wasn't long before Naslund took Rejean Houle's spot with Pierre Mondou and Mario Tremblay on what turned out to be a very effective line.

"I think we fit really well together," Naslund said. "Mario was a really tough grinder and Pierre was so good defensively. And they were both were right-handed shots, so they fed me on the left wing. So we were a pretty good line, yeah."

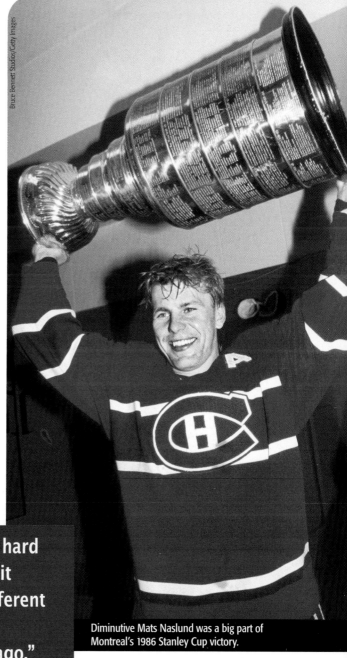

Bruce Bennett Studios/Getty Images

"It really wasn't that hard to adapt, but maybe it would have been different for me if I played in Philadelphia or Chicago."

Diminutive Mats Naslund was a big part of Montreal's 1986 Stanley Cup victory.

Naslund did set a record with 67 assists in 1985-86, which is still the franchise standard for left wingers. His 110-points that season earned him a second-team all-star berth and he added 22 points in 17 playoff games for the only Stanley Cup of his career.

It all seemed rather unlikely when Naslund, just 5-foot-7 and 160 pounds, arrived in Montreal after a sterling career in the Swedish Elite League. The NHL was just beginning to become obsessed with big players, but Naslund was aided by the fact the Canadiens had seen the value in small, skilled players over the years.

"I think guys like Henri Richard and Yvan Cournoyer helped with that," Naslund said. "It really wasn't that hard to adapt, but maybe it would have been different for me if I played in Philadelphia or Chicago. I had a lot of respect for the NHL, but I didn't have too much. I always knew I could play there." ●

Bruce Bennett Studios/Getty Images

Bert **OLMSTEAD**

No Nonsense Allowed

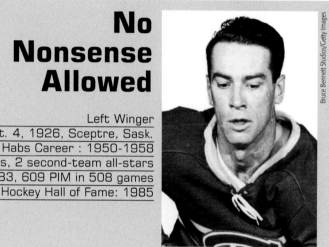

Bruce Bennett Studios/Getty Images

Left Winger
Born: Sept. 4, 1926, Sceptre, Sask.
Habs Career : 1950-1958
4 Stanley Cups, 2 second-team all-stars
103-280-383, 609 PIM in 508 games
Hockey Hall of Fame: 1985

It's something Bert Olmstead likes to call, "the human element." Its logic lies in the notion it's inevitable that, while enduring the rigors of a season, a hockey player is going to let up a little bit during a few games and practices now and then.

Just because Olmstead could recognize it doesn't mean he ever subscribed to it. Olmstead forged his Hall of Famer career with a combination of talent, belligerence and leadership, along with an ability to bring out the best in the players around him. Letting up, even in one practice a season, simply wasn't something he would ever do.

"I was always that way," Olmstead said. "I grew up on a farm and I learned early how to work hard. I played ball hard and I played hockey hard and it was a great way to play. I just seemed to get into the habit of doing it. I wanted to keep the standard as high as possible."

When the Canadiens were searching for a replacement for Toe Blake to play the left side with Elmer Lach and Rocket Richard,

> "I grew up on a farm and I learned early how to work hard."

they found it in Olmstead, who had been traded to Detroit from Chicago, then flipped to the Canadiens in 1950. Olmstead played well with Richard and Lach, but had his best years playing on a line with youngsters Jean Beliveau and Bernie Geoffrion.

> "I think I could always evaluate my teammates pretty well and I think I was pretty good at helping them get the best out of themselves."

In his 1970 book, *Strength Down the Middle,* Beliveau described the indelible mark Olmstead had on his career.

"He didn't stand any nonsense from us," Beliveau wrote. "If he met me in the left corner, he'd growl at me, 'Get the hell out of here. You get in front of the net,' he'd say and I did what he said because Bert was about the best left wing I ever saw when it came to fighting for possession of the puck. And if I was where he wanted me, parked in front of the net, his pass would be perfect. Playing with Bert, I always felt that he got the best out of me, that he made me do smarter things than I would have done myself."

"I knew what his strengths were and I wanted to keep it that way. I knew he couldn't score from the corner," Olmstead said. "I think I could always evaluate my teammates pretty well and I think I was pretty good at helping them get the best out of themselves."

Olmstead gained a reputation over the years for being cantankerous and bitter, but during a telephone call in the spring of 2008 at age 81, he was delightful, engaging, funny and insightful. When asked whether he was proud of the fact he still shares the Canadiens record for most points in a game (eight) with Richard, Olmstead said it wasn't something that got a lot of attention when he accomplished the feat in 1954.

There were other triumphs, such as setting an NHL single-season record for assists with 56 in 1956. That was the second consecutive year Olmstead led the league in helpers. After winning the first three of five straight Cups with the Canadiens, he was sent to the Toronto Maple Leafs, where he won another Cup in 1962.

"The last game I played for Montreal I won the Cup and the last game I played for Toronto I won the Cup," Olmstead said. "So there you go." ●

Tom **JOHNSON**

A Blueline Beauty

Bruce Bennett Studios/Getty Images

Defenseman	
Born: Feb. 18, 1928, Baldur, Man.	
Died: Nov. 21, 2006	
Habs Career : 1948-1963	
6 Stanley Cups, 1 first-team all-star,	
1 second-team all-star, 1 Norris Trophy	
47-183-230, 897 PIM in 857 games	
Hockey Hall of Fame: 1970	

The story goes that early in his career, a young and dashing Tom Johnson once invited four single girls to the same game with the promise that he'd meet each one afterward.

When Johnson emerged from the dressing room at The Forum to find four women waiting for him, he pulled up his collar and sneaked out the back door.

"I'll say this, he knows some beautiful girls," teammate Doug Harvey once said of Johnson. "Not plain girls. Lovely, sophisticated women with intelligence."

As fetching as Johnson was off the ice, he was more than content to be overshadowed on the ice by a dashing lineup of high-flying scorers. In fact, as Harvey's defense partner, he was often overlooked by those who focused on the sublime skills of Harvey.

But Johnson was always appreciated by those for whom and with he played. In a piece in *Sport* magazine in the 1950s, Canadiens coach Toe Blake said of Johnson: "He's one of the most courageous players I've ever coached. And one of the best."

Canadiens GM Frank Selke, who paid $2,000 to get Johnson on the club's protected list after he was not named among the 18 protected players on the Maple Leaf-sponsored Winnipeg Monarchs team in 1947, was even more effusive in his praise of Johnson.

"That was probably the best investment I ever made," Selke once said of acquiring Johnson.

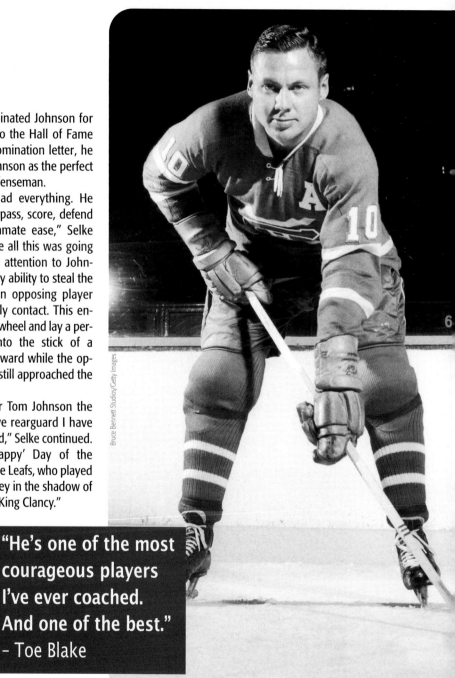

Selke nominated Johnson for induction into the Hall of Fame and in his nomination letter, he described Johnson as the perfect defensive defenseman.

"Harvey had everything. He could shoot, pass, score, defend with consummate ease," Selke wrote. "While all this was going on, few paid attention to Johnson's uncanny ability to steal the puck from an opposing player without bodily contact. This enabled him to wheel and lay a perfect pass onto the stick of a Canadien forward while the opposing team still approached the Habitant net.

"I consider Tom Johnson the best defensive rearguard I have ever managed," Selke continued. "Another 'Happy' Day of the Toronto Maple Leafs, who played his best hockey in the shadow of the dynamic King Clancy."

Bruce Bennett Studios/Getty Images

"He's one of the most courageous players I've ever coached. And one of the best."
– Toe Blake

Tom Johnson, right, was once described as the perfect defensive defenseman.

In his 13 seasons with the Canadiens, Johnson managed to score 10 goals only once, in 1958-59 when he broke Harvey's stranglehold on the Norris Trophy, largely because Harvey was injured much of the season. But offense was never Johnson's forte. He was at his best when the Canadiens were shorthanded. He had speed and skill to go with an ability to play well in the corners. He was a deft passer and while he took his share of penalties, not many of them were of the foolish variety.

And opponents, for the most part, reviled him. During Johnson's rookie season, one in which he would record a career-high 128 penalty minutes, Paul Chandler of the Detroit *News* had this to say about Johnson: "Tom Johnson is a villain. He's a new defenseman in the league this season whom such a calloused veteran as John Ross Roach describes as one of the, 'cruder wood-choppers to appear here in some time.'"

The next season, Johnson got into a penalty box brawl with Ted Kennedy of the Toronto Maple Leafs in which the police were called and Johnson was fined $75.

But Johnson learned to tame his ways as his career progressed. After his career in Montreal, Johnson was claimed by the Boston Bruins in the waiver draft that started a 36-year relationship between the Bruins and Johnson as a player, coach, GM and front-office executive. ●

> "I consider Tom Johnson the best defensive rearguard I have ever managed."
> - Frank Selke

Claude **PROVOST**

Champion Checker

Right Winger
Born: Sept. 17, 1933, Montreal, Que.
Died: April 17, 1984
Habs Career : 1955-1970
9 Stanley Cups, 1 first-team all-star,
1 Masterton Trophy
254-335-589, 469 PIM in 1,005 games

A hockey writer once noted that when Claude Provost skated, he looked like, "a drunken sailor walking on a ship's deck during a hurricane."

Provost didn't earn many style points over the course of his career, but might have been the most underrated and proficient two-way player of his era. To be sure, Provost was Bobby Hull's personal nemesis, often checking the Chicago star into submission. In Montreal's seven-game victory over the Black Hawks in 1965, Provost blanketed Hull and held the Golden Jet to just two goals, both of them coming in one game.

It was often said Provost made his reputation in the NHL by shadowing Hull, but Provost was an excellent defensive player before Hull came along. It should also be noted Provost was also a very good scorer and one gets the sense he could have even been better at it had he put his mind to focusing more on offense.

> **Provost might have been the most underrated and proficient two-way players of his era.**

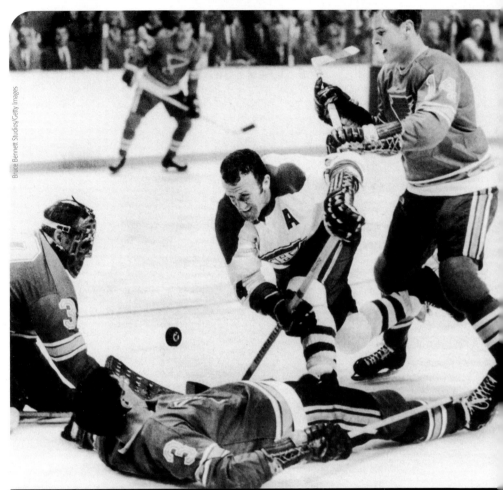

Bruce Bennett Studios/Getty Images

Claude Provost earned a reputation as a checker, but could put the puck in the net, too.
Here he tries to beat former teammate Jacques Plante in the 1969 Stanley Cup final, a series Montreal swept.

In 1961-62, Provost stunned the hockey world by scoring 33 goals, sharing second place in goal scoring with Gordie Howe and Frank Mahovlich and behind Hull, who scored 50.

"I got all those goals, but my checking was lousy," Provost told *Hockey World* magazine. "I'd rather check more and score less. It's better for the team."

Words like those would have NHL people salivating these days, but in the 1950s and '60s, defensive work wasn't as appreciated. Certainly if there had been a Selke Trophy in existence when Provost played, he would have given Bob Gainey a stiff challenge as most decorated defensive forward.

Just 5-foot-8 and 175 pounds, Provost kept himself in tremendous physical condition and was about as easy to move as a fire hydrant. That made him difficult to fend off as a checker and just as difficult to knock off the puck when he was carrying it.

> **"Provost is the hardest working player I've ever seen in my life."**
> – Henri Richard

Bruce Bennett Studios/Getty Images

"Provost is the hardest working player I've ever seen in my life," Henri Richard, Provost's center for much of his career, once said.

Remarkably, Provost won Cups each of the first five years of his career, as did Henri Richard and Jean-Guy Talbot. Provost finished his career with nine Cups and scored at least 50 points five times, all the while filling the role as the team's top penalty killer and shut-down forward.

Provost is one in a long line of superior checkers the Canadiens have employed over the years. It would have been extremely difficult for Provost to usurp Rocket Richard or Boom-Boom Geoffrion at right wing when he broke into the league, but coach Toe Blake liked Provost so much because of his two-way game.

"He scores because he checks," Blake once said of Provost. "It's only logical that when you check you get possession of the puck and that's bound to lead to goals. I'll bet he gets as many opportunities during a game as Yvan Cournoyer does." ●

Chris **CHELIOS**

(40)

An American Becomes a Canadien

Bruce Bennett Studios/Getty Images

Defenseman
Born: Jan. 25, 1962, Chicago, Ill.
Habs Career : 1983-1990
1 Stanley Cup, 1 first-team all-star, 1 Norris Trophy
72-237-309, 783 PIM in 402 games

Long before he became one of the greatest defensemen of his generation, long before he became the NHL's oldest player, long before his crusade helped bring down the leader of the NHL Players' Association, Chris Chelios was a cocky college kid with a wild streak who had no idea what kind of world he was entering.

That was the world of the Canadiens in 1984 and Chelios knew almost nothing about it. In fact, he had only been to Montreal once in his life, for an exhibition game with the U.S. Olympic team in 1983.

"I got absolutely blindsided," Chelios said. "Growing up in Chicago, hockey wasn't on TV much and the only memories I had of Montreal was in '71 when the Black Hawks lost to Montreal in the Stanley Cup final. But trust me, I learned quickly being around guys like Guy Lafleur, Bob Gainey and Larry Robinson and going to Henri Richard's brasserie to drink with him. It wasn't tough to figure out once I got there that there was something special about playing for that organization."

It wasn't tough to figure out there was something special about Chelios, too. Almost from the start, he played defense with the offensive flair of Guy Lapointe, combined with the junkyard dog mentality of Ken Reardon. Chelios had some spectacular offensive seasons with the Canadiens, some of the best of his career, in part because he was so gifted, but also because of the mentoring he received and the fact he was paired with fellow American Craig Ludwig on the blueline.

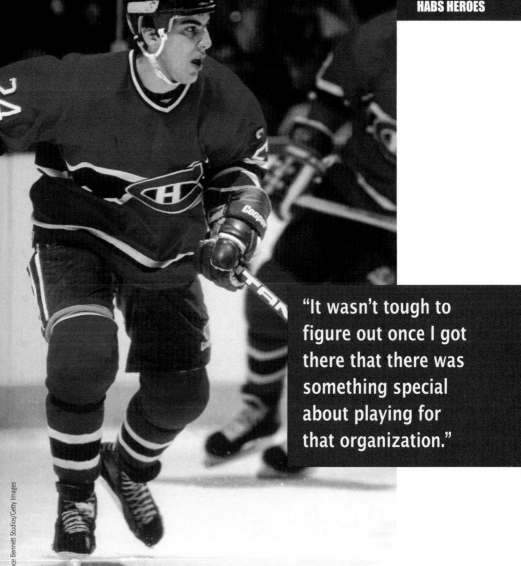

"It wasn't tough to figure out once I got there that there was something special about playing for that organization."

Bruce Bennett Studios/Getty Images

Chelios remembers how he always used to talk with Yvan Cournoyer after games and how he and his teammates would also go to Cournoyer's bar, when they weren't going to Henri Richard's bar.

"He was one guy who was just so proud to be a Canadien," Chelios said of Cournoyer. "It was a mentality that really rubbed off on me."

Chelios and Ludwig enjoyed the nightlife Montreal had to offer, occasionally a little too much, but both were lynchpins of the Canadiens' defense on the ice. Chelios won the first of his three Norris Trophies and earned the first of his five first-team all-star berths with the Canadiens in 1989 when

Chris CHELIOS

"When I went to Chicago, I didn't feel the burden I felt in Montreal."

he scored 73 points, a total he would hit only one more time during his career. The year before, he posted the only 20-goal season of his career.

The one dark cloud for Chelios came in 1989-90 when the Canadiens named him captain along with Guy Carbonneau to replace the retired Bob Gainey. Chelios acknowledged he had a lot of trouble dealing with replacing an icon and the pressure the captaincy brought with it and didn't handle it particularly well. His play suffered, he said, and when the Canadiens traded him to the Blackhawks for Denis Savard in the summer of 1990, he welcomed the deal.

"When I went to Chicago, I didn't feel the burden I felt in Montreal," Chelios said. "I think that being the captain really affected the way I played. I wasn't comfortable with it and I was young. I felt more responsible for the losses. I wish they had given me another year or two and had been a little more patient with me and allowed me to mature a little more, but everything happens for a reason." ●

Saku **KOIVU**

Captain Courageous

Andre Ringuette/NHLI via Getty Images

Center
Born: Nov. 23, 1974, Turku, Finland
Habs Career : 1995-2008*
1 Masterton Trophy
175-416-591, 579 PIM in 727 games
(*still a member of the Habs through August, 2008)

When Saku Koivu stepped on the Bell Centre ice for a game against the Toronto Maple Leafs Nov. 3, 2007, he made history. It wasn't exactly the kind he'd prefer to make, but it placed him firmly in the annals of team lore.

That night marked Koivu's 663rd career game as a Canadien, making him the longest-serving player in franchise history not to win a Stanley Cup. Prior to that night, the designation belonged to Shayne Corson, who was along for the ride when the Canadiens won the Cup in 1986, but was not on the roster and did not meet the requirements to have his name etched on the trophy.

That, however, should not tarnish Koivu's legacy as a Canadien. Whether or not he ever wins a Stanley Cup, Koivu and his career in Montreal will be defined by so many other things. He hasn't always been the Canadiens' best player, but there has never been any question

> On Nov. 3, 2007, he became the longest-serving player in franchise history not to win a Stanley Cup.

Saku Koivu has always meant more to the Canadiens and the community than what shows up on the scoresheet.

about his level of dedication and commitment to the game. And, of course, his most important triumph as a player and a person came when he survived non-Hodgkins lymphoma and returned to the team in 2001-02.

"Did I ever think we would lose him?" Canadiens doctor David Mulder told legendary Montreal hockey writer Red Fisher in 2007. "Well, you have to look at the statistics…"

But Koivu's game has never been about statistics. After finishing his treatment in 2002 and with the threat of a recurrence of the disease hanging over him for the next five years, Koivu continued to give back to the Canadiens on the ice and in the community. He is considered cancer-free now, but will never forget how the team and the city rallied around him during his time of need.

Robert Laberge /Allsport

"The support I got from everybody and the way the team helped me and my family made me feel even more of a Canadien," Koivu said in 2006. "Even before I felt it, but especially after, I felt like I wanted to make them feel that I'm giving something back."

Koivu has done that both by his effort on the ice and the establishment of the Saku Koivu Foundation, which raised $2.5 million of the $8 million needed to purchase a PET/CT scanner for the Montreal General Hospital, the same machine that was used for Koivu's final tests before he was declared cancer-free in January, 2007.

There have been other setbacks, the most prominent of which occurred in the 2006 playoffs when an errant high stick by Justin Williams damaged Koivu's eye so badly it left him with a blind spot and a cataract in the eye. The injury knocked Koivu out of the playoffs and changed the complexion of the series. When Koivu was injured, the Canadiens were ahead 2-0 in games and were leading Game 3 of the first round series, which the Carolina Hurricanes went on to capture en route to winning the Stanley Cup.

Koivu may never get the tangible recognition of having his name on the Stanley Cup, but he will always be seen as a winner by the Canadiens. ●

> "The support I got from everybody and the way the team helped me and my family made me feel even more of a Canadien."

Gilles **TREMBLAY**

Port-side Speedster

Bruce Bennett Studios/Getty Images

Left Winger	
Born: Dec. 17, 1938, Montmorency, Que.	
Habs Career : 1960-1969	
3 Stanley Cups	
168-162-330, 161 PIM in 509 games	

When Gilles Tremblay speaks, he sounds like a man who is perpetually out of breath. In fact, he can barely get through a 10-minute conversation without taking a break to cough and wheeze his way back to a regular breathing pattern.

"I'm still taking cortisone every day, I will never be able to stop taking cortisone," Tremblay said. "And there are side effects. I don't have any muscles and I'm not the same man anymore.

"But it could be worse."

It has been 40 years since Tremblay was forced to retire from the Canadiens in the prime of his career because of the asthma and respiratory problems that continue to debilitate him today. Tremblay was just 30 when he played his last NHL game and by that time was considered one of the top two-way left wingers in the NHL. From Dickie Moore to Tremblay to Bob Gainey, the Canadiens have always had strong two-way players on the port side and Tremblay isn't out of place in that group.

Much of his career with the Canadiens was spent checking the best right wingers in the game. As a left winger, he almost always lined up against Gordie Howe and there were nights when he would outplay the Detroit Red Wings legend. Other nights, such as the one when Howe tied Maurice Richard's record of 544 goals right at the Montreal Forum, Tremblay was not as effective.

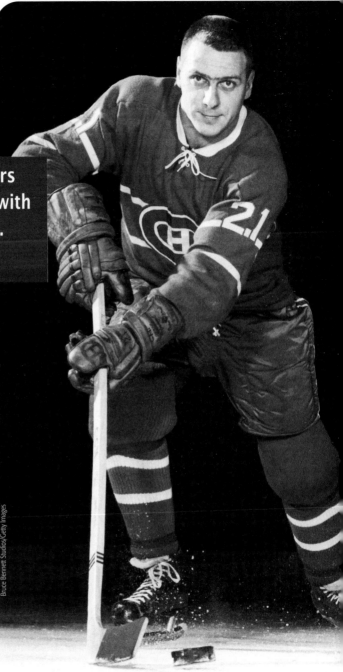

> "That's 41 years in hockey, all with the Canadiens. Not bad."

Bruce Bennett Studios/Getty Images

But he clearly enjoyed the challenge of going against the best players in the game. What's even more impressive when it comes to Tremblay is he managed to post five 20-goal seasons in the nine years he played with the Canadiens.

"It took about one year for Howe to really respect me," Tremblay said. "But when I played against Howe, I played the game the way it was meant to be played, not just following him around wherever he went. I could really skate and sometimes I forced him to cover me. He told me he didn't like playing against me because I forced him to skate all the time."

167

Gilles Tremblay figures he could have played another seven or eight years had his career not been shortened by respiratory problems.

> "When I played against Howe, I played the game the way it was meant to be played, not just following him around wherever he went."

Tremblay possessed the things it took to counter players such as Howe – lots of upper-body strength, a solid core and terrific speed. And he used all three of them to benefit his game at both ends of the ice.

Tremblay was indeed one of the fastest skaters in the league, probably the second fastest left winger behind Bobby Hull. At one point, Tremblay played on a unit with Jean Beliveau and Yvan Cournoyer and Beliveau recalled the line created all sorts of chances with the speed of its two wingers. Beliveau said he would often throw the puck up the left side of the ice where Tremblay would take it in full stride and when that happened, there were few defenders in the league who could catch him.

In his book, *My Life in Hockey,* Beliveau said the loss of Tremblay, "robbed the NHL of one of its most exciting players." The Canadiens turned down numerous opportunities to trade Tremblay and coach Toe Blake was once quoted as saying he wouldn't trade Tremblay straight up for Frank Mahovlich.

Had Tremblay not been afflicted with asthma, he figures he could have played another seven or eight years at least, which would have given him several more Cups with the Canadiens and, perhaps, a chance to make some real money in the World Hockey Association. Instead, he joined *La Soiree du Hockey* as a color analyst and saw the Canadiens win eight more Cups as a broadcaster.

"That's 41 years in hockey, all with the Canadiens," Tremblay said. "Not bad." ●

Ralph **BACKSTROM**

Third in Command

Bruce Bennett Studios/Getty Images

Center
Born: Sept. 18, 1937, Kirkland Lake, Ont.
Habs Career : 1956-1971
6 Stanley Cups, 1 Calder Trophy
215-287-502, 348 PIM in 844 games

Ralph Backstrom's days of not exactly being fully appreciated by the Montreal Canadiens started quite early, in 1954 to be exact, when assistant GM Ken Reardon showed up at Backstrom's home in Kirkland Lake to convince the 17-year-old to sign with the Canadiens.

"My dad was a gold miner and he didn't make very much money and Kenny came in and pulled out five $100 bills," Backstrom recalled. "As he was putting on his coat and his scarf and his fedora, he pulled out another $500 and slapped it in front of my nose. He said he had authorization to go up to $1,000 and said, 'I'll see you in Montreal.'"

Then early in his career, Backstrom celebrated the birth of his first child by buying a box of cigars and heading to The Forum for practice. When he offered one to coach Toe Blake, the crusty coach accepted his and said, "Good, now maybe you'll get off your ass and play some hockey."

> "Kenny (Reardon) came in and pulled out five $100 bills."

Bruce Bennett Studios/Getty Images

Despite being slotted for much of his career as a third-line center, Ralph Backstrom, right, was a formidable foe who got close attention from the likes of New York's Brad Park.

Backstrom faced the same dilemma many great young players who joined the Canadiens faced throughout their careers. Playing almost all his career as the third-line center behind Jean Beliveau and Henri Richard, Backstrom probably would have garnered more personal accolades elsewhere, but not even close to the same number of Stanley Cups.

Given his druthers, Backstrom will take the Cups, even if it means carrying the reputation as one of the greatest third-line centers the Canadiens ever had. He did receive a measure of personal recognition in 1958-59 when he won the Calder Trophy as rookie of the year and despite seeing al-

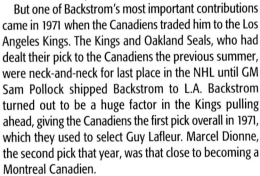

> "In those days there were only six teams in the NHL and you did everything you could to stay there. You played hard and you kept your mouth shut."

most no time on the power play and reduced ice time, registered five 20-goal seasons.

"There were a lot of games where I was told, 'I don't care if you don't even get one shot on goal, just make sure the guy you're checking doesn't score,' " Backstrom said. "On the one hand, playing behind Henri and Jean all those years saved me a little bit of wear and tear, but on the other hand I think my stats could have been significantly higher. But in those days there were only six teams in the NHL and you did everything you could to stay there. You played hard and you kept your mouth shut."

The lack of personal recognition was replaced in a big way by championships. Backstrom was there for the last two years of the late 1950s dynasty and was on four more Cup winners in the 1960s, a team many refer to as The Forgotten Dynasty.

But one of Backstrom's most important contributions came in 1971 when the Canadiens traded him to the Los Angeles Kings. The Kings and Oakland Seals, who had dealt their pick to the Canadiens the previous summer, were neck-and-neck for last place in the NHL until GM Sam Pollock shipped Backstrom to L.A. Backstrom turned out to be a huge factor in the Kings pulling ahead, giving the Canadiens the first pick overall in 1971, which they used to select Guy Lafleur. Marcel Dionne, the second pick that year, was that close to becoming a Montreal Canadien.

After his playing days, Backstrom remained in the game and was an in-line skating pioneer. Before retiring, he owned the Colorado Eagles of the Central League, a team that set a minor-league record in 2008 with 195 straight sellouts. ●

Doug **JARVIS**

Iron and Steal

Bruce Bennett Studios/Getty Images

Center	
Born: March 24, 1955, Brantford, Ont.	
Habs Career : 1975-1982	
4 Stanley Cups	
91-154-245, 151 PIM in 560 games	

It certainly wasn't the first time, or the last, that Sam Pollock had fleeced one of his NHL counterparts. This time, the victim was Toronto Maple Leafs GM Jim Gregory and the player involved was Doug Jarvis.

With Robin Sadler, Pierre Mondou and Brian Engblom already in the fold with his first three picks in the 1975 entry draft, Pollock peddled off minor leaguer Greg Hubick to the Maple Leafs in exchange for Jarvis, who had been selected 24th overall by the Maple Leafs.

In Jarvis, the Canadiens got a top-notch defensive center who would go on to play 560 consecutive games for them and win four Stanley Cups before being traded to the Washington Capitals. In Hubick, the Leafs got a player who would play one season for them and score 14 points in 72 games.

There were fears Jarvis would sign with the Houston Aeros of the World Hockey Association, but Gregory said that wasn't the main motivation for trading Jarvis, who would go on to establish the

> **He won four Stanley Cups before being traded to the Washington Capitals.**

Bruce Bennett Studios/Getty Images

"Stepping into that lineup was almost like going to the University of Hockey."

league's ironman mark by playing 964 consecutive games with the Canadiens, Capitals and Hartford Whalers.

"Our scouts thought we needed somebody with a little more size and Hubick had played a couple of years in the American League," Gregory said. "But it certainly isn't great to have to remember a trade like that."

If nothing else, Jarvis had a great sense of timing, both as a premier faceoff man and in terms of his tenure with the Canadiens. Starting his career on the fourth line with Bob Gainey and Jimmy Roberts, Jarvis arrived in 1975-76, just in time to win the first of four straight Stanley Cups with a team that some think was the most formidable in the history of the NHL.

"For a young guy like me, there was certainly no better place to start a career," Jarvis said. "Stepping into that lineup was almost like going to the University of Hockey."

Jarvis never scored more than 20 goals or 48 points in a season with the Canadiens, and that was in his last year, but he did provide a defensive and penalty-killing presence in a lineup that was loaded with players who had offensive Hall of Fame credentials. And it wasn't as though Jarvis was a no-talent slug who was forced into a defensive role. In his last season with the Peterborough Petes, he recorded 45 goals and 133 points in 64 games.

Bruce Bennett Studios/Getty Images

But his coach that season was Roger Neilson, who prepared him well for the career path he was about to take with the most star-studded team in hockey. Neilson drilled into Jarvis the importance of a strong defensive game, something that was further emphasized by Canadiens coach Scotty Bowman.

"Sam Pollock told me right away that they had room on the roster for a checking center who could play a specific role," Jarvis said. "He said there was basically one spot open on the team and that the players competing for it were myself, Pierre Mondou and Ron Andruff. We all went on to have pretty decent careers." ●

45 Gump **WORSLEY**

An Off-Broadway Hit

Bruce Bennett Studios/Getty Images

Goaltender
Born: May 14, 1929, Montreal, Que.
Died: Jan. 26, 2007
Habs Career : 1963-1970
4 Stanley Cups, 1 first-team all-star,
1 second-team all-star, 2 Vezina Trophies
92-44-25, 2.42 GAA, 16 shutouts
Hockey Hall of Fame: 1980

A writer for THN once mused that Gump Worsley looked like a guy who worked at Jiffy-Lube and there has never been a more apt comparison in the history of hockey. Worsley never carried the classy, dignified, square-jawed air that personified Canadiens goalies, but not many of them tended goal as well as he did.

Worsley is the only one of the Canadiens' all-time great goaltenders who wasn't developed from within the organization. When he came to the Canadiens in a trade in 1963, he had already played 10 years in the league for the moribund New York Rangers.

And while he developed sterling credentials with the Rangers – including the Calder Trophy as rookie of the year in 1953 – he was never recognized for his brilliance until he starred in Montreal, largely because the Rangers were dismal with the exception of their goalie. Once when asked which team gave him the most trouble, he responded by saying the Rangers.

> A writer for THN once mused that Gump Worsley looked like a guy who worked at Jiffy-Lube.

Bruce Bennett Studios/Getty Images

"You could argue he was the best goalie in the league when he was with the Rangers," said Bob Duff, a hockey historian who co-authored a book on goalies titled *Without Fear*. "They didn't keep save percentages then, but hockey historians have gone back and figured them out and he led the league in save percentage almost every year with the Rangers."

Worsley came to the Canadiens and while he tried to portray an air of ambivalence, many think he struggled with the pressure of playing in Montreal at first. He arrived at his first camp overweight and played just eight games before being dispatched to the minors, where he spent much of the next two seasons.

In fact, the Canadiens held Worsley out as trade bait in 1964 and the Red Wings almost made a deal to get him. Wings GM Sid Abel wanted to see how 22-year-old Roger Crozier would do, knowing he could get Worsley from Montreal if Crozier faltered. Crozier led the league in wins that season and won the Calder Trophy, so Worsley stayed a Canadien.

Midway through the '64-65 season, Worsley was called up and played, then platooned with Charlie Hodge in the playoffs. But he suffered a ligament injury in the final and missed Games 4, 5 and 6 against the Black Hawks. Canadiens coach Toe Blake gambled and played Worsley in Game 7 and Worsley responded with a 4-0 shutout to clinch the Cup.

That was the good news. That bad news, Duff said, is that Worsley used a liniment called DMSO, which is used on horses and one of the side effects is brutally bad breath.

"I don't think his teammates wanted to get too close to him after that," Duff said.

The Canadiens would win two more Cups with Worsley in the nets and another with him playing a backup role before dealing him to the Minnesota North Stars in 1970. The combination of the pressure of playing in Montreal and a severe fear of flying triggered a near nervous breakdown in 1967-68.

Once on a flight, the plane dipped and Jean Beliveau ended up with coffee all over himself. When the attendant told Beliveau to bill his dry-cleaning to Air Canada, Worsley responded, "What about my shorts?"

> "You could argue he was the best goalie in the league when he was with the Rangers."
> – Bob Duff

On a turbulent flight to Los Angeles in November, 1968, Worsley left the plane on a Chicago stopover and took the train back to Montreal. He took a month off, but returned to lead the Canadiens to the Stanley Cup, his last as a No. 1 goalie. ●

Bruce Bennett Studios/Getty Images

Gump Worsley may have been the best goalie in the NHL before joining Montreal, but it wasn't until he was a Hab he started to be recognized for his brilliance.

Bobby **ROUSSEAU**

Born to Be a Canadien

Right Winger

Born: July 26, 1940, Montreal, Que.

Habs Career : 1961-1970

4 Stanley Cups, 1 second-team all-star, 1 Calder Trophy

200-322-522, 317 PIM in 643 games

Perhaps the passage of time has something to do with Bobby Rousseau's view on his life as a Montreal Canadien. Few have stared down the kind of pressure and stress Rousseau faced during his hockey career in Montreal and, by all accounts at that time, it took a heavy toll on him.

Rousseau was so anxious to make the team in 1960 he developed stomach ulcers. Later in his career, he picked up *The Power of Positive Thinking* by Dr. Vincent Norman Peale when the Canadiens were playing an exhibition game in Fort Wayne, Ind., and adopted it as his personal bible, flipping through the pages for inspiration every time he felt unsure of himself.

"I've always been a pessimist and looked on the dark side of things, even when I was doing well," Rousseau told a reporter in 1966. "This book has convinced me to look at the bright side of life."

But to hear Rousseau talk about it almost 40 years later, you'd think he breezed through his career, living the charmed life of a Montreal kid who ended up playing for the team he loved.

"I absolutely did not feel the pressure one bit and I'm being very honest about that," Rousseau said in the spring of 2008. "If I could go back and do my career all over again, I would play for the Montreal Canadiens again and take all the pressure that comes with it."

Graphic Artist/HHOF Images

Goalies such as Toronto's Johnny Bower needed to be alert when talented Bobby Rousseau was on the ice.

> **"I was born to be a hockey player. And I was born to play for the Montreal Canadiens."**

Whether Rousseau actually felt the pressure or not, it was certainly omnipresent. One of 12 children from the Montreal suburb of St-Hyacinthe, Rousseau had already seen two of his older brothers try to catch on with the Canadiens and fail, although older brother Guy played sparingly with the Canadiens and assisted on Maurice Richard's 400th career goal. When Rousseau was a player, he acknowledged he felt an obligation to do his family proud and he was worried about letting it down.

179

Bruce Bennett Studios/Getty Images

If that wasn't enough, the Canadiens first noticed Rousseau when he was playing Jr. B hockey in St-Jean, only to find the team was sponsored by the Detroit Red Wings and Rousseau wasn't available. So, the Canadiens proceeded to buy the team and the rights to all the players just to get Rousseau.

Then, after scoring just 10 points in his first 35 games of his rookie season of 1961-62, Rousseau scored at a point-per-game pace for the next 35 to take the Calder Trophy. An excellent golfer born with abnormally large wrists, Rousseau had a hard, accurate shot and scoring potential that reminded some people of Rocket Richard.

"First, the Canadiens come up with Maurice Richard, then they get Jean Beliveau and Dickie Moore and Bernie Geoffrion and Henri Richard," Detroit Red Wings goalie Terry Sawchuk lamented to THN in 1962. "Now it looks as if Rousseau is going to make me lose more sleep before I quit this game."

Rousseau didn't ever reach that level, but he did lead the Canadiens in scoring in 1965-66 and '66-67, the only two seasons he finished among the top 10 scorers in the NHL. He won four Cups with the Canadiens, but his playoffs were generally far less spectacular than his regular seasons and over the course of his career, Rousseau developed a reputation for avoiding physical contact. Those in Montreal vehemently opposed the theory and future teammates with the Minnesota North Stars and New York Rangers lauded Rousseau for his courage.

"I was born to be a hockey player," Rousseau said. "And I was born to play for the Montreal Canadiens." ●

Doug **RISEBROUGH**

The New Breed

Bruce Bennett Studios/Getty Images

	Center
	Born: Jan 29, 1954, Guelph, Ont.
	Habs Career : 1974-1982
	4 Stanley Cups
	117-185-302, 959 PIM in 493 games

It's safe to say that in his eight seasons with the Montreal Canadiens, Doug Risebrough gained a definitive appreciation for the organization's winning philosophy. Of course winning a Stanley Cup, on average, every other season will have that effect on a guy.

But it wasn't until Risebrough was dealt to the Calgary Flames in 1982 that it was cemented in his psyche.

"When I got to Calgary, I couldn't believe how far away they were from winning," Risebrough said. "That was not as much a reflection on the Flames as it was on the Canadiens."

It's very difficult for other organizations to compete with the Canadiens and their legacy, something Risebrough realized when he moved on. And while his individual numbers were more robust in Calgary, the lessons Risebrough learned as a Canadien guide him still as GM of the Minnesota Wild.

Risebrough actually came to the Canadiens at a very interesting time. The league was changing and so were the Canadiens. More of a premium was being placed on smashmouth hockey and while the Canadiens were loathe to join the fray, they knew they had to gain more fractiousness in their lineup. That's why with a mind-boggling five of the first 15 picks in the 1974 draft, they selected Cam Connor, Risebrough, Rick Chartraw, Mario Tremblay and Gord McTavish.

Gritty Doug Risebrough, who set a team record for penalty minutes early in his career, represented a change in philosophy for the Habs.

> **"I don't think you ever felt safe in the lineup, even as a checking forward, unless you scored 15 to 20 goals."**

None was considered an elite offensive player, but all possessed competitive natures and an ability to play a far more physical, grinding game. After starting the 1974-75 season in the minors, Risebrough was called up when Henri Richard hurt his ankle, an injury that would keep Richard out of most of that season, the last of his Hall of Fame career.

Risebrough seized the center spot on the fourth line and proved his worth immediately. Not only did he score an impressive 47 points in 64 games, he accumulated what was then a team-record 198 penalty minutes (a mark that isn't even in the top 10 anymore thanks in large part to Chris Nilan and Lyle Odelein) and followed that up with seasons of 44 and 60 points and 182 and 130 PIM.

"You have to remember, they hadn't won in two years and that was a long time for them in those days," Risebrough said of breaking in with the Canadiens in 1974-75. "The team that had won the year before was the Broad Street Bullies and I don't think the people in Montreal believed that was the way to go, but I think they believed there had to be some element of that. The Canadiens weren't going to be a dump-and-chase teams, they had to find elements of that."

Risebrough found his spot on a line with Tremblay and Yvon Lambert, which turned out to be one of the league's most effective checking/energy lines because all three had an ability to score as well.

"As much as (the Canadiens) believed in a little more bite and grind, they still believed that, at the end of the day, you had to score more goals," Risebrough said. "I don't think you ever felt safe in the lineup, even as a checking forward, unless you scored 15 to 20 goals. There were always guys coming from behind, too. That was always the thing in Montreal, there was always somebody else." ●

183

Stephane **RICHER**

The Next Great Hope

Jim Leary/Getty Images

Right Winger
Born: June 7, 1966, Ripon, Que.
Habs Career : 1985-1991, 1996-98
1 Stanley Cup
225-196-421, 399 PIM in 490 games

Early in his career, Stephane Richer posed for the cover of a magazine published by The Hockey News in which a huge portrait of Rocket Richard in full flight was in the background.

It was fitting since, as the one-time next great French Canadian offensive superstar for the Canadiens, Richer could never escape the shadows of players such as Richard, Jean Beliveau, Boom-Boom Geoffrion and Guy Lafleur.

He did try. In fact, Richer remains the last player in Canadiens history to score 50 goals in a season, something he did twice during his first tour of duty with the Canadiens. He also won a Stanley Cup and was a plus or even player every season during that initial six-year stint, from 1985-91.

But somehow, when compared to the other French Canadian greats who played in Montreal over the years, Richer never measured up. It didn't help that he grew up in Ripon, Que., which is about six miles down the road from Lafleur's hometown of Thurso. And sometimes he didn't take it very well.

"I probably didn't make all the sacrifices I should have," Richer said.

After playing his rookie season in 1985-86 and helping the Canadiens win the Stanley Cup, Richer was sent to the minors. At one point after being benched for the third period of a game in the American League, Richer left the team and threatened to retire,

Robert Laberge /Allsport

"(Lemaire and Robinson) made me a better player and a better person."

just as he did once in junior hockey. "I've lost my taste for playing hockey," Richer said at the time. Prior to sending him down, coach Jean Perron essentially threw up his hands over Richer. "He's a special case," Perron said at the time. "I tried everything with him."

Although sometimes it doesn't seem so, Richer, who was traded to New Jersey in 1991 then reacquired in '95, insists he enjoyed most of his time with the Canadiens. Certainly, he never scored with anyone else the way he did with Montreal.

"I have to say I really enjoyed the parade until all the bullshit started," Richer said. "'I'm gay, I'm on drugs, I'm a party guy...blah, blah, blah.' Every bad thing that could be said about a person was said about me. If I was such a party guy, how was it that I was able to play 18 years in the NHL? If I hadn't hurt my foot those last couple of years, I probably would have played 20 or 21 years."

Robert Laberge/Getty Images

When Richer came to Montreal, he had never scored more than 39 goals in three seasons of major junior and Richer acknowledges he was much more a set-up man than goal-scorer prior to his days in Montreal. But early in Richer's NHL career, GM Serge Savard suggested to Perron he move Richer to right wing. Savard reasoned that with the Canadiens already strong down the middle, where Bobby Smith, Guy Carbonneau and Brian Skrudland were fixtures, Richer's size, skating ability and shot could be better exploited on the right side.

A trade to New Jersey in 1991, essentially for Kirk Muller, worked out for both teams and allowed Richer later to be reunited with Jacques Lemaire and Larry Robinson.

"That was the best thing for me and I'm so thankful for that," Richer said. "(Lemaire and Robinson) made me a better player and a better person." ●

Dick **DUFF**

Two-team Champ

Graphic Artist/HHOF Images

Left Winger
Born: Feb. 18, 1936, Kirkland Lake, Ont.
Habs Career : 1964-1970
4 Stanley Cups
87-85-172, 166 PIM in 305 games
Hockey Hall of Fame: 2006

A couple weeks after he was acquired by the Canadiens from the New York Rangers in 1964, Dick Duff was walking down Sainte-Catherine Street on a Sunday afternoon. It was there he had a chance meeting with Canadiens coach Toe Blake, who smiled and politely asked him how things were going.

Duff told him he was thrilled to be in Montreal, that his new teammates were wonderful, he was pleased with his play and that generally, things were going great.

"Well, if you don't start playing better, things will be going (expletive) great somewhere else," Blake said before walking away.

"I thought I was playing all right, you know," Duff said. "I think it was part of his strategy to keep guys thinking all the time."

Duff did manage to pick up his play and won four Stanley Cups with the Canadiens to go with the two he won with the Maple Leafs. In doing so, Duff joined Bert Olmstead as the only players to win Stanley Cups with both the Leafs and the Canadiens, a group that grew by one when Frank Mahovlich joined the Habs in 1971.

> "To you from failing hands we throw the torch... I'm up there, they told me that."

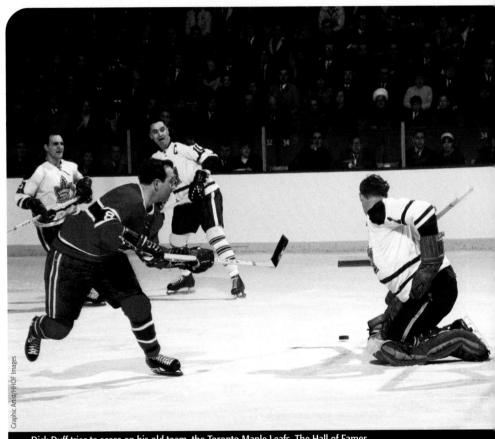

Dick Duff tries to score on his old team, the Toronto Maple Leafs. The Hall of Famer won two Stanley Cups in Toronto and four more with Montreal.

"I'm really glad I got into the Hall of Fame, but even if I hadn't, I had some great experiences in the league," Duff said. "How many guys can say they won the Cup with Montreal and Toronto? I really liked Montreal, though. I loved the fact that hockey meant something to them."

When Duff came to the Canadiens in a deal for Bill Hicke, Blake did not mince words when he said, "we expect him to play better hockey than he did for the Rangers." After three straight 20-goal seasons in Toronto, Duff tailed off, part of the reason for which he attributed to conditioning.

In Montreal, Duff found a system that was more to his liking and he responded with two 20-goal seasons and a 19-goal campaign. He could be used on any line and play any role. In 1969, his last playoff with the Canadiens, Duff led the team in goals with six and finished second to Jean Beliveau in points with 14 and also finished second to Serge Savard in voting for the Conn Smythe Trophy.

"How many guys can say they won the Cup with Montreal and Toronto?"

Not all of the times were good in Montreal for Duff, however. Although he managed to complete his university degree in political science while playing for the Canadiens, there were some dark days. During his playing career, he invested heavily in an electronics company and lost about $60,000, including about $28,000 in one day when the stock plummeted from $43 to $15.

The Canadiens dispatched Duff to the Los Angeles Kings in 1969-70 and he finished out his career with the Buffalo Sabres, where rookie Richard Martin idolized Duff so much he would tape Duff's sticks.

Duff said his body went to Los Angeles and later to Buffalo, but he felt like his heart never left Montreal and was thrilled to learn he and Patrick Roy had been added to the Canadiens Hall of Famers who adorn the team's dressing room.

"To you from failing hands we throw the torch…I'm up there, they told me that," Duff said. "Aye, aye, aye. How's that for a kid from Kirkland Lake?" ●

Duff, attempting to put one past Chicago's Glenn Hall as teammate Bobby Rousseau crashes the crease, said his heart never really left Montreal after he was traded away.

Bruce Bennett Studios/Getty Images

Gerry **McNEIL**

Coulda', Woulda', Shoulda'

Goaltender	
Born: April 17, 1926, Quebec City, Que.	
Died: June 17, 2004	
Habs Career : 1947-1954, 1957	
2 Stanley Cups, 1 second-team all-star	
119-105-52, 2.36 GAA, 28 shutouts	

Gerry McNeil was a product of the Canadiens' powerful recruiting and developing system of the 1940s, but he may have been the biggest victim of it as well.

In fact, McNeil might be the most forgotten big-time goalie the Canadiens have ever had if not for the notable goals he allowed. First, he surrendered Bill Barilko's overtime winner in Game 5 of the Stanley Cup final that gave the Leafs the Cup and helped vault Barilko, who died on a fishing trip later that summer, into immortality.

Then in 1954, the Canadiens were trailing 3-1 in the Stanley Cup final and McNeil replaced Jacques Plante in the nets. He got them to overtime of Game 7 before a harmless Tony Leswick shot deflected off Doug Harvey's glove and into the Montreal goal.

McNeil won two Cups with Montreal, but it could have been so different. He arrived in Montreal in 1943 and in camp was every bit as good as Bill Durnan. To some observers, he was even better. But the Canadiens decided to go with the more experienced Durnan and McNeil had to wait seven years while Durnan piled up Stanley Cups and Vezina Trophies. The Canadiens were also in the Stanley Cup final each of the four seasons he was their No. 1 goalie.

Perhaps McNeil's worst turn of luck was that his tenure as a Canadiens goalie was bookended by Durnan and Jacques Plante.

> "I have a nervous temperament and I want to do something that involves less worry."

Bruce Bennett Studios/Getty Images

"The guy before you wins six Vezinas and the guy after you wins six Vezinas," said hockey historian Bob Duff, "it's pretty easy to be forgotten."

What also makes McNeil's story remarkable is that he was a high-scoring winger who led his team in scoring in bantam hockey before switching to the goaltending position. That didn't stop him from becoming a top prospect a few years later when Canadiens player/scout Mike McMahon discovered him in Quebec City.

And while McNeil never won a Vezina Trophy for the Canadiens, he had a huge hand in Durnan's last one in 1950. With Durnan out because of an infection caused by a gash to his forehead and leading the Vezina race by just four goals, McNeil came in and allowed just nine goals in six games. Durnan won the Vezina – which in those days was given to the goalie on the team that allowed the fewest goals – by 14 goals over Harry Lumley of Detroit.

The Hockey News was effusive in its praise of McNeil in its March 18, 1950 issue. "Bill Durnan and the entire Montreal squad owe McNeil a handsome vote of thanks for his sparkling work in the pinch. In fact, they ought to vote him a slice of that Vezina and Stanley Cup money coming up!" THN wrote in a front-page story.

The good times did not last for McNeil and, like Durnan, he left the game seemingly at the prime of his career because of bad nerves. Some say the Leswick goal, which wasn't his fault because Harvey stuck out his hand to stop it, put McNeil over the edge.

"I have a nervous temperament," he said at the time, "and I want to do something that involves less worry."

McNeil didn't play for a year and then came back to play in the minors. The only exception was a nine-game stint with the Canadiens in 1956-57 when Plante was injured. ●

Jean-Guy **TALBOT**

Seven Cups and a Sweat Suit

Defenseman
Born: July 11, 1932,
Cap-de-la-Madeleine, Que.
Habs Career : 1955-1967
7 Stanley Cups, 1 first-team all-star
36-209-245, 884 PIM in 791 games

It is one of hockey's all-time injustices that Jean-Guy Talbot is known better by many fans for his unfortunate fashion faux pas of wearing a cheesy polyester track suit behind the bench of the New York Rangers and his part in ending Scotty Bowman's playing career than for his accomplishments as a player.

And they were many, particularly in his 12 seasons with the Canadiens. During that time, Talbot established himself as an excellent passer who also provided a high level of physical play in his own zone.

In fact, he was a key component of seven Stanley Cup teams with the Canadiens and is one of only 12 players who played on all five Cup-winning teams from 1956 through 1960. Only eight players in NHL history have won more Cups than Talbot.

Talbot's best season was the 1961-62 campaign in which he led all defensemen in scoring with 47 points and was named to the first all-star team along with former Canadien Doug Harvey.

> **Only eight players in NHL history have won more Cups than Talbot.**

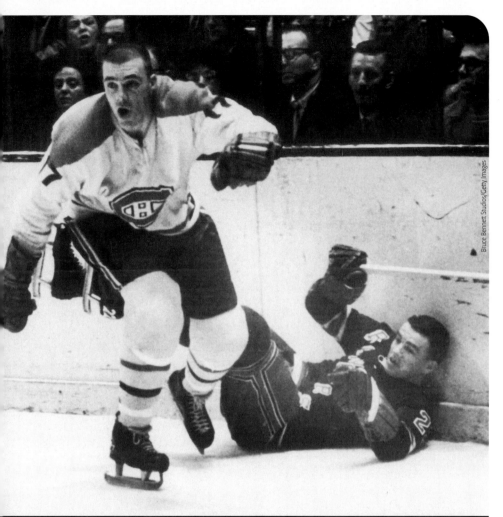

Physical play was part of Jean-Guy Talbot's arsenal, a fact Ted Hampson of the Rangers discovered after absorbing a bodycheck.

Talbot's stick to Bowman's head in junior hockey in 1952 did ultimately end Bowman's playing career and started him on the path to coaching, but it wasn't as dramatic as it was made out to be.

The story goes that Bowman suffered a crushed skull and had to have a plate inserted into his head. The reality is, he received a cut that required 14 stitches and missed only one game. But the hit did leave Bowman with recurring headaches and tentativeness as a player which led to the expiration of his career.

Bowman didn't hold any grudges. In fact, he ended up being Talbot's coach when the Blues claimed Talbot on waivers in 1968. ●

Pit **LEPINE**

Second in Command

Center
Born: July 30, 1901,
Ste-Anne-de-Bellevue, Que.
Died: Aug. 2, 1955
Habs Career : 1925-1938
2 Stanley Cups
143-98-241, 392 PIM in 526 games

The only blemishes on Pit Lepine's record with the Canadiens is he coached them to their worst statistical season ever and is the only person in the history of the franchise to both play for and coach a Canadiens team that finished last overall in the NHL.

The Canadiens have only done that twice in their history. Lepine played for the 1925-26 team that finished seventh in a seven-team NHL and coached the team that finished with a 10-33-5 mark to finish last in the league in 1939-40.

Fortunately for Alfred Pierre Lepine, his on-ice credentials are much more solid. Lepine played 526 games for the Canadiens – no small feat considering the seasons were much shorter – and proved himself to be a very useful two-way player. Playing on a team with offensive stars such as Howie Morenz and Aurel Joliat, Lepine was a fine complement to the big scorers.

> "He was the guy, I guess you could say, who invented secondary scoring."
> – Ernie Fitzsimmons

"He was the guy, I guess you could say, who invented secondary scoring," said hockey historian Ernie Fitzsimmons. "He was a brainy sort of player who knew how to keep the opposition from scoring and he could get some points, too."

Lepine was also one of the first in a long line of superior checkers for the Canadiens.

"Back in those days if you got more than one penalty, you just kept going off," said hockey historian Bob Duff. "If you got four penalties, you played four men short. There was a game against the Maroons where they had a big scuffle and it ended up there was one player and the goalie for each team and they put (Lepine) on because he was their best defensive player." ●

HHOF Images

Eric **DESJARDINS**

Hat Trick Hero

Defenseman	
Born: June 14, 1969, Rouyn, Que.	
Habs Career : 1988-1995	
1 Stanley Cup	
43-136-179, 351 PIM in 405 games	

Marty McSorley gets asked a lot about the illegal stick that probably cost the Los Angeles Kings a chance to win their only Stanley Cup in 1993. Eric Desjardins gets a lot of questions about that night, but for an entirely different reason.

It was Desjardins who was on the euphoric side of McSorley's blunder the evening of June 3, 1993.

That's because it was Desjardins who scored all three goals in the Canadiens' 3-2 overtime win in Game 2. In doing so, he became the first defenseman in NHL history to score a hat trick in a Stanley Cup final game.

"Every time I meet people in Montreal, that's all they want to talk about," Desjardins said. "That was a special game and the highlight of my career in Montreal, that's for sure."

It was a Habs career that was remarkably short, given that Desjardins had established himself as a very reliable two-way defenseman in his first six years in Montreal. But nine games into the lockout-shortened 1995 season, the offense-starved Canadiens traded Desjardins, John LeClair and

> **"I never wanted to leave Montreal, but... I wasn't bitter about it."**

Gilbert Dionne to the Philadelphia Flyers for Mark Recchi and a third round pick in a trade that is regarded as one of the most lopsided of all-time.

"When things don't go well, I'm not the kind of person who wants to go somewhere else and think it's going to be better," Desjardins said. "I never wanted to leave Montreal, but I understand why they made the trade and I wasn't bitter about it."

Desjardins was steady in Montreal, but established himself as an elite defenseman with the Flyers. As great as things were in Montreal, Desjardins identifies himself more as a Flyer than a Canadien.

"Lots of people can't understand that," he said. "They think that when you leave Montreal, you stop playing." ●

Robert Laberge/Getty Images

197

Bobby **SMITH**

Maturation in Montreal

Center
Born: Feb. 12, 1958, North Sydney, N.S.
Habs Career : 1983-1990
1 Stanley Cup
172-310-482, 430 PIM in 505 games

Not many players go to Montreal to escape the pressures of hockey, but that's what Bobby Smith did when he joined the Canadiens in 1983. And not surprisingly, it made him a better player and, ultimately, a Stanley Cup champion.

When Smith was drafted first overall by the Minnesota North Stars in 1978, he was coming off a 192-point season and no less an authority than Scotty Bowman predicted he would become the best player in the league before long. During Smith's second season, North Stars' coach Glen Sonmor said, "Bobby Smith has what it takes to become the best hockey player in the world."

Smith never quite met those projections, but arrived with the Canadiens at the age of 25 a much more mature player and one who was surrounded by more veteran talent, albeit on a team that was still in the midst of GM Serge Savard's five-year plan.

"We weren't a great team when I got there," Smith said. "I was brought in to bring some offense to the team, but I didn't see myself as, 'Thursday night in St. Louis…Bobby Smith and the Montreal Canadiens,' where that was the case my first couple of years in Minnesota."

> "I didn't see myself as, 'Thursday in St. Louis… Bobby Smith and the Montreal Canadiens.'"

Photo by Brian Miller/Getty Images

"We weren't a great team when I got (to Montreal)."

Bobby Smith, left, excelled in Montreal in part because he wasn't viewed as 'The Franchise'.

For the most part, with the exception of a couple playoffs, Smith was a very productive player for the Canadiens, posting three seasons of 80-plus points and becoming a better all-around player.

"I definitely think I was a better player (in Montreal)," Smith said. "Playing for Jacques Lemaire, I learned so much from him. I don't think I would have played 15 years in the league if I hadn't had the chance to play for him during that period." ●

Charlie **HODGE**

The 'Lucky' Understudy

Goaltender
Born: July 28, 1933, Lachine, Que.
Habs Career : 1954-1967
4 Stanley Cups, 2 second-team all-stars, 2 Vezina Trophies
117-71-39, 2.46 GAA, 21 shutouts

There may not be another man who better exemplifies the vagaries of pre-expansion goaltending than Charlie Hodge.

"I've been lucky basically all my life," Hodge said from his home in British Columbia and, well, that's one way of looking at it.

For example, his name is on the Stanley Cup four times with the Canadiens, but he played just three Cup final games and 16 playoff games for the team throughout his entire career. And he's right to point out he stuck in the NHL where goalies just as good as he was were stuck in the minors.

With just six teams and five of them basically having the same goaltender for the better part of a decade – Jacques Plante in Montreal, Gump Worsley in New York, Terry Sawchuk in Detroit, Glenn Hall in Chicago and Johnny Bower in Toronto – there was little room for Hodge, so he made the best of his situation.

And most of the time, that required him to be ready to perform for the Canadiens when Plante came down with one of his mystery illnesses or injuries.

"Whenever Plante was ready to come back, it wasn't a case of him having to earn his job back," Hodge said. "He automatically got it back. It didn't matter how well you played and I think that's what was most frustrating."

> **"I've been lucky basically all my life."**

Bruce Bennett Studios/Getty Images

Hodge had a good run with the Canadiens in the mid-1960s, winning the Vezina Trophy outright in 1964 and sharing it with Worsley in 1965-66. He was also a second-team all-star in 1964 and '65. But the emergence of Rogie Vachon once again squeezed Hodge out and he was taken by the Oakland Seals in the expansion draft.

"I guess you can never say I was as good as those guys (Plante, Bower, etc.) because they were the cream of the crop," Hodge said, "but I'd like to think I was at least in the ballpark." ●

201

Ken **MOSDELL**

Pain Man

	Center
	Born: July 13,1922, Montreal, Que.
	Died: Jan. 5, 2006
	Habs Career : 1944-1956, 1957-1959
	4 Stanley Cups, 1 first-team all-star,
	1 second-team all-star
	132-155-287, 449 PIM in 627 games

They used to say Ken Mosdell's body was held together with stitches and screws. THN writer Vince Lunny opined in 1953 Mosdell's bones were, "as brittle as peppermint sticks."

The body was often unable for the tireless Mosdell, but the spirit was always willing beyond belief. In the summer of 1953, one of the few in which he was unencumbered by any serious injuries that needed mending, Mosdell took a job building box cars at the Canadian Car plant in Montreal. He'd wake up at 5:30 a.m. for the drive into the city, work all day doing heavy labor at the car plant, then return to the cottage exhausted at 7:30 in the evening.

And the man who was previously best known as a penalty killer and checker responded by scoring 44 goals and 100 points the next two seasons, being named to the first all-star team in 1954 and the second team in 1955.

"Moe is the most consistent forward on the team," Canadiens' coach Dick Irvin told THN in 1953. "I can always depend on him never to play a bad game."

> **Mosdell's bones were, "as brittle as peppermint sticks."**
> – Vince Lunny

> "I can always
> depend on him
> never to play
> a bad game."
> – Dick Irvin

After playing for the New York Americans early in his career, Mosdell joined the Canadiens after serving two years for the Royal Canadian Air Force in World War II and won four Cups with them. He was sold to the Chicago Black Hawks in 1956, but returned to the Canadiens a year later, playing most of the rest of his career in the minors. He managed to win his last Cup in 1959 when he replaced Jean Beliveau, who cracked two vertebrae in his back after getting crushed into the boards in the first round of the playoffs.

When he appeared in the playoffs that year, Mosdell became the last member of the New York Americans to play in the NHL. ●

Bruce Bennett Studios/Getty Images

203

Vincent DAMPHOUSSE

Hometown Hero

Center
Born: Dec. 16, 1967, Montreal, Que.
Habs Career : 1992-1999
1 Stanley Cup
184-314-498, 559 PIM in 519 games

You look back and it makes you wonder how Serge Savard pulled it off. Then the Canadiens' GM, Savard managed to get one of the most purely talented and versatile players in the NHL during the prime of his career when he acquired Vincent Damphousse from the Edmonton Oilers in 1992 in exchange for Shayne Corson.

"It was the best year of my life," Damphousse said. "We won the Stanley Cup and I got to play at home."

Damphousse was probably ready to bust out regardless of the team for which he played, but his seven seasons in Montreal were undoubtedly the best of his career. Three times Damphousse led the Canadiens in scoring and three more times he finished second. And while Patrick Roy receives the bulk of the credit for the Canadiens run to the Stanley Cup in 1993, Damphousse himself had a monster playoff.

Not only did he collect the first of a remarkable 10 overtime goals the Canadiens netted that spring, but he also led the team

> "I was counted on to score some big goals and make big plays"

in scoring with 11 goals and 23 points. In fact, only Frank Mahovlich, Guy Lafleur and Yvan Cournoyer have ever recorded more points in one playoff year for the Canadiens.

"I was counted on to score some big goals and make big plays and we had two very good offensive lines," Damphousse said. "I was playing with (Stephan) Lebeau and (Mike) Keane and a lot of the attention was on Kirk Muller and Brian Bellows and John LeClair, so our opponents didn't really know who to cover. And I was the set-up man, so I got a lot of points on the power play."

Damphousse continued his productive ways with the Canadiens and was eventually made team captain before being traded to the San Jose Sharks during the 1998-99 season, the first of three in a row in which the Canadiens would miss the playoffs. ●

Robert Laberge / Allsport

205

Johnny **GAGNON**

A Charmed 'Black Cat'

Right Winger	
Born: June 8, 1905, Chicoutimi, Que.	
Died: March 22, 1984	
Habs Career : 1930-1940	
1 Stanley Cup	
115-137-252, 286 PIM in 406 games	

History often views Johnny Gagnon as the third wheel on the Montreal Canadiens powerhouse line with Howie Morenz and Aurel Joliat, but that is selling the man far too short, both in terms of talent and his colorful character.

Gagnon was just 5-foot-5 and 140 pounds, but legend has it he put 10 pounds of rocks in his pocket for his first weigh-in with the Canadiens. Gagnon came from a family of 11 children that lived in poverty and his father was so upset with his passion for hockey he apparently broke his sticks whenever he saw his son playing.

Gagnon joined the Canadiens in 1930-31 and took Billy Boucher's spot on the big line with Morenz and Joliat. While his linemates got most of the accolades, Gagnon proved he was a legitimate star in his own right. In fact, the Society for International Hockey Research (SIHR) designated him the Conn Smythe Trophy winner as playoff MVP in 1931.

That spring, Gagnon led the Canadiens with six playoff goals, including four goals and two assists in the Stanley Cup final as the Canadiens beat the Chicago Black Hawks 3-2 in a best-of-

> **"He'd be like the guy who played with Gretzky and Kurri."**
> – Bob Duff

> "Morenz and Joliat could do it all, but he was more of a pure goal-scorer."
> – Bob Duff

five final. He was a consistent scorer throughout his career and forged a reputation as a player who played his best when the most was on the line. He earned the nickname 'Black Cat' because of his thatch of thick jet-black hair.

"He'd be like the guy who played with (Wayne) Gretzky and (Jari) Kurri," said hockey historian Bob Duff. "But he scored a lot of money goals, a lot of overtime goals. He was definitely a finisher, that was his strength. Morenz and Joliat could do it all, but he was more of a pure goal-scorer." ●

Phil **GOYETTE**

The Splendid Splinter

	Center
	Born: Oct. 31, 1933, Lachine, Que.
	Habs Career : 1956-1963
	4 Stanley Cups
	62-120-182, 44 PIM in 375 games

Because he was so tall and lean, Phil Goyette earned the nickname 'The Splendid Splinter.' He was one of the league's most gifted stickhandlers, but he was too far down the Canadiens' depth chart to exploit them to their fullest.

"I guess you could say I was pretty handy with the puck," Goyette said. "My game was to try to control the play, then give the puck to one of my teammates."

But the Canadiens were loaded with talented centermen, so Goyette spent most of his career in Montreal playing on the third line with Claude Provost and Andre Pronovost, both of whom were supreme defensive players. For his sacrifice, Goyette was rewarded with Stanley Cups in each of his first four seasons with the Canadiens.

"There wasn't much you could do with a team like that," Goyette said. "Sometimes when somebody would get injured, I would get a chance. It was the same with the power play. They had so many great players and you could only put five of them out there."

> "I guess you could say I was pretty handy with the puck."

> "Sometimes when somebody would get injured, I would get a chance."

Phil Goyette, right, and 'Rocket' Richard ham it up for photographers – with a bowl of spaghetti below – during a photo shoot. On the ice, Goyette was a serious stickhandler.

It was only after Goyette left Montreal that he achieved any sort of significant individual recognition. In his first season after being traded to the New York Rangers in 1963, Goyette finished eighth in NHL scoring, the first of three times he would finish in the top 10. In 1969-70, at 37, he finished fourth in NHL scoring playing for the St. Louis Blues and also won the Lady Byng Trophy.

Even though Goyette had far more individual success with the Rangers, he'll always consider himself a Canadien.

"I grew up in their system," Goyette said, "and that's where I won all my Cups." ●

Kirk **MULLER**

Filling Big Skates

	Left Winger
	Born: Feb. 8, 1966, Kingston, Ont.
	Habs Career : 1991-1995
	1 Stanley Cup
	104-143-247, 292 PIM in 267 games

Before Kirk Muller had even stepped on the ice for the first time as a Montreal Canadien, the player he replaced had already begun to make things a little uncomfortable for him.

"The New Jersey Devils had played that afternoon," Muller said. "I came into the dressing room and Mike Keane said to me, 'Hey, no pressure, but Richer scored two goals this afternoon. But right away (coach) Pat Burns pulled me aside and said, 'Kirk, we got you here for a reason. Don't worry and just go out and play your game.' "

Like a guy needs any more pressure going to the Canadiens, not to mention replacing a guy who was supposed to be the franchise's next French Canadian superstar. Just two weeks before the 1991-92 season opened, the Canadiens had acquired Muller as the centerpiece in a deal with the New Jersey Devils for two-time 50-goal scorer Stephane Richer.

Muller played fewer than four years for the Canadiens, but for three of those he provided a solid two-way presence, including posting back-to-back 35-goal seasons. In the Canadiens' unlikely run to the Stanley Cup in 1993, he finished second to Vincent Damphousse in playoff

> "I felt really good about my game in Montreal and I loved playing there."

goals with 10 and posted 17 points in 20 games. It was by far Muller's best playoff, with three of his goals counting as game-winners.

"I felt like those were really my prime years in the NHL," Muller said. "I was playing on the first power play and killing penalties. I really felt like I was in my prime. I felt really good about my game in Montreal and I loved playing there." ●

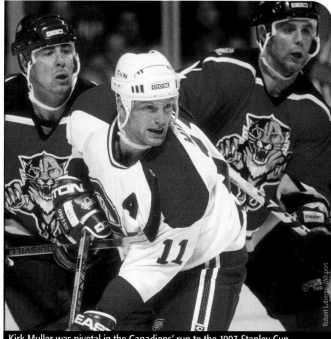

Kirk Muller was pivotal in the Canadiens' run to the 1993 Stanley Cup, scoring three-game winners among his 10 post-season goals.

211

Pierre **MONDOU**

Offensive Flair, Defensive Care

Center
Born: Nov. 27, 1955, Sorel, Que.
Habs Career : 1977-1985
3 Stanley Cups
194-262-456, 179 PIM in 548 games

Pierre Mondou was on fire, well on his way to leading the AHL in goals in just his first professional season, when Nova Scotia Voyageurs' coach Al MacNeil called Mondou into his office one day after practice.

It was that day Mondou received his indoctrination into Montreal Canadiens hockey.

"I was the leading scorer and I thought he was going to tell me how happy he was with me," Mondou said. "Instead, he told me, 'I'll teach you how to play hockey.' "

MacNeil must have done a marvelous job because by the time he reached the Canadiens, Mondou was NHL-ready and impeccably prepared for his role as one of many great two-way centers in the history of the organization.

Mondou never really lived up to the hype as an offensive force, but it's pretty tough to do that when teammates such as Serge Savard are saying, "He can be as good as Guy Lafleur. He has moves I haven't seen before."

> "(Mondou) can be as good as anyone."
> – Guy Lafleur

In fact, Lafleur himself told The Hockey News in 1980 that, "(Mondou) can be as good as anyone."

Bruce Bennett Studios/Getty Images

"In those days, it was all team bonuses and the biggest one was always for goals against."

Mondou did managed to post three 30-goal seasons in eight years with the Canadiens, but his real value to the team was his work at both ends of the ice. A star scorer in junior and the minors, Mondou developed into a terrific and responsible player and a key contributor to the Canadiens' defensive juggernaut.

Mondou, though, admitted he also had an ulterior motive.

"In those days, nobody got individual bonuses, it was all team bonuses," Mondou said, "and the biggest one was always for goals against."

Mondou's career was cut short at age 29 by an eye injury late in the 1984-85 season, but not before he got his name on the Stanley Cup three times. ●

Yvon **LAMBERT**

Out of the Blue

Left Winger
Born: May 20, 1950, Drummondville, Que.
Habs Career : 1973-1981
4 Stanley Cups
181-234-415, 302 PIM in 606 games

To be sure, there have been better players in the history of the Montreal Canadiens, but none who came from more humble beginnings than Yvon Lambert.

First of all, Lambert didn't learn to skate until he received a pair of blades for Christmas at the age of 13 and didn't play his first organized game of hockey until he was 15. At 16 and 17, he was playing industrial league hockey in Drummondville.

"I was born and raised on a farm," Lambert said. "There was never time for me to play hockey. I was the oldest of eight kids and we had to take care of the farm."

The lack of polish and experience didn't prevent Lambert from becoming a very good two-way left winger and from being a stalwart on one of the best and longest-lasting checking lines the Canadiens have ever had, along with Doug Risebrough and Mario Tremblay.

> "I went to my first (Canadiens) camp and and I said to myself, 'I'll never make this team.'

In fact, Lambert is one of the few players in history who has won a Turner Cup (championship of the defunct International League), a Calder Cup and a Stanley Cup.

It was after the Turner Cup in 1971 Lambert stopped in Detroit after a vacation in Florida and met with Red Wings GM Ned Harkness.

"He told me to stay in shape because I'd have a great chance to make the team the next year," Lambert said. "Then I read in the paper I had been traded to Montreal and I was so disappointed. I went to my first camp and I see Henri Richard, Yvan Cournoyer, Jacques Lemaire and Pete Mahovlich and I said to myself, 'I'll never make this team.' "

After two years in the minors, he did make it and was a key part of the Canadiens four Stanley Cups. A six-time 20-goal scorer, Lambert scored his biggest goal in overtime of Game 7 of the semifinal against the Boston Bruins in 1979. ●

"I was born and raised on a farm. There was never time for me to play hockey."

215

Sprague **CLEGHORN**

Ready to Rumble

Defenseman
Born: March 11, 1890, Montreal, Que.
Died: July 11,1956
Habs Career : 1921-1925
1 Stanley Cup
42-31-73, 248 PIM in 98 games
Hockey Hall of Fame: 1958

The Montreal Canadiens' plan to get tougher in the 1920s could have started and ended with Sprague Cleghorn, the meanest, nastiest and dirtiest player of his era.

Acquired from Ottawa in 1921, Cleghorn forced three of his former Senators teammates to be helped off the ice in a game following the trade. Referee Lou Marsh gave Cleghorn, who'd committed a couple stick fouls and delivered a vicious check, a match penalty and recommended he be banished from the league, but Cleghorn was saved by the fact the motion did not receive unanimous approval.

"Sprague Cleghorn was well-known as a great dresser. He would show up at the games all slicked up in a three-piece suit," said author and historian Chrys Goyens. "He'd take it off, put on the equipment and spear the first guy who came near him."

Today, Cleghorn would likely be described as someone with anger management issues. His attack on Lionel Hitchman of the Senators in the 1923 playoffs was so offensive Habs owner Leo Dandurand suspended his star defenseman, saying his actions were, "befitting an animal."

> ### "(His actions were) befitting an animal."
> – Leo Dandurand

Cleghorn was essentially hockey's first policeman and caused a fair bit of mayhem with defense partner Billy Coutu, but he could also play. In four years with the Canadiens, he scored 42 goals – huge numbers for a defenseman – including 17 in 1921-22. His leadership skills were also held in high regard. He was named captain of the Canadiens the year after he arrived and held the post for three years.

"(Cleghorn) was just a terrible man to play against," King Clancy was quoted as saying in the book, *The Mad Men of Hockey*. "A terrific stickhandler, a master of the butt end and tough, holy Jesus he was tough." ●

Mario **TREMBLAY**

A Fiery Fan Favorite

	Right Winger
	Born: Sept. 2, 1956, Alma, Que.
	Habs Career : 1974-1986
	5 Stanley Cups
	258-326-584, 1,043 PIM in 852 games

Give the Montreal Canadiens four picks in the first 12 in a draft and about 15 years later you can usually count on having a couple of Hall of Famers on your hands.

But when they were faced with that very prospect in 1974, the Canadiens went in a decidedly different direction. They took Cam Connor fifth, Doug Risebrough seventh, Rick Chartraw 10th and Mario Tremblay 12th.

The Canadiens wanted to add some grit to their shine and it turned out to be a terrific decision. Both Risebrough and Tremblay, along with linemate Yvon Lambert, evolved into key components for a team that might have been the most dominant in the history of the league.

> **Tremblay was the emotional spark on one of the top third lines in the history of the game.**

And while Tremblay might have been more of an offensive player had things gone differently, he wouldn't have had it any other way.

"I'll tell you, I'd rather be a third-liner on a team that wins the Stanley Cup like we did than be a first- or second-liner on a team that never wins," Tremblay said. "I know that players like Guy Lafleur and Yvan Cournoyer really appreciated what we did."

They should have because Tremblay was the emotional spark on one of the top third lines in the history of the game. Tremblay, another big

Mario Tremblay, looking for a rebound off the pads of Hartford's Mike Liut, didn't score a ton of goals, but was a crucial contributor.

scorer in junior who sacrificed his offensive game to play for the Canadiens, still managed four 30-goal seasons and five of 25 or more. When he scored his first career goal in 1974, Tremblay picked up the puck himself and kissed it.

"I couldn't believe it," he said at the time.

Tremblay's style of play – not to mention his wonderful assist on Lambert's goal in overtime of Game 7 against the Boston Bruins in the 1979 semifinal – always endeared him to the fans in Montreal. It all came to an end late in the 1985-86 season when a separated shoulder ended his career and forced him to watch his fifth Stanley Cup from the sidelines. ●

> "I'd rather be a third-liner on a team that wins than be a first-liner on a team that never wins."

219

Dollard **ST-LAURENT**

Fighting for High Stakes, Filling Big Skates

Defenseman	
Born: May 12, 1929, Verdun, Que.	
Habs Career : 1952-1958	
4 Stanley Cups	
19-82-101, 306 PIM in 383 games	

It should come as no surprise Dollard St-Laurent was one of the driving forces behind the formation of a union that evolved into the NHL Players' Association.

In fact, St-Laurent could have joined the Canadiens in 1951, but refused to accept what was essentially a two-way contract, which would have allowed the Canadiens to farm him out to the minors at a severely reduced wage. Only when the Canadiens relented and guaranteed him an NHL salary did he sign with the team.

Even casual fans know Ted Lindsay was exiled to Chicago for his involvement in the union, but so was St-Laurent, who was dealt to the Black Hawks in 1958 for a minor-leaguer and cash, despite the fact he was coming off his best season and the Canadiens were in the midst of their run of five straight Stanley Cups.

He did, however, manage to add another Cup in Chicago in 1961 to the four he had won in Montreal.

"I think we did the right thing at the time," St-Laurent told the Montreal *Gazette* in 2003. "We wanted to know what pension plans there were for our group. We found out baseball and football and many other sports had better pension plans than us."

> One of the driving forces behind the formation of a (players') union.

On the ice, St-Laurent spent much of his career with the Canadiens as Doug Harvey's defense partner and was seen at the time as a throwback to Kenny Reardon, another physical, two-way presence on the blueline.

The former stickboy for the Montreal Jr. Canadiens earned a tryout with the junior team in 1947 and was given skates that belonged to Butch Bouchard that were three sizes too big.

"But I was so proud to be wearing Bouchard's skates that I put on several pairs of extra stockings and said nothing about it," St-Laurent told THN years later. "You see, Bouchard has been my boyhood idol and I figured that his skates would give wings to my feet." ●

Bruce Bennett Studios/Getty Images

221

Claude **LEMIEUX**

King of Spring

Right Winger	
Born: July 16, 1965, Buckingham, Que.	
Habs Career : 1984-1990	
1 Stanley Cup	
97-92-189, 576 PIM in 281 games	

Though he has proved it time and again, Claude Lemieux disagrees with the notion he was a "money player" through much of his NHL career.

"They don't take the playoffs into account in arbitration," Lemieux cracked. "So it's the guys who do great in the regular season who are the money players."

Lemieux will then have to be content to be known as one of the greatest clutch players in history. He did it constantly throughout his career, the first time coming in 1986 when his crunch-time play was an integral reason why the Canadiens won the Stanley Cup that year. Following a season in which he was sent to the minors after training camp and scored just one goal in 10 regular season games, Lemieux collected 10 goals and 16 points in 20 playoff games, including four winners, two of them in overtime.

Although Lemieux had always displayed a penchant for playing well in big games, that year he displayed a knack for being a petulant jerk. He was so frustrated he smashed a window in his car when he was sent down and spent much of the year sulking. He was just 20.

> "They don't take the playoffs into account in arbitration."

> "I was a cocky kid and I spent a lot of time pouting and complaining."

Bruce Bennett Studios/Getty Images

"I was a cocky kid and I spent a lot of time pouting and complaining that I was getting cheated out of a job," Lemieux said. "Then after Christmas I decided to play the way I knew I was capable. I guess they really broke me down, but it worked out pretty well for everybody."

Lemieux had four more seasons with the Canadiens before moving on to the New Jersey Devils, where he won a Cup. He won No. 3 with Colorado in 1996; No. 4 back with the Devils in 2000.

He can't fully explain his success in the playoffs, but said he definitely got more motivated for the bigger games.

"I know for sure that the way I played in the playoffs, there's no way I would have been able to play 82 games in the season the same way," he said. ●

Claude Lemieux had a penchant for passion – and scoring big goals.

223

Rejean **HOULE**

A Good Company Man

	Right Winger
Born: Oct. 25, 1949, Rouyn, Que.	
Habs Career : 1969-1973, 1976-1983	
5 Stanley Cups	
161-247-408, 395 PIM in 635 games	

The year was 1969 and the Canadiens were losing their iron-clad grip on the best French Canadian prospects, but not before they took Rejean Houle and Marc Tardif with the first two picks of that year's entry draft.

The Canadiens had extremely high hopes for both players, since both Houle and Tardif had been spectacular scoring stars for the Montreal Jr. Canadiens. In his last year of junior, Houle scored 53 goals in 54 games and had established himself as the most promising prospect in a draft that included a diabetic buzzsaw from western Canada named Bobby Clarke.

The Canadiens surely envisioned Houle and Tardif as the next great native sons for the Canadiens, but both found stardom in the World Hockey Association they never were able to achieve in the NHL. But when Houle returned to the Canadiens from the WHA in 1976, he found his niche as a very good, serviceable player on a powerhouse team.

Even Houle admitted he expected more from his NHL career, at least on an individual level.

"I would have liked to have done better," Houle told THN after retiring in 1983. "When I graduated from the Jr. Canadiens scoring all

> "Scoring all those goals (in junior), I thought I could do the same thing in professional hockey."

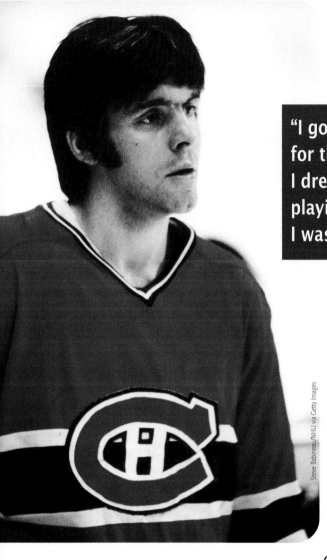

Steve Babineau/NHLI via Getty Images

"I got to play
for the team
I dreamed about
playing for since
I was a boy."

those goals, I thought I could do the same thing in professional hockey."

After recording just 34 goals in his first three seasons, Houle left for the WHA, where he tripled his salary and became a confident 50-goal scorer. When he returned to the Canadiens, he found himself as more of a role player on a team filled with superstars. He won two Stanley Cups with the Canadiens before he left and three more after he came back.

Ever the company man, Houle served as the team's GM from 1996 to 2000 and his tenure has been generally panned. He now serves as director of alumni relations for the Canadiens.

Houle acknowledges he was better in his second tenure, but enjoyed the first one just as much.

"I got to win a Stanley Cup with Jean Beliveau," Houle said. "And I got to play for the team I dreamed about playing for since I was a boy." ●

Floyd **CURRY**

From Scorer to Stopper

	Right Winger
	Born: Aug. 11, 1925, Chapleau, Ont.
	Died: Sept. 16, 2006
	Habs Career : 1947-1958
	4 Stanley Cups
	105-99-204, 147 PIM in 601 games

Some 35 years before Guy Carbonneau came to the same conclusion, Floyd Curry showed up at the Canadiens' training camp and made a crucial, career-altering decision.

He could always score and had done so with ease and regularity in both junior and senior hockey. But he looked out onto the ice in 1947 and saw a lineup that included Maurice Richard, Boom-Boom Geoffrion, Jean Beliveau and Doug Harvey and knew immediately his success would revolve around his ability to adapt.

"When I first came out of junior hockey I was known as a scorer," Curry once said. "But when I arrived in Montreal I knew right away I could not compete with the likes of some of the stars they had there, so I made a conscious effort to change my game to a defensive style."

> ## "When I first came out of junior hockey I was known as a scorer."

Very wise move. Every successful Canadiens team had its embarrassment of riches when it came to offensive stars, but there was also a strong defensive conscience and Curry was just that for 10 years. Had the Selke Trophy been in existence in those days, Curry would have been a perennial con-

> "I made a conscious effort to change my game to a defensive style."

tender. Despite the fact he had to check some of the game's biggest stars, Curry was also a very clean player. In 1956, he finished as the runner-up for the Lady Byng Trophy after earning just 10 penalty minutes.

But it's interesting to ponder what might have been had Curry not decided to become a defensive player. When Richard was suspended in the playoffs in 1955, Curry moved to his spot on right wing and had a monster post-season, scoring eight goals and 12 points, including five goals in the Stanley Cup final as the Canadiens lost to the Detroit Red Wings in seven games.

"I wasn't playing any differently, that's for sure," Curry told THN. "But I was getting on the ice more often." ●

Bruce Bennett Studios/Getty Images

Ryan **WALTER**

Strength Under Pressure

Center/Left Winger
Born: April 23, 1958,
New Westminster, B.C.
Habs Career : 1982-1991
1 Stanley Cup
141-208-349, 419 PIM in 604 games

Imagine being traded to one of the most demanding cities in the NHL and before you even get there, fans and media are referring to the day you were acquired as "Black Friday."

That's what Ryan Walter and Rick Green faced when they were dealt to the Canadiens from the Washington Capitals for Rod Langway, Brian Engblom, Doug Jarvis and Craig Laughlin in September, 1982.

> "Rocket Richard's picture was right across from me, like he was staring right at me."

Walter and Green were both very good players and the deal would ultimately turn out to be a terrific one for both teams, but fans in Montreal weren't exactly welcoming to the two new players.

"I don't think people had a real sense of what was coming," Walter recalled, "but they certainly had a sense of what was going. There was a lot of pressure from the outside, but from the inside, the guys were great with us."

Walter made a good first impression, scoring 29 goals and 75 points in his first season. Although he never approached those kinds of numbers again, he developed a reputation as a

"There was a lot of pressure, but the guys were great."

Bruce Bennett Studios/Getty Images

versatile player who could be depended on to produce on the first line or the fourth.

It's fair to say Walter would never have experienced the team success he had in Montreal had he stayed in Washington. Part of that comes from the culture surrounding the Canadiens and the pressure to perform that comes with it.

"Where I sat in the dressing room, Rocket Richard's picture was right across from me," Walter said. "And it was almost like he was staring right at me all the time." ●

Jack **LAVIOLETTE**

Mr. Everything

Defenseman/Right Winger	
Born: July 27, 1879, Belleville, Ont.	
Died: Jan. 10, 1960	
Habs Career : 1909-1918	
1 Stanley Cup	
48-19-67, 174 PIM in 156 games	
Hockey Hall of Fame: 1962	

> "By today's standards, you could probably count on (him) for 20-to-30 goals and 150-to-200 penalty minutes."
> – Ernie Fitzsimmons

Twelve men have both played for and coached the Montreal Canadiens and four Canadiens players have served as the team's GM. But none of them did it while they were playing for the team the way Jean-Baptiste 'Jack' Laviolette did.

When Ambrose O'Brien secured financing to establish a French-Canadian team in Montreal in 1909, he hired Laviolette to manage, coach and play for the team. Laviolette played 10 years with the Canadiens, but was also something of a charismatic bon vivant and used that to attract both investors and players to the new National Hockey Association organization.

Known as 'The Speed Merchant,' Laviolette formed the basis of 'The Flying Frenchmen' along with linemates Newsy Lalonde and Didier Pitre. As a player, Laviolette never put up spectacular numbers, largely because

Laviolette's numbers don't reveal his true worth.

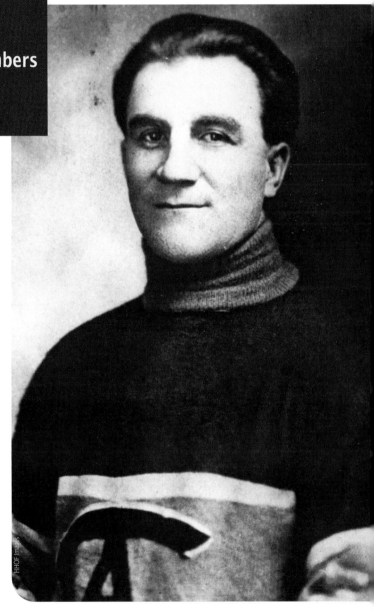

he was a player who started plays and dug the puck out of the corners for Lalonde and Pitre. Because assists were almost impossible to come by in those days, Laviolette's numbers don't reveal his true worth.

"By today's standards, he was a guy you could probably count on for 20-to-30 goals and 150-to-200 penalty minutes," said hockey historian Ernie Fitzsimmons.

Laviolette was a dashing sort who also drove race cars in the summer. While tuning a car for a tour of Quebec in the summer of 1918, Laviolette was involved in an accident and lost his right foot. That didn't stop him from doing some refereeing after that, including a game that was held in his honor later that year. ●

HHOF Images

Andrei **MARKOV**

A Russian Revelation

Defenseman
Born: Dec. 20, 1978, Voskresensk, Russia
Habs Career : 2000-2008*
62-203-265, 289 PIM in 493 games
(*still a member of the Habs
through August, 2008)

The Canadiens drafted 10 players in 1998 and hit the mark on four of them. Mike Ribeiro and Francois Beauchemin have gone on to have productive careers elsewhere and Michael Ryder had some good seasons before bottoming out in 2007-08.

But the team's scouting staff knocked one right out of the park with the 162nd pick that year when it selected defenseman Andrei Markov from Voskresensk of the Russian League.

After a couple years marred by injury and inconsistent play, Markov has developed into a star for the Canadiens and is one of the steadiest two-way defensemen in the game today. In 2007-08, Markov scored a career-high 58 points and tied for the league lead among defensemen in power play goals with 10.

"Everybody knows about Markie's skills and world-class talent," defense partner Mike Komisarek told the Montreal *Gazette* in 2008. "He's really come into his own the past few years."

> "Everybody knows about Markie's skills and world-class talent."
> – Mike Komisarek

> "(Players) shake their heads in awe of the passes he makes through sticks and skates."
> – Mike Komisarek

And he has been well compensated for it. Prior to 2007-08, Markov signed a four-year deal worth $5.75 million per season, making him the Canadiens' top-paid player and among the top 10 paid defensemen in the league at the time.

Markov has done some of his best work on the power play, but plays an all-around smart game with an offensive bent to it.

"There's a tremendous respect for what Markie does and the skills he brings," Komisarek told the *Gazette*. "Sometimes you see him out there on the power play and the guys on the bench will just shake their heads in awe of the passes he makes through sticks and skates and the seams he'll find to open guys." ●

Steve Babineau/NHLI via Getty Images

Rod **LANGWAY**

A Warrior in the Making

Defenseman
Born: May 3, 1957, Maag, Formosa
Habs Career : 1978-82
1 Stanley Cup
26-101-127, 347 PIM in 268 games
Hockey Hall of Fame: 2002

B efore he became the Secretary of Defense in Washington, Rod Langway was a foot soldier for the Canadiens, learning his craft under the tutelage of field generals such as Larry Robinson, Guy Lapointe and Serge Savard.

The Canadiens' Big Three was in the twilight of its dominance as a group and Langway joined them from the World Hockey Association in 1979, in time to win the last of the Canadiens' four straight Stanley Cups. And he recalled it didn't take him long to understand the pressures that came with playing for the Canadiens.

The dynasty was beginning to show signs of decay to be sure, but the Canadiens still managed to finish second overall in the league and win the Cup.

"The team had already won three Cups, but in the previous two years they lost a total of 18 games," Langway said. "Well, that year we lost 17 and everybody was saying we had a bad year."

> "Right from the day I was traded, I knew I was leaving something great."

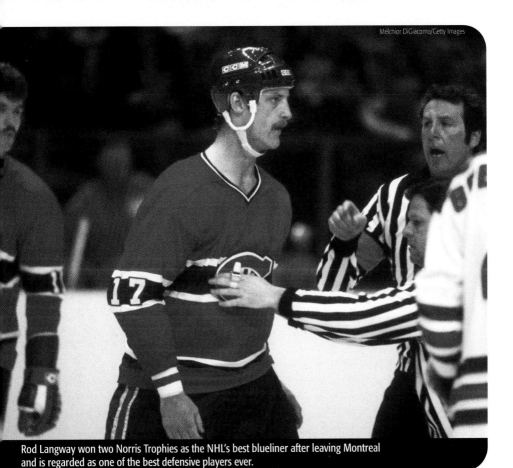

Melchior DiGiacomo/Getty Images

Rod Langway won two Norris Trophies as the NHL's best blueliner after leaving Montreal and is regarded as one of the best defensive players ever.

Langway's stay in Montreal was not long. He played just four years, demanding a trade in 1982, citing the tax burden on Americans working in Canada as the primary reason. But more than 25 years later, Langway acknowledged much of his motivation was to try to extract a more lucrative deal from the Canadiens.

"I never really wanted to leave," he said. "I did my own negotiations then and I was playing hardball to see if they would take care of me. But they weren't coming off their number for what I thought was a pretty reasonable offer."

Langway went on to a fine career as one of the league's best-ever defensive defensemen with the Capitals and won the Norris Trophy in each of the first two seasons after the trade. But he still thinks of the Canadiens wistfully.

"No question," he said, "right from the day I was traded, I knew I was leaving something great." ●

Georges **MANTHA**

A Versatile Winner

Defenseman/Left Winger
Born: Nov 29, 1908, Lachine, Que.
Died: Jan. 25, 1990
Habs Career : 1928-1941
2 Stanley Cups
89-102-191, 148 PIM in 488 games

Perhaps it was because he was overshadowed by his Hall of Fame brother Sylvio or that he was one of the few beacons of hope on some shockingly bad Canadiens teams, but Georges Mantha rarely seems to receive his due as a legitimate contributor to the franchise's history.

"He certainly wasn't a dominant scorer, but he did play for some first-place and Stanley Cup teams," said hockey historian Ernie Fitzsimmons. "Obviously he was a winner, but to me, he's no star."

> ## There was a time he was an integral part of the team's fortunes.

Unfortunately, that's the legacy Mantha leaves, but there was a time he was an integral part of the team's fortunes. Not only was Mantha a tireless worker, but he was a versatile player who could play both forward and defense. A solid defensive forward, Mantha combined with linemates Pit Lepine and Wildor Larochelle to shut down a powerhouse Boston Bruins team in the Stanley Cup final in 1930.

That Bruins team finished the season with a 38-5-1 record and posted the best winning percentage in NHL history (.875). They led

HHOF Images

the league with 179 goals, but Mantha's line held them to just three in the best-of-three final, which the Canadiens won in two games. The next season the Canandiens won the Stanley Cup again and Mantha finished second in playoff goals with five.

But it was a precipitous decline for the Canadiens after that. The team bottomed out and was among the worst in the league for the better part of a decade, but Mantha continued to produce. In 1937-38, he finished fourth in NHL scoring, but was quickly cut loose, along with most of the rest of the team with the exception of Elmer Lach and Ray Getliffe, when Tom Gorman took over as GM in 1940-41. ●

237

Albert **LEDUC**

Crash and Crunch

Defenseman	
Born: Nov. 22, 1902, Valleyfield, Que.	
Died: July 31, 1990	
Habs Career : 1925-1933, 1934-1935	
2 Stanley Cups	
57-32-89, 574 PIM in 341 games	

The name says it all – Albert 'Battleship' Leduc was a nasty, tough defenseman who made life for opponents difficult and life for his teammates a little easier.

Leduc played eight years for the Canadiens, primarily as a defenseman, and quickly made himself a favorite with The Forum faithful because of his energetic play and bone-crushing hits. He was also a decent scorer; his 10 goals in his first season with the Canadiens in 1925-26 would be equivalent to a 30-goal season today.

"He started off there in his first year and they were in last place," said hockey historian Ernie Fitzsimmons, "and after that, they just got better and better and he just got better and better."

Leduc was a stalwart on the Canadiens teams that won the Stanley Cup in 1930 and '31, the two Cups that came before 'The Great Darkness,' a period in which the team went 13 seasons without a Cup and teetered on the brink of irrelevance.

> A favorite with The Forum faithful because of his energetic play and bone-crushing hits.

> "He was the kind of guy every team needs."
> – Bob Duff

At 5-foot-9 and 180 pounds, Leduc was considered a big, imposing and physical defenseman. The years in which the Canadiens won their two Cups, he posted PIM totals of 90 and 82 in 44 games each season, which would be the equivalent to close to 200 PIM by today's standards.

"He was nothing spectacular, just a physical, stay-at-home, solid guy," said hockey historian Bob Duff. "He was the kind of guy every team needs, but never seems to get the same credit as a lot of other guys on the team." ●

HHOF Images

239

Billy **REAY**

More Than a Fedora

	Center
	Born: Aug. 21, 1918, Winnipeg, Man.
	Died: Sept. 23, 2004
	Habs Career : 1945-1953
	2 Stanley Cups
	103-162-265, 202 PIM in 475 games

You're certainly not alone if your only visions of Billy Reay are of him pacing behind the Chicago Black Hawks' bench wearing a fedora.

Much of Reay's legacy in hockey comes from the 13 seasons he spent as the Black Hawks' coach, but prior to that he forged one as a very useful two-way center for the Canadiens in the 1940s. Reay book-ended his Canadiens career with Stanley Cups and is one of the few players in history to win a Memorial Cup, Allan Cup and Stanley Cup.

> **One of the few players to win a Memorial Cup, Allan Cup and Stanley Cup.**

Reay spent much of his career playing a supporting role to Elmer Lach, who was the Canadiens first-line center, but managed to hit the 20-goal plateau twice and scored 19 once. Reay began his career with the Detroit Red Wings, but played only four games in two seasons with them before being dealt to Montreal in 1945. He quickly found a home with the Canadiens and spent his career as an industrious player and quality penalty killer who played the game cleanly.

The one exception came in a game during the 1949-50 season when he was fined $125 for receiving a 10-minute misconduct and for hitting referee Hugh McLean in a game in Detroit.

> **"Sure, I hit the guy, but I should have never got the first misconduct."**

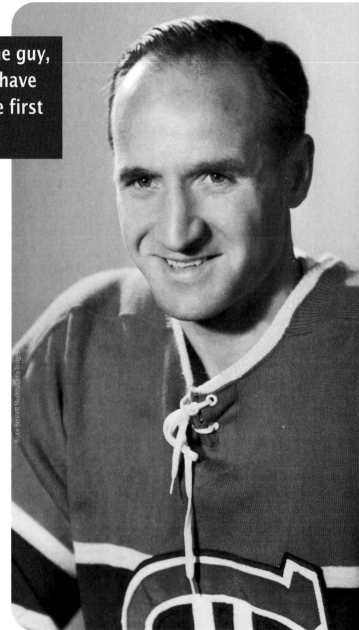

Bruce Bennett Studios/Getty Images

Doug Harvey had been clipped in the nose by Ted Lindsay and received a minor penalty. Canadiens' coach Dick Irvin, thinking Lindsay hat gotten off lightly, jumped over the boards and started chasing McLean with the rulebook in his hand. Reay also vehemently disputed the call and received his misconduct, then reached around teammate Butch Bouchard and hit McLean.

"Sure, I admit I hit the guy," Reay told THN, "but I should have never got the first misconduct." ●

Claude **LAROSE**

A Valuable Foot Soldier

	Right Winger
	Born: March 2, 1942, Hearst, Ont.
	Habs Career : 1962-1968, 1970-1974
	5 Stanley Cups
	117-123-240, 544 PIM in 529 games

The history of the Canadiens is littered with players who could have been stars on almost any other team in the league, but were more foot soldiers than elite players on clubs that made a regular habit of winning the Stanley Cup.

Claude Larose was one of those players, an individual who had to go elsewhere to prove he could make an impact as an offensive player, but also one who had his greatest team success playing for the Canadiens.

"That's just the way it was," Larose said. "That's the way you learned with the Canadiens right from the minor leagues. I remember we played against all the big lines. We would play against (Johnny) Bucyk and (Ken) Hodge in Boston, and Bobby and Dennis Hull in Chicago. Playing against Vic Hadfield was always a war."

> "Playing against Vic Hadfield was always a war."

Playing on a line with Ralph Backstrom at center and John Ferguson at left wing early in his career and with Jacques Lemaire and Marc Tardif later, Larose had to learn how to curb his temper as a young NHLer.

Bruce Bennett Studios/Getty Images

Larose had to learn how to curb his temper as a young NHLer.

He managed to do that after his first couple of years and went on to play two stints with the Canadiens, winning four Cups. Larose was traded to Minnesota with Danny Grant in 1968 and went on to be the North Stars' captain and MVP one season.

Larose's biggest offensive outburst in Montreal came in 1973-74 when he scored nine goals in three games. After three in one game and four in the next, Larose was on the precipice of becoming the first player in NHL history to record hat tricks in three straight games. In the third game, against Oakland, he scored one goal in the first period and another in the second and despite having nine shots in the game and two breakaways, he couldn't get the third.

"I missed all sorts of chances," Larose said. "I hit the post a couple of times and I missed at least one open net. I'll never forget that." ●

Don **MARSHALL**

Supreme in Support

Left Winger	
Born: March 23, 1932, Montreal, Que.	
Habs Career : 1952-1963	
5 Stanley Cups	
114-140-254, 81 PIM in 585 games	

Don Marshall recalled attending a reception in Ottawa in 2007 for the surviving members of all five of the Canadiens' Stanley Cup-winning teams from 1956 to 1960 and the first thing he noticed was how small the group was.

Out of a possible 12 players, just six were still alive and Tom Johnson died soon after. "But we did figure out that we were all still on our first wives," Marshall said.

> "He's a guy you just don't dare give a first-string job to."
> – Toe Blake

Marshall was one of the ultimate foot soldiers on that dynasty, an understudy who performed in a reduced role and stepped into the spotlight when needed. It might have been different had Marshall not broken his leg in training camp in 1955 when he was penciled in to be the center between Maurice Richard and Bert Olmstead. He was out until December and never got his place on the top line.

"That kind of set me back," Marshall said. "But you have to earn your job."

Instead, Marshall adapted his game and became a top penalty killer and defensive player and switched to play left wing. The

Frank Prazak/HHOF Images

> "But we did figure out that we were all still on our first wives."

transformation was an easy one because he was such a versatile player before he got to Montreal. He often killed penalties for the entire two minutes, which sometimes left little time or energy to contribute offensively.

But he could never seem to crack the upper echelons of the lineup as long as Toe Blake was coaching the team.

"He's a guy you just don't dare give a first-string job to," Blake once said of Marshall. "As a spare forward, filling in for injured players, he's a top scorer. But as soon as I put him on a regular line, he stops scoring. Maybe he's the sort who responds to emergencies." ●

Petr **SVOBODA**

Living the Dream

Defenseman
Born: Feb. 14, 1966, Most, Czech.
Habs Career : 1984-1992
1 Stanley Cup
39-190-229, 761 PIM in 534 games

It's not entirely true the Montreal Canadiens were the only team that knew Petr Svoboda had defected from the former Czechoslovakia and that's why they were able to get him in the 1984 draft.

It was certainly dramatic, though, with GM Serge Savard announcing the Canadiens had picked Svoboda fifth overall – four picks after Mario Lemieux – and watching the jaws drop in the Montreal Forum as Svoboda came to the podium to shake hands with Savard.

Other teams were well aware Svoboda had defected during the European Championship in the former West Germany months before. It's just the Canadiens did such a good job of hiding him, the other teams lost track of him and had no guarantees they'd ever see him play in the NHL.

"They hid me for a couple of days in Montreal," Svoboda recalled. "It was pretty good because they treated me very well. (Team president) Ronald Corey and Serge Savard put me up in

> "Playing in Montreal was a dream, even for a guy from behind the Iron Curtain."

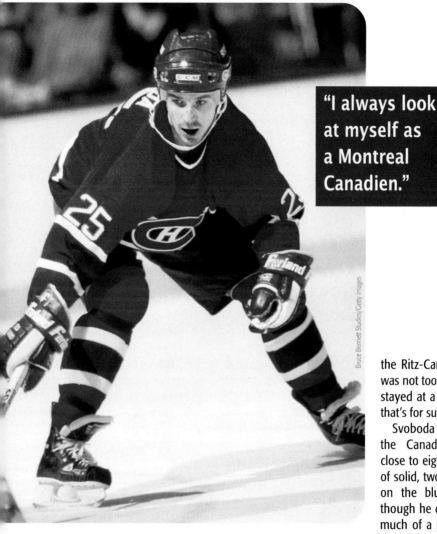

Bruce Bennett Studios/Getty Images

> "I always look at myself as a Montreal Canadien."

the Ritz-Carlton, so it was not too bad. I had stayed at a lot worse, that's for sure."

Svoboda rewarded the Canadiens with close to eight seasons of solid, two-way play on the blueline. Although he didn't play much of a prominent role in the playoffs that year, he was a member of the 1986 team that won the Stanley Cup, the only one of his career.

"Playing in Montreal for eight years was a dream come true, even for a guy who was from behind the Iron Curtain," said Svoboda, who also suited up for Buffalo, Philadelphia and Tampa Bay during his NHL career. "I always look at myself as a Montreal Canadien. Not to take anything away from the other teams I played for, but I see myself as a Canadien." ●

Brian **ENGBLOM**

Weathering the Storm

Defenseman	
Born: Jan. 27, 1955, Winnipeg, Man.	
Habs Career : 1977-1982	
2 Stanley Cups	
14-87-101, 298 PIM in 316 games	

F ans in Montreal often got on Brian Engblom for defensive errors early in his career. Little did they know they were helping to scare the living daylights out of him.

"I was so intimidated," Engblom said. "In fact, I was more intimidated by the guys I was playing with than the guys I was playing against. These guys just never made mistakes and when I made one, it seemed to stand out so much."

Fortunately, Engblom recovered and went on to have a good career with the Canadiens before being dealt to the Washington Capitals in 1982. After joining the Canadiens organization, Engblom won two Calder Cups in the American League, then two Stanley Cups his first two years in the NHL.

But there were difficult times to be sure. Engblom had come from the University of Wisconsin where he was a star, to an organization that was chin-deep in quality defensemen.

"There were times early in my career when I was extremely frustrated because I could see guys I played with all around

> "I know a lot of guys who never won. I'm glad the way things turned out."

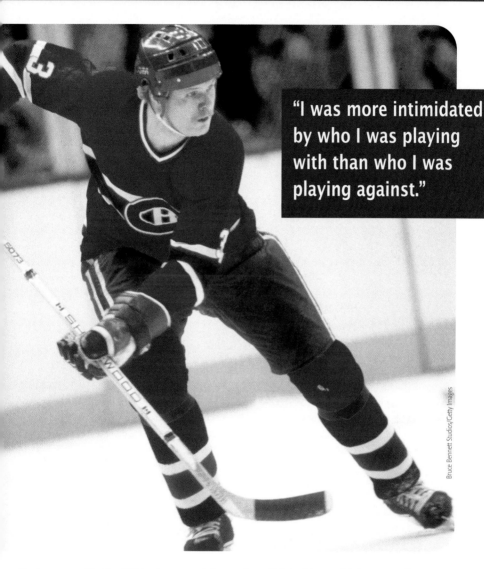

"I was more intimidated by who I was playing with than who I was playing against."

Bruce Bennett Studios/Getty Images

the league and in the WHA who were doing really well," Engblom said. "I was getting very antsy. I thought, 'Should I make some noise and say enough is enough or do I hang in there and see what happens?' "

Engblom decided on the latter course of action and while he played just five years in Montreal, he posted some respectable offensive numbers and learned lessons from the Canadiens' veteran defensemen that would serve him well later in his career.

"Sometimes you wonder what would have happened in another organization," he said. "But I know a lot of guys who never won anything. I'm really glad the way things turned out." ●

Rogie VACHON

Following His Heart

Goaltender	
Born: Sept. 8, 1945, Palmarolle, Que.	
Habs Career : 1966-1971	
3 Stanley Cups, 1 Vezina Trophy	
110-56-31, 2.65 GAA, 13 shutouts	

Throughout their history, the Canadiens have had a plethora of players who sacrificed individual glory in exchange for a jewelry box full of Stanley Cup rings.

Rogie Vachon was not one of those players. He felt he was best if he played and that was not going to happen in Montreal, particularly after some college kid named Ken Dryden came onto the scene in 1971.

> "It probably cost me a few Cups, but you have to be happy."

"It probably cost me a few Cups, but you have to be happy," Vachon said of his decision to ask for a trade. "I could have been the backup there for a lot of years, but I was young and I was healthy and I wanted to play and sitting on the bench was not good enough for me."

Vachon endured his share of ups and downs in parts of six seasons with the Canadiens. During that time, the Canadiens won three Cups, but Vachon was a key player in just one of them, in 1968-69 when he went 7-1 in the playoffs after Gump Worsley broke his finger in the first round. Two years before that, the Habs entered the final against the

"I could have been the backup there, but I wanted to play."

Toronto Maple Leafs as the prohibitive favorite with Vachon in goal, but lost the series and Vachon was pulled in Game 5 for Worsley.

Prior to the series, Leafs GM-coach Punch Imlach referred to Vachon as a Jr. B goalie, but Vachon said the comments never bothered him.

"I just laughed about it," Vachon said. "He was right. I was just a couple of years removed from Jr. B."

It seemed Vachon could never measure up in Montreal, a situation made worse by the fact the Canadiens chose him over Tony Esposito and allowed Esposito to go to Chicago in an intraleague draft in 1969. But Vachon established himself as a No. 1 goalie with the L.A. Kings and was named MVP of the Canadian team in the 1976 Canada Cup. ●

Mark **RECCHI**

Piercing the Darkness

Right Winger	
Born: Feb. 1, 1968, Kamloops, B.C.	
Habs Career : 1995-1999	
120-202-322, 222 PIM in 346 games	

During Mark Recchi's five-year tenure in Montreal, the Canadiens finished out of the playoffs twice and won only one playoff round. It also stung that he was dealt to the Canadiens in exchange for Eric Desjardins, a player who continued an upward trajectory, and John LeClair, who suddenly morphed into a 50-goal scorer.

In those years, the Canadiens went through three coaches, two GMs, lost Patrick Roy and emerging star Mathieu Schneider, didn't draft and develop players particularly well and endured considerable financial hardship.

But Recchi, to his credit, did his part. He continued to score at a very productive clip given the players around him and, more importantly, didn't allow the situation to affect his effort on the ice.

"I think that's what I'm most proud of with the Canadiens," Recchi said. "We had some lean years, but I think all the guys on that team played hard all the time. We tried to hold up the tradition and give the fans a team that at least they could say competed."

Recchi won a Stanley Cup before he got to Montreal and another after he left, but never came close with the

> **"We had some lean years, but I think all the guys on that team played hard all the time."**

Robert Laberge /Allsport

Bruce Bennett Studios/Getty Images

Despite some dark times for the team, Mark Recchi's intensity never waned in Montreal, a fact not lost on Philadelphia's Chris Therien.

struggling Canadiens. He led the team in points and goals three times, twice scoring 30-plus goals on a team that had trouble generating offense and one that was playing in the early days of the NHL's Dead Puck Era.

"I'm still so glad I got a chance to play there," Recchi said. "It's a very different world and you can either embrace it or let it get you down and I did everything to embrace it when I was there." ●

Jose **THEODORE**

Hart Times, Hard Times

Goaltender
Born: Sept. 13, 1976, Laval, Que.
Habs Career : 1996-2006
1 second-team all-star, 1 Hart Trophy,
1 Vezina Trophy, 1 Roger Crozier
Saving Grace Award
141-163-30, 2.62 GAA, 23 shutouts

The Canadiens goaltending torch was effectively passed from Patrick Roy to Jose Theodore. Theodore held it very high for a short time, then fumbled it before being dealt for a career backup.

But as great as Roy was and as inconsistent as Theodore was as a Canadien, Theodore accomplished something Roy never did. He won the Hart Trophy as the NHL's most valuable player in 2001-02, becoming only the second Canadiens netminder to ever be named MVP. He had a save percentage of .931 that season, the highest ever for a Canadien since the statistic has been recorded.

Coincidentally, Theodore also beat Roy out for the Vezina Trophy that year. It was the closest voting for both awards in history. Theodore was tied in voting points with Calgary's Jarome Iginla for the Hart and with Roy for the Vezina, but won both by virtue of having more first-place votes. (One Montreal writer had Iginla as his fifth choice for the Hart. Had he been one place higher, Iginla would have won the trophy.)

> "The Hart was never a trophy I was looking for because there are so many players and it's hard for a goalie to get."

Charles Laberge/Getty Images

"When I was a kid, I was thinking about the Vezina, not the Hart," Theodore said that night. "The Hart was never a trophy I was looking for because there are so many players and it's hard for a goalie to get."

Theodore's fall from grace came almost as quickly and as dramatically as his ascension. After signing a three-year deal worth $16 million in 2005, things began to fall apart. There were a number of off-ice issues – his father and stepbrothers were charged in a loansharking scheme and he tested positive for a banned substance that was linked to a hair-restoration drug – and his play began to suffer.

With the Canadiens satisfied with the play of Cristobal Huet, they dealt Theodore to Colorado in 2006, where he had varying degrees of success before signing with Washington in 2008. ●

Glen **HARMON**

Defensive Demon

Defenseman
Born: Jan. 2, 1921, Holland, Man.
Died: March 9, 2007
Habs Career : 1942-1951
2 Stanley Cups, 2 second-team all-stars
50-96-146, 334 PIM in 452 games

During the 1940s, Canadiens' coach Dick Irvin used to like to challenge his defensemen in practice. One of his tricks was to send The Punch Line of Elmer Lach between Toe Blake and Maurice Richard out against defensemen Glen Harmon and Frank Eddolls and goalie Bill Durnan and bet the other players the talented trio couldn't score two goals.

"And he usually won," Harmon recalled on one occasion.

That Harmon and Eddolls could shut down the best line in hockey was no surprise to Irvin or the rest of the NHL. In his 10 seasons with the Canadiens, Harmon established himself as one of the best two-way defensemen in the game. Standing just 5-foot-9 and weighing 165 pounds, Harmon found a way to stop some of the game's best scorers while putting up some very respectable offensive numbers at the same time.

Harmon was a second-team all-star in 1945 and '49 and was a key defensive anchor for Stanley Cup-winning teams in 1944 and '46. He was part of the wave of players brought in by GM Tom

> Despite his size, Harmon was a terrific bodychecker who played a fearless brand of hockey.

Gorman and Irvin that was instrumental in returning the Canadiens to respectability after years of organizational decay. He had an immediate impact, finishing second in Calder Trophy balloting to Gaye Stewart in 1943.

Despite his size, Harmon was a terrific bodychecker who played a fearless brand of hockey. And while he was able to put up points at a fairly consistent pace, it was his ability to defend that was his main calling card.

In fact, in 1944-45 Harmon and Eddolls were playing a regular shift and did not allow a goal to be scored against them in 34 straight games. Prior to a game against the Toronto Maple Leafs, Irvin bragged to the press how good his team was defensively and in the subsequent game, Harmon and Eddolls were on the ice for seven goals against.

After his career, Harmon sold cars for 30 years in Montreal and settled in the Toronto area. He died of Alzheimer's disease in 2007. ●

Bruce Bennett Studios/Getty Images

Rick **GREEN**

Quiet Excellence

Defenseman	
Born: Feb. 20, 1956, Belleville, Ont.	
Habs Career : 1982-1990	
1 Stanley Cup	
10-79-89, 183 PIM in 399 games	

When Rick Green was dealt to the Canadiens from the Washington Capitals in 1982, he went from a team that just hoped to make the playoffs – and didn't until after he left – to one that considered the season a failure if it didn't have a championship banner to show for it.

Green had been able to handle the pressure of living up to the expectations placed on a No. 1 overall pick in his six seasons with the Washington Capitals, such as they were in Washington. But there's little that can prepare you for the kind of pressure you face in Montreal, particularly when you're the centerpiece of a trade with which the locals weren't exactly thrilled. (The Habs dealt Rod Langway, Brian Engblom, Doug Jarvis and Craig Laughlin to the Caps for Rick Green and Ryan Walter.)

> **"I don't think there was any doubt I played the best hockey of my career in Montreal."**

"The great thing about going there, though, was the guys on the team were great," Green recalled. "It was just a great atmosphere for hockey and I think it brought out some good things in me."

Green struggled with injuries for long stretches with the Canadiens, but was available and played well when the Canadiens needed him most in the playoffs. He was limited to just seven games in 1983-84, but played valiantly

Bruce Bennett Studios/Getty Images

in the playoffs as the Habs made an unlikely run to the Wales Conference final. Two years later, he played just 46 games during the regular season, but again performed well in the playoffs as the Canadiens won the Stanley Cup.

Green's quiet defensive presence was key to the Canadiens through the 1980s. He was so good at the role that he merited inclusion on the NHL team at Rendez-vous '87.

"I don't think there was any doubt I played the best hockey of my career in Montreal," said Green, who was an assistant coach with the Canadiens after his playing days. "It was just a great experience." ●

Pierre **LAROUCHE**

The Ultimate Victory

	Center
	Born: Nov. 16, 1955, Taschereau, Que.
	Habs Career : 1977-1981
	2 Stanley Cups
	110-126-236, 59 PIM in 236 games

The headline in The Hockey News in 1977 when the Canadiens acquired Pierre Larouche from the Pittsburgh Penguins was a stinging indictment.

"Penguins swap losers for winners," accompanied the story about the trade of Larouche to the Canadiens for Pete Mahovlich and Peter Lee on Nov. 29, 1977.

Larouche certainly didn't feel like a loser with the Canadiens. He won two Cups, albeit with minimal playoff contribution, and scored 50 goals in 1979-80.

But it was in Montreal that Larouche and his wife, Cindy, scored the biggest victory of their lives. Shortly after arriving in Montreal, Cindy was diagnosed with cancer in her lymph nodes and had surgery in Montreal and spent most of the next couple of years in chemotherapy treatments.

> "It was great – I got 50 and Guy got 50 that year."

"They said 80 per cent of the people who get the cancer she had die," Larouche said. "We kept it private. My teammates knew about it, but we didn't tell anybody. The doctors in Montreal saved her life."

It was in 1979 that Larouche had his greatest individual season as a Canadien. Buoyed by the departure of Scotty Bowman as coach and Jacques Lemaire's decision to play in Switzerland, Larouche was put on the top line with Guy Lafleur and Steve Shutt. He

Bruce Bennett Studios/Getty Images

scored 50 goals in 1979-80, becoming the first player to collect 50 for two different teams and also the first and, entering 2008-09, the only Canadiens' center to hit the coveted mark.

"It was great – I got 50 and Guy got 50 that year," Larouche said. "Steve got 47 and we tried so hard to get him 50. He must have had 14 shots in our last game against Detroit that year."

By the midway point in the 1981-82 season, Larouche had clashed with coach Bob Berry, GM Irving Grundman and teammates and was dealt to Hartford. ●

Pierre Larouche became the first player to score 50 goals for two different teams and is the only Habs center to reach the coveted mark.

261

Alexei **KOVALEV**

The Comeback Kid

Right Winger
Born: Feb. 24, 1973, Togliatti, USSR
Habs Career : 2004-2008*
1 second-team all-star
77-122-199, 236 PIM in 236 games
(*still a member of the Habs through August, 2008)

Prior to the 2007-08 season, Alexei Kovalev sat down to have a little chat with his agent. The man who was supposed to be Kovalev's most trusted advisor essentially told Kovalev he had to lower the bar on his personal expectations because he was no longer an elite NHL player.

> "I haven't felt this good since my days in Pittsburgh. I'm proud of what I have done."

Kovalev hadn't done much in Montreal to dispel that notion. In theory, Kovalev was one of the most purely talented players the Canadiens have ever had – and that's saying something. But in two-plus seasons, Kovalev had been nothing much more than a point-per-game contributor at best, an underachieving and inconsistent player at worst.

But then came 2007-08, one in which Kovalev enjoyed a spectacular renaissance and vaulted himself into the top 100 players in franchise history. In the regular season, Kovalev led the Canadiens with 35 goals and 84 points. Both totals were the second-best of his career and earned him The Hockey News' designation as NHL Comeback Player of the Year.

Alexei Kovalev and the Habs were pleasant surprises in 2007-08, a joy ride that ended when Mike Knuble and the Philadelphia Flyers knocked them out in the second round of the playoffs.

By the end of that season, when captain Saku Koivu missed the last several games with an injury, Kovalev was wearing the 'C' on his sweater.

"I'm a very proud person and to hear that from my agent was difficult," Kovalev said. "I knew I could be a better player. When somebody says something like that, it kills you a little bit. It's hard to accept."

In that one season, however, Kovalev won back the hearts of a skeptical fan base and re-emerged as a leader both on the ice and in the dressing room.

"I haven't felt this good since my days in Pittsburgh," Kovalev said. "I'm proud of what I have done." ●

Ted **HARRIS**

The Nose Buster

Defenseman
Born: July 18, 1936, Winnipeg, Man.
Habs Career : 1964-1970
4 Stanley Cups, 1 second-team all-star
18-95-113, 576 PIM in 407 games

It should come as no surprise that at 72, Ted Harris was working five days a week as the manager of a Benjamin-Moore paint outlet in suburban Philadelphia.

After all, Harris never had an aversion to heavy lifting. It took him until he was 28 to gain full-time employment in the NHL and before joining the Canadiens in the early 1960s, he played four seasons for the notorious Eddie Shore in Springfield.

So when the Canadiens were looking to change their identity and to stop their skilled players from being pushed around, they got players such as John Ferguson and Harris and suddenly they weren't so skilled and scared anymore.

"They were looking for a guy who was willing to get his nose busted," Harris said. "And God knows I got mine busted enough."

More often, though, it was Harris who was at the other end of the nose busting. A notoriously tough player in the minors, Harris had 100 or more penalty minutes three times in seven years with the Canadiens.

"John Ferguson gets a lot of the credit for the toughness on those teams in the 1960s," said former

> "They wanted a guy who wasn't afraid to get his nose busted."

Canadiens broadcaster Dick Irvin, "but I thought Ted Harris played that role every bit as well as Ferguson did, maybe better sometimes."

Harris won four Cups with the Canadiens in the 1960s, then played in Minnesota, Detroit and St. Louis before capping his career with a fifth Stanley Cup with the Philadelphia Flyers in 1974-75.

"Just like with Montreal, it was a case of being in the right place at the right time," Harris said. ●

Bruce Bennett Studios/Getty Images

Bob **TURNER**

Eight Goals, Five Rings

Defenseman
Born: Jan. 31, 1934, Regina, Sask.
Died: Feb. 7, 2005
Habs Career : 1955-1961
5 Stanley Cups
8-46-54, 235 PIM in 339 games

> "The Canadiens had a lot of superstars, but they had a lot of guys who could do a lot of things and Turner was that kind of player."
> – Dick Irvin

He's there in every team picture from 1956 through 1960, usually in the back row and to the right.

Of all the players who were part of the Canadiens' dynasty that won five straight Cups, none was as quiet and anonymous as a defensive defenseman named Bob Turner. In six seasons, he scored eight goals for the Canadiens, which would have been a good week for teammates such as Maurice Richard, Jean Beliveau and Bernie Geoffrion.

Turner is one of 12 players who played for all five Cup-winning teams and while his contributions aren't terribly prominent for those who watched the team casually, they were valued by those with whom he played.

"Bob Turner was a defenseman, but what a lot of people don't realize is that (coach Toe) Blake used to use him as a forward to kill penalties," said former Canadiens' broadcaster Dick Irvin. "The Canadiens had a lot of superstars, but they had a lot of guys who could do a lot of things and Turner was that kind of player."

If nothing else, Turner had an incredible sense of timing. After starting the 1955-56 season with the Shawinigan Cataractes of the Quebec Senior League, Turner was called up to the Canadiens at mid-season and basically replaced captain Butch Bouchard, who was in his last season and wasn't playing very much. Turner never relinquished his spot and won five Stanley Cups before being traded to the Chicago Black Hawks in 1961-62.

After his career, Turner returned to his native Regina and coached the Regina Pats to the Memorial Cup in 1974. ●

Bruce Bennett Studios/Getty Images

Mathieu **SCHNEIDER**

From Soaring to Souring

Defenseman	
Born: June 12, 1969, New York, N.Y.	
Habs Career : 1988-1995	
1 Stanley Cup	
63-136-199, 364 PIM in 360 games	

Prior to Mathieu Schneider's first season with the Canadiens, The Hockey News posed the question in its Season Preview edition whether Schneider would one day win a Norris Trophy.

The answer was yes, given time. Schneider never did win that Norris Trophy in Montreal or any of the other stops in his career, but he did provide the Canadiens with a very solid presence on the blueline for five-plus seasons.

Particularly after the trade of Chris Chelios in 1990, Schneider became the kingpin on the Canadiens defense corps and scored 20 goals and 52 points in 1993-94.

But when it came down to a choice between Schneider and superstar goalie Patrick Roy the next season, the Canadiens chose to ship out Schneider. There were reports of a rift in the dressing room and while most Canadien players worked out together in suburban Montreal during the 1994 lockout, Schneider skated with the McGill University team.

He became increasingly withdrawn from teammates and things came to a head when he got into a fight with Roy between periods of a game and had to be separated by teammates.

> "Schneider became the kingpin on the Canadiens defense corps."

Rick Stewart/Stringer

Neither player denied the fight had taken place, but both later downplayed its significance. Soon after, Schneider was dealt to the New York Islanders with Kirk Muller and Craig Darby for Pierre Turgeon and Vladimir Malakhov.

"It was nothing special, I had nothing against Mathieu," Roy later told THN. "He was a good guy to me. It was no big deal to me. He wasn't happy in Montreal and it's good to see him leave." ●

Terry **HARPER**

Once a Canadien, Always a Canadien

Defenseman	
Born: Jan. 27, 1940, Regina, Sask.	
Habs Career : 1963-1972	
5 Stanley Cups	
14-112-126, 805 PIM in 554 games	

> **"They pretty much had me from the time I first tied up my skates when I was five years old."**

Terry Harper dreamed of playing for the Montreal Canadiens from the time he was a young child. He grew up desperately hoping to follow in the footsteps of his heroes Bob Turner and Ed Litzenberger, two Saskatchewan boys who went on to play for the Habs.

That was a good thing because it wasn't like he had much of a choice in the matter.

"They pretty much had me from the time I first tied up my skates when I was five years old," Harper said.

The Canadiens basically had a monopoly on players from Regina and Harper caught their eye early. In fact, Harper said when he was about to accept a scholarship to play at the University of Michigan in the late 1950s, the Canadiens told the NCAA they had previously paid for his room and board in Regina and that rendered him ineligible.

Melchior DiGiacomo/Getty Images

So, Harper signed a C Form and played for the Regina Pats and became a full-time Canadien in 1963-64. In the nine full seasons he played with the Canadiens, he won five Stanley Cups, including four in five years in the 1960s. Not a bad haul for any player, but Harper thinks it should have been even more impressive.

"We should have won it every year I was there," Harper said. "We sure had the team to do it."

Harper played much of his career as Jean-Guy Talbot's defense partner and said Talbot's speed and skill was a perfect marriage with his penchant for staying back.

"I was a tall, lanky guy who could reach around and get into the face of the guys who would go after (Talbot)," Harper said. "It was great for me to play with somebody who had his speed and moxie with the puck." ●

Brian SKRUDLAND

Buried Treasure

Center
Born: July 31, 1963, Peace River, Alta.
Habs Career : 1985-1993
1 Stanley Cup
78-139-217, 592 PIM in 475 games

Brian Skrudland clearly remembers the day he made the final cut with the Canadiens in the fall of 1985. After congratulating all the rookies, Chris Nilan brought them into a separate room for a little chat.

"He told us, 'I want one thing to be clear. You guys are going to set the pace in practice,'" Skrudland recalled. "Then he said, 'There are a few guys around here who want one thing before they retire and that's the Stanley Cup.' And lo and behold, May 24 we're skating around with the Stanley Cup over our heads."

A big reason why they were was Skrudland, who got the Canadiens even in the final series against Calgary with an overtime goal that won Game 2. It came nine seconds into the extra period and still stands as the fastest playoff overtime goal in NHL history. That goal propelled the Canadiens to a 4-1 series victory over the Flames and gave Skrudland a Calder Cup and a Stanley Cup in two years work.

Not bad for a player who had never been drafted and was one of the last cuts from the 1984 Canadian Olympic team. In

> "I can't believe sometimes that I was part of this organization. I still have to pinch myself."

Otto Greule Jr. /Allsport

fact, the Canadiens had a contract ready for him they didn't want him to sign because they wanted him to play in the Olympics. As soon as he was cut, a devastated Skrudland called the Habs, went to Saskatoon to pack his things and left for Montreal, where he would be a solid checking forward and character guy for the next eight-plus seasons.

"I was just at an event with Hockey Canada where I was representing the Canadiens with Yvan Cournoyer," Skrudland said. "I can't believe sometimes that I was part of this organization. I still have to pinch myself." ●

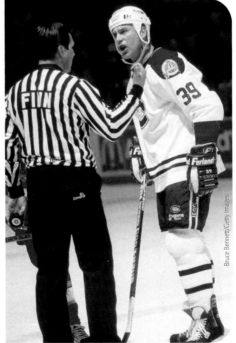

Bruce Bennett/Getty Images

92 Patrice **BRISEBOIS**

Helpers and Hollers

	Defenseman
Born: Jan 27, 1971, Montreal, Que.	
Habs Career : 1990-2004, 2007-08	
	1 Stanley Cup
82-271-353, 527 PIM in 834 games	

When Patrice Brisebois signed with the Canadiens for his second tour of duty in the summer of 2007, he surprised a number of people with his decision.

"(Canadiens GM Bob Gainey) was the first to call," Brisebois said at the time, "and I knew right away this is where I want to be."

> "I knew right away this is where I want to be."

You could excuse people for wondering whether Brisebois had lost his senses, or at least his sense of recall. In his 13 seasons on the Canadiens' blueline the first time around, Brisebois was often the fans' whipping boy for his defensive gaffes. Fans and the media often referred to Brisebois as "Breeze-by" because of his penchant for having opposing forwards blow by him on the rush.

Despite his defensive deficiencies, Brisebois has always put up very good numbers. His 353 career points and 271 assists with the Canadiens as of the end of 2007-08 put him sixth in franchise history among blueliners on both lists behind only Larry Robinson, Guy Lapointe, Doug Harvey, Serge Savard and J-C Tremblay.

Andre Ringuette/NHL via Getty Images

It should also be noted Brisebois was one of the better players to come out of a weak 1989 draft and was by far the best player of the 13 the Canadiens took that year. In fact, if not for Brisebois (30th overall), the 1989 draft would have been a complete wipeout for the Canadiens, since he was the only player they chose who ended up having a career as a full-time NHL player.

After leading the Laval Titan to three straight Memorial Cup appearances as a major junior player, Brisebois won a Stanley Cup in his first full NHL season, 1992-93, and appeared in all 20 playoff games the Canadiens played that spring. ●

Steve Babineau/NHL via Getty Images

Murph **CHAMBERLAIN**

'Old Hardrock'

	Left Winger
	Born: Feb. 14, 1915, Shawville, Que.
	Died: May 8, 1986
	Habs Career : 1940-42, 1943-1949
	2 Stanley Cups
	66-97-163, 540 PIM in 323 games

"A guy like that you're never going to see in the leading scorers, but someone has to go in and do the hammering and digging."

– Ernie Fitzsimmons

There's a very good reason why Murph Chamberlain was known as 'Old Hardrock,' and it had nothing to do with the fact he played for mining teams in Noranda, Que., South Porcupine, Ont., and Sudbury, Ont., before he joined the NHL.

Erwin Groves Chamberlain was one of the most devastating hitters and fighters of his time. During his eight seasons with the Canadiens in the 1940s, he was the sandpaper that complemented the more skilled likes of Rocket Richard, Elmer Lach and Toe Blake. In fact, it speaks volumes for Chamberlain that one of the first things Dick Irvin did when he came to the Canadiens from the Maple Leafs in 1940 was to convince GM Tom Gorman to get Chamberlain from the Leafs.

"A guy like that you're never going to see in the leading scorers, but someone has to go in and do the hammering and digging," said hockey historian Ernie Fitzsimmons. "He was sort of like (Bert) Olmstead later on. He was a guy who would crash along the boards. He would have been an excellent winger in today's game."

The Canadiens loaned Chamberlain twice, first to the Brooklyn Americans in 1942 and to the Boston Bruins for the 1942-43 season. But once he returned to the Canadiens, he began to have a very significant impact on the team's fortunes. Playing a second-line role behind the famed Punch Line, Chamberlain scored 47 points in 47 games and added five playoff goals to help the Canadiens to their first Stanley Cup in 13 seasons in 1944. One more Cup would follow two years later.

Chamberlain retired after the 1948-49 season, but not before being an integral, albeit unheralded, cog in the franchise's rebirth as a contender. ●

Buddy **O'CONNOR**

A Star-in-Waiting

Center
Born: June 21, 1916
Died: Aug. 24, 1977
Habs Career : 1941-1947
2 Stanley Cups
78-155-233, 22 PIM in 271 games
Hockey Hall of Fame: 1988

Herbert 'Buddy' O'Connor had to leave Montreal to earn star status in the NHL, but that should in no way minimize what he contributed to the Montreal Canadiens.

Like Murph Chamberlain, O'Connor was an important piece in the Canadiens' climb back to respectability in the 1940s. The only problem was O'Connor was always destined to be a second-liner because of the presence of Elmer Lach. A scoring star with the Montreal Royals before joining the Canadiens, O'Connor posted some pretty impressive numbers for the Habs, but was never able to usurp their top-tier scorers.

"He's one of those guys who didn't quite blossom as well as he might have in Montreal because they had a lot of stars," said hockey historian Eric Zweig.

There is little documentation that would explain why the Canadiens traded O'Connor to the New York Rangers in 1947, but there is no doubt

> ## "He's one of those guys who didn't quite blossom as well as he might have in Montreal because they had a lot of stars,"
>
> – Eric Zweig

they regretted the move. In his first season in New York, O'Connor scored 60 points and became the first player in league history to win the Hart and Lady Byng Trophies in the same season. He was also named Canada's athlete of the year for 1948.

That was his best season as an NHLer, but O'Connor also had consecutive seasons of 58 and 54 points with the Canadiens, largely because of his playmaking skills.

"In his first full season, he finished 10th in NHL scoring, which isn't bad," said hockey historian Ernie Fitzsimmons. "He gave them depth and he was a playmaking, checking centerman who never gave up." ●

HHOF Images

Herb **GARDINER**

The Original Ironman

Defenseman
Born: May 8, 1891, Winnipeg, Man.
Died: Jan. 11, 1972
Habs Career : 1926-1929
1 Hart Trophy
10-9-19, 52 PIM in 96 games

> Not only did he play every minute of every game in 1926–27 to win the Hart Trophy at the age of 35, he also went nine years without skating at all.

We can't say for sure, but we're fairly confident Herb Gardiner was some kind of freak of nature. Not only did he play every minute of every game in 1926-27 to win the Hart Trophy at the age of 35, he also went nine years without skating at all. Five of those were spent with the Canadian Forces in World War I.

Gardiner became the Canadiens first ever Hart Trophy winner when he took the award in '26-27, one of only two seasons he played for the Habs. Just a couple months shy of his 36th birthday, he is the second oldest player to win the Hart, behind only Eddie Shore. Wayne Gretzky is the only other player in league history to win the Hart in his first NHL season.

He earned the nickname 'The Ironman of Hockey' by playing every minute of every game and forming a solid defense tandem with fellow Hall of Famer Sylvio Mantha.

Gardiner caught the Canadiens' attention two years before that when Montreal defeated Gardiner's Calgary Tigers in the 1924 Stanley Cup final. Gardiner joined the Tigers of the Western Canadian Hockey League – a league that was on par with the NHL in the 1920s – shortly after serving in the war and only joined the Canadiens because pro hockey had collapsed in western Canada.

"He didn't really think about hockey as a career," said Gardiner's grandson Jim Rhodes, explaining Gardiner's emergence as a star late in his career.

Gardiner played one more season with the Canadiens before being loaned to the Chicago Black Hawks, but returned to the Canadiens for the playoffs in 1929. Gardiner ultimately ended up coaching minor pro hockey for the Philadelphia Arrows of the Can-Am Hockey League and settled there, becoming the first-ever season-ticket holder for the Philadelphia Flyers. ●

HHOF Images

Billy **COUTU**

Dude With a 'Tude

Defenseman	
Born: March 1, 1892, North Bay, Ont.	
Died: Feb. 28, 1978	
Habs Career : 1916-1920, 1921-1926	
1 Stanley Cup	
24-16-40, 357 PIM in 198 games	

Somewhere along the line, Billy Couture became Billy Coutu, but one thing that remained the same was the man's temper and penchant for taking it out on his opponents.

That included referees. In fact, Coutu became the first and only player to be banned from the NHL for life after he assaulted referee Jerry LaFlamme during the 1927 Stanley Cup final between the Boston Bruins and Ottawa Senators. The suspension was lifted after two years at the insistence of Canadiens' GM Leo Dandurand, who earlier had Coutu for nine years with the Canadiens.

By all accounts, Coutu was a combustible player who was once fined $200 by his own team for reckless play. In fact, he might have been considered even more notorious had he not been paired on the

> **"He was one of those guys people thought, 'Gee, you'd better not bother him because there's no telling what's going to happen.' "**
>
> – Ernie Fitzsimmons

Canadiens' defense corps with Sprague Cleghorn, who was even meaner than Coutu.

"He might get overlooked because he played with Cleghorn, in terms of how dirty and nasty a player he was," said hockey historian Bob Duff.

"He was a rough, rough dude," said hockey historian Ernie Fitzsimmons, "and I think a lot of people steered clear of him. He was one of those guys people thought, 'Gee, you'd better not bother him because there's no telling what's going to happen.' He was a pretty good player, but while the others were doing the the rushing, he was staying back and doing the dirty work."

Coutu was one of five players hospitalized with Spanish influenza in 1919 when the Canadiens traveled to Seattle to play the Stanley Cup final. Teammate Joe Hall died because of complications of the illness, but Coutu survived the ordeal. ●

Jimmy **ROBERTS**

Working-Class Winner

	Right Winger
	Born: April 9, 1940, Toronto, Ont.
	Habs Career : 1963-1967, 1971-1977
	5 Stanley Cups
	63-100-163, 299 PIM in 611 games

E arly in Jimmy Roberts' career, Toronto Maple Leafs GM Conn Smythe described him as, "a hewer of wood and a hauler of water," and there may not have ever been a more apt description applied to any player in NHL history.

"I couldn't really argue with that," Roberts said. "That's pretty much what I was and that's what kept me in the league."

Unlike many Canadiens who played a defensive role on an offensive juggernaut, Roberts was not a big scorer as a younger player who had to adapt his game when he joined the Canadiens. Thanks in large part to the influence Scotty Bowman had over him, first with the Peterborough Petes in junior hockey and then with the Ottawa-Hull Canadiens in the Eastern Pro League, Roberts arrived in Montreal in 1964 with a solid background in sound defensive hockey.

Roberts was one of the few players in Canadiens history to win Cups with the organization, then get traded and come back to Montreal to win more Cups. In all, he won five with the Canadiens and in 16 years in the NHL, played in the Stanley Cup final 10 times.

> "I think they wanted to get a little bit of that old-school mentality back in there."

Jimmy Roberts, right, engages Boston's
Andre Savard with his typical all-out effort.

One of the first things Bowman did as coach of the expansion St. Louis Blues in 1967 was get Roberts in the expansion draft and managed to get him back from the Blues shortly after taking over as coach of the Canadiens in 1971-72.

"I think they wanted to get a little bit of that old-school mentality back in there," Roberts said.

Roberts not only played a valuable shut-down role for the Canadiens in his second stint, but was also instrumental in mentoring future defensive greats Bob Gainey and Doug Jarvis. ●

285

Murray **WILSON**

Putting 'D' in Dynasty

Left winger	
Born: Nov. 7, 1951, Toronto, Ont.	
Habs Career : 1972-1978	
4 Stanley Cups	
83-80-163, 148 PIM in 328 games	

Imagine you're Murray Wilson and it's June 10, 1971. You're sitting at the Queen Elizabeth Hotel and you've just been selected 11th overall by the Canadiens.

You know the Canadiens have just won the Stanley Cup...again. You look down the draft list and you see the Canadiens have already taken Guy Lafleur first overall and Chuck Arnason seventh. Between them, they scored 209 goals and 373 points in junior hockey the previous season.

"I was there at the Queen Elizabeth Hotel and I thought I was going to go to Philadelphia because they had the eighth and ninth picks," Wilson said. "When Montreal took me I turned to my parents and said, 'Shit, I guess I'm going to Muskegon for a long time.'"

What Wilson would soon realize, though, is that as powerful as the Canadiens have been throughout their history, they've always had a strong defensive presence and Wilson fit that requirement perfectly. After just one year in the minors, Wilson joined the Canadiens for good in

> "The Canadiens never asked guys like me to score 50 goals."

Bruce Bennett Studios/Getty Images

1972-73 and was a terrific two-way forward on four Stanley Cup-winning teams in just six seasons.

"The best thing for me was that we had six guys who had played in the Summit Series," Wilson said. "That allowed me to play a lot of exhibition games in 1972 and I showed I could play and I scored 18 goals that first year. The Canadiens never asked guys like me to score 50 goals, but if you could stop a 50-goal scorer, whether it be Mickey Redmond or Mike Bossy, we were doing our job…and I think we were pretty damn good at it." ●

Pierre **TURGEON**

Points and... Poof!

Center
Born: Aug. 29, 1969, Rouyn, Que.
Habs Career : 1995-1996
50-77-127, 50 PIM in 104 games

All Pierre Turgeon ever did in his short time in a Montreal Canadiens uniform was produce.

All Pierre Turgeon ever did in his short time in a Montreal Canadiens uniform was produce. But in the end, that wasn't enough to keep him in Montreal for more than one full season.

In just 104 games for the Canadiens, Turgeon scored 50 goals and 127 points. His points-per-game average of 1.22 is second in franchise history behind Guy Lafleur among players who have played 100 or more games for the Canadiens.

The Canadiens were the third stop in Turgeon's career, despite the fact he had yet to reach his 26th birthday when he was dealt to Montreal. Turgeon produced immediately in 1994-95, but the Habs failed to make the playoffs in the lock-out-shortened season.

The Canadiens named Turgeon captain when Mike Keane was dealt to Colorado in the Patrick Roy trade and he led the team with 96 points, but was vilified by fans after his performance in the

Sprawling Islanders defenseman Mathieu Schneider tries to stop super set-up man Pierre Turgeon from collecting another point.

playoffs. The Canadiens were ousted by the New York Rangers in six games and while Turgeon had respectable 2-4-6 totals, he failed to register a point in the first two games and didn't score a goal until Game 4.

The next season, with the Canadiens having no trouble scoring and having Saku Koivu and Vincent Damphousse as their top two centers, they first asked Turgeon to accept a checking role – which he did not – then traded him to the St. Louis Blues with Rory Fitzpatrick and Craig Conroy for Shayne Corson and Murray Baron.

"This trade makes us a bigger, tougher team," GM Rejean Houle told THN. "It's a trade for the second half and the playoffs." ●

289

Joe **MALONE**

The Illusionist

Center/Left Winger
Born: Feb. 28, 1890, Quebec City, Que.
Died: May 15, 1969
Habs Career : 1917-1919, 1922-24
1 Stanley Cup, 2 Art Ross Trophies
52-6-58, 35 PIM in 58 games
Hockey Hall of Fame: 1950

They call him 'Phantom' Joe Malone in deference to his ability to vaporize when there was a scoring chance, but the moniker could just as easily be applied to Malone's tenure with the Canadiens.

Malone recorded arguably the greatest goal-scoring season in hockey history with the Canadiens, then never came close to duplicating it again in a Montreal uniform.

Malone's tenure with the Canadiens was short – to be sure his Hall of Fame career was more forged with the Quebec Bulldogs, who loaned him to the Canadiens after the franchise went dormant – but that magical season of 44 goals in 20 games in 1917-18 gave Malone the highest single-season goals-per-game mark in history and represented the NHL's highest single-season total 27 years later.

Malone played just eight games with the Canadiens, scoring seven goals, the next season. By that time, Malone had secured a good job with a bank and was a part-time player. After scoring five goals in the NHL playoffs, Malone begged off going to Seattle to play in the Stanley Cup final because of work commitments. The final was cancelled because of an influenza epidemic that killed Canadiens defenseman Joe Hall, with the

> "He scored goals like a crazy man."
> – Ernie Fitzsimmons

series tied 2-2 and one game suspended after two periods of overtime could not break a 0-0 tie.

Canadiens great Newsy Lalonde claimed for years Malone would have been the difference, but that's debatable. The Canadiens' two losses were by scores of 7-0 and 7-2 so Malone would have had to provide the difference in the scoreless overtime game for the Canadiens to have won the Cup.

"He scored goals like a crazy man," said hockey historian Ernie Fitzsimmons. ●

Bruce Bennett Studios/Getty Images

Off-Ice
HEROES

If success begins at the top, it's easy to see why the Canadiens have been so prosperous in their 100-year history.

There have been great players to be sure, but the Canadiens have also produced a Murderers' Row of coaches and GMs, the top 10 of whom are chronicled here in alphabetical order:

Pictorial Parade/Hulton Archive/Getty Images

TOE **BLAKE** – coach, 1955-1968:

Blake certainly wasn't the unanimous choice to coach the team in 1955, but no coach has ever come close to his accomplishments with the Canadiens.

Arguably the best bench coach the game has ever seen, Blake amassed 500 wins and eight Stanley Cups. Both are franchise highs.

What is more impressive was he won five consecutive Cups in the late 1950s with a team loaded with skill, then won three more in the 1960s guiding a team that was much more a triumph of the collective over the individual.

2006 Getty Images

"In the 1960s we had a very good team, but we were not head and shoulders above the rest of the league as we had been in the 1950s," Jean Beliveau said in the book *Lions in Winter*. "The difference was that we had the very best coach in hockey and a man who could get the best out of his players at all times."

SCOTTY BOWMAN – coach, 1971-79

A head injury in junior hockey derailed Bowman's career as a player, but it started him on the path to become one of the greatest coaches in NHL history.

Bowman's .744 winning percentage is by far the best of any coach in Canadiens history and his six Stanley Cups is second only to Blake's eight.

Bowman was a protégé of Sam Pollock and coached junior teams and scouted for the Canadiens before becoming the team's head coach.

LEO DANDURAND – owner/GM, 1921-35; coach, 1921-26 and 1934-35

A dashing and charismatic entrepreneur, Dandurand was born in Illinois, but came to Montreal as a teenager and fashioned a career as one of the top sports businessmen of his day.

In 1921, he purchased the Canadiens along with Joseph Cattarinich and Louis Letourneau for $11,000 and turned the Canadiens into a thriving business and on-ice success. With stars Howie Morenz and Aurel Joliat leading the way, the Canadiens won Cups in 1924, 1930 and 1931.

He was also coach of the team that won in 1924.

TOM GORMAN – GM, 1940-46

The only man in NHL history to win Stanley Cups as GM of four different teams, Gorman's accomplishments with the Canadiens have been minimized over the years, but he was instrumental in saving the Canadiens from near extinction after a disastrous period in the 1930s.

Gorman took over the Canadiens in 1940 as they were coming off what remains the worst season in franchise history. He almost immediately blew up the roster, leaving only Toe Blake and Ray Getliffe, and set about to rebuild the team. He hired Dick Irvin as his coach and won two Stanley Cups before leaving the organization in 1946.

DICK IRVIN – coach, 1940-55

Like Blake, Irvin had a Hall of Fame career as a player before forging one as a coach.

Long after leading the Toronto Maple Leafs to their first Stanley Cup, Irvin came to Montreal along with Tom Gorman in 1940 and the two began the process of building a dynasty. Irvin presided over Cup-winning teams in 1944, 1946 and 1953 before turning the job over to Blake.

GEORGE KENNEDY – owner/GM, 1910-21

Also known by his given name of George Kendall, Kennedy co-founded the Club Athletique Canadien in 1908, a popular French-speaking sports club in Montreal.

Kennedy leveraged the name "Canadien" to take control of the Canadiens in 1910 and he set about to build the first Canadiens team to win the Stanley Cup in 1916 with stars such as Jack Laviolette, Didier Pitre, Georges Vezina and Newsy Lalonde.

AL MACNEIL – coach, 1970-71

Henri Richard drove a stake in MacNeil's coaching career in Montreal by calling MacNeil, "the worst coach I ever had," after MacNeil benched him in Game 5 of the Stanley Cup final in 1971, but the truth is MacNeil was a brilliant coach.

Not only did he play a hunch that resulted in Ken Dryden's spectacular run in the '71 playoffs, but ask any member of the Canadiens' dynasty of the 1970s who played in the minors and he'll tell you MacNeil had an enormous impact on his career.

MacNeil coached the Canadiens' farm teams in the late 1960s and early 1970s and helped develop a plethora of talent. Some of the more notable players coached by MacNeil in the minors were Larry Robinson, Guy Lapointe, Yvon Lambert, Pete Mahovlich, Pierre Bouchard, Bill Nyrop, Brian Engblom and Pierre Mondou. MacNeil also won three Calder Cups as a coach.

SAM POLLOCK – GM, 1964-78

Arguably the greatest GM in the history of the game, Pollock was an incredibly astute judge of players and a formidable negotiator. While NHL teams were finding their way through the new drafting system, Pollock continued to devise inventive ways to continue the flow of top players to the Canadiens.

In 14 years as GM of the Canadiens, he won nine Stanley Cups and prior to that, built Canadien-affiliated teams that won Memorial Cups and Eastern and Central Pro League championships. He also assembled the Canadian team that won the first Canada Cup in 1976 and was one of the integral organizers when the league expanded from six to 12 teams.

SERGE SAVARD – GM, 1983-1995

Only Frank Selke and Pollock had longer tenures as GM of the Canadiens. And while they won several more Stanley Cups than Savard did, Savard's impact on the franchise should not be minimized.

When Savard took the Canadiens over in 1983, the roster had fallen into a state of disrepair, but within three years he built a team that won the Canadiens 23rd Stanley Cup.

Savard made a number of very key acquisitions for the Canadiens, but his biggest contribution was presiding over the draft. Under Savard in 1984, the Canadiens had one of the best drafts in history when they selected Petr Svoboda, Shayne Corson, Stephane Richer and Patrick Roy.

FRANK SELKE – GM, 1946-64

After leaving the Toronto Maple Leafs in 1946, Selke continued Gorman's work and built the Canadiens into a powerhouse. He assembled teams for the Canadiens that won both Memorial and Allan Cups along with six Stanley Cups, including five in a row from 1956-60.

Selke was largely responsible for building a formidable network of scouts that helped produce a seemingly endless supply of top players to Montreal.

By the numbers Canadiens' All-Time Leaders
Points

#	Player	Points
1	Guy Lafleur	1,246
2	Jean Beliveau	1,219
3	Henri Richard	1,046
4	Maurice Richard	965
5	Larry Robinson	883
6	Yvan Cournoyer	863
7	Jacques Lemaire	835
8	Steve Shutt	776
9	Bernie Geoffrion	759
10	Elmer Lach	623
11	Mats Naslund	612
12	Dickie Moore	594
13	Saku Koivu	591
14	Claude Provost	589
15	Mario Tremblay	584
16	Guy Lapointe	572

Bruce Bennett Studios/Getty Images

Guy Lafleur

17	Pete Mahovlich	569	**34**	Bert Olmstead	383
18	Guy Carbonneau	547	**35**	J.C. Tremblay	363
19	Toe Blake	527	**36**	Patrice Brisebois	353
20	Bobby Rousseau	522	**37**	Ryan Walter	349
21	Ralph Backstrom	502	**38**	Gilles Tremblay	330
22	Bob Gainey	501	**39**	Mike McPhee	324
23	Vincent Damphousse	498	**40**	Mark Recchi	322
24	Bobby Smith	482	**41**	Frank Mahovlich	310
25	Aurel Joliat	460	**42**	Chris Chelios	309
26	Pierre Mondou	456	**43**	Mark Napier	304
27	Doug Harvey	447	**44**	John Ferguson	303
28	Shayne Corson	423	**45**	Doug Risebrough	302
29	Stephane Richer	421	**46**	Martin Rucinsky	297
30	Howie Morenz	417	**47**	Ken Mosdell	287
31	Yvon Lambert	415	**48**	Brian Savage	285
32	Serge Savard	412	**49**	Jacques Laperriere	282
33	Rejean Houle	408	**50**	Mike Keane	269

Robert Laberge/Getty Images

Vincent Damphousse

By the numbers
Canadiens' All-Time Leaders
Games played

1	Henri Richard	1,256
2	Larry Robinson	1,202
3	Bob Gainey	1,160
4	Jean Beliveau	1,125
5	Claude Provost	1,005
6	Maurice Richard	978
7	Yvan Cournoyer	968
8	Guy Lafleur	961
9	Serge Savard	917
10	Guy Carbonneau	912
11	Doug Harvey	890
12	Steve Shutt	871
13	Tom Johnson	857
14	Jacques Lemaire	853
15	Mario Tremblay	852
16	Ralph Backstrom	844

Melchior DiGiacomo/Getty Images

Henri Richard

17	Patrice Brisebois	834
18	J.C. Tremblay	794
19	Jean-Guy Talbot	791
20	Butch Bouchard	785
21	Guy Lapointe	777
22	Bernie Geoffrion	766
23	Saku Koivu	727
24	Jacques Laperriere	691
25	Elmer Lach	664
26	Shayne Corson	662

27	Aurel Joliat	655
28	Dickie Moore	654
29	Craig Rivet	653
30	Bobby Rousseau	643
31	Rejean Houle	635
32	Ken Mosdell	627
33	Mats Naslund	617
34	Jimmy Roberts	611
35	Yvon Lambert	606
36	Ryan Walter	604
37	Floyd Curry	601
38	Craig Ludwig	597
39	Don Marshall	585
40	Pete Mahovlich	581
41	Mike McPhee	581
42	Toe Blake	569
43	Doug Jarvis	560
44	Terry Harper	554
45	Pierre Mondou	548
46	Sylvio Mantha	538
47	Petr Svoboda	534
48	Claude Larose	529
49	Pit Lepine	526
50	Chris Nilan	523

Patrice Brisebois

Bill Wippert/NHLI via Getty Images

By the numbers
Canadiens'
All-Time Leaders
Goals

1	Maurice Richard	544
2	Guy Lafleur	518
3	Jean Beliveau	507
4	Yvan Cournoyer	428
5	Steve Shutt	408
6	Bernie Geoffrion	371
7	Jacques Lemaire	366
8	Henri Richard	358
9	Aurel Joliat	270
10	Mario Tremblay	258
11	Howie Morenz	256
12	Claude Provost	254
13	Dickie Moore	254
14	Mats Naslund	243
15	Bob Gainey	239
16	Toe Blake	235

1950 Getty Images

Maurice Richard

17	Stephane Richer	225
18	Pete Mahovlich	223
19	Guy Carbonneau	221
20	Ralph Backstrom	215
21	Elmer Lach	215
22	Bobby Rousseau	200
23	Larry Robinson	197
24	Pierre Mondou	194
25	Vincent Damphousse	184

Points Per Game
(min. 100 GP)

1	Guy Lafleur	1.297
2	Pierre Turgeon	1.221
3	Frank Mahovlich	1.179
4	Jean Beliveau	1.084
5	Pierre Larouche	1.000
6	Mats Naslund	0.992
7	Bernie Geoffrion	0.991
8	Maurice Richard	0.987
9	Pete Mahovlich	0.979
10	Jacques Lemaire	0.979
11	Vincent Damphousse	0.960

12	Bobby Smith	0.954
13	Elmer Lach	0.938
14	Mark Recchi	0.931
15	Toe Blake	0.926
16	Kirk Muller	0.925
17	Dickie Moore	0.908
18	Howie Morenz	0.907
19	Yvan Cournoyer	0.892
20	Steve Shutt	0.891
21	Brian Bellows	0.875
22	Buddy O'Connor	0.860
23	Stephane Richer	0.859
24	Denis Savard	0.852
25	Henri Richard	0.833

Pete Mahovlich

Steve Babineau/NHLI via Getty Images

By the numbers Canadiens' All-Time Leaders
Penalty Minutes

1	Chris Nilan	2,248
2	Lyle Odelein	1,367
3	Shayne Corson	1,341
4	Maurice Richard	1,285
5	John Ferguson	1,214
6	Mario Tremblay	1,043
7	Doug Harvey	1,042
8	Jean Beliveau	1,029
9	Doug Risebrough	959
10	Henri Richard	928
11	Tom Johnson	897
12	Jean-Guy Talbot	884
13	Butch Bouchard	863
14	Guy Lapointe	812
15	Terry Harper	805
16	Craig Rivet	795

Bruce Bennett Studios/Getty Images

Mario Tremblay

Goalie **Wins**

Shut**outs**

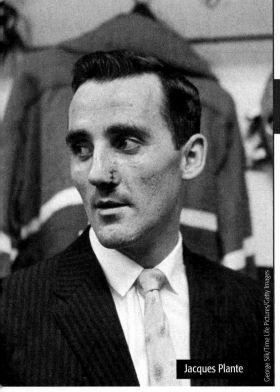

Jacques Plante

George Silk/Time Life Pictures/Getty Images

By the numbers
Canadiens'
All-Time Leaders
Goals-Against
Average (min. 100 GP)

1	George Hainsworth	1.78
2	Jacques Plante	2.23
3	Ken Dryden	2.24
4	Gerry McNeil	2.36
5	Bill Durnan	2.36
6	Gump Worsley	2.42
7	Charlie Hodge	2.46
8	Jeff Hackett	2.53
9	Cristobal Huet	2.53
10	Jose Theodore	2.62

Dave Sandford/Getty Images

Jose Theodore

By the numbers
Canadiens'
All-Time Leaders
Stanley Cup
Winners

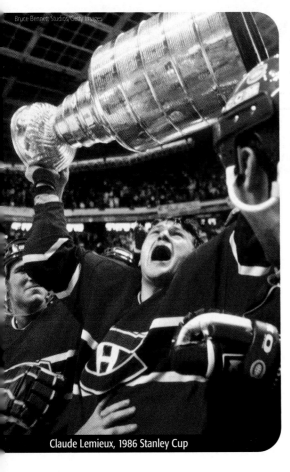

Bruce Bennett Studios/Getty Images

Claude Lemieux, 1986 Stanley Cup

Bruce Bennett Studios/Getty Images

Kirk Muller, 1993 Stanley Cup

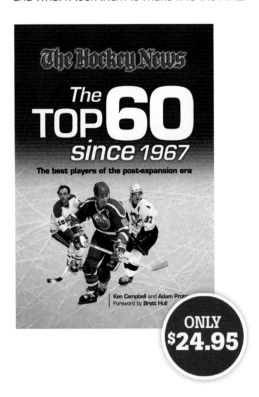
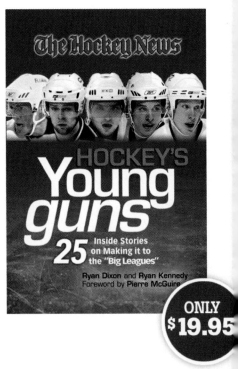